The Liminal
and The Luminescent

The Liminal
and The Luminescent

Jungian Reflections on Ensouled Living
Amid a Troubled Era

TERRILL L. GIBSON
Foreword by John Allan

WIPF *&* STOCK · Eugene, Oregon

THE LIMINAL AND THE LUMINESCENT
Jungian Reflections on Ensouled Living Amid a Troubled Era

Wipf & Stock
An Imprint of Wipf and Stock Publishers
199 W. 8th Ave., Suite 3
Eugene, OR 97401

www.wipfandstock.com

PAPERBACK ISBN: 978-1-6667-2414-1
HARDCOVER ISBN: 978-1-6667-2016-7
EBOOK ISBN: 978-1-6667-2017-4

DECEMBER 1, 2021 2:44 PM

For those who suffer and seek.

CONTENTS

Foreword by JOHN ALLAN | ix

Preface | xiii

Acknowledgments | xv

PRELUDE | 1

PILGRIMAGE | 56

PERFORMANCE | 86

POLITICS | 122

POSTLUDE | 171

Bibliography | 193

FOREWORD

DR. GIBSON'S BOOK, "THE Liminal and the Luminescent: Jungian Reflections on Ensouled Living Amid a Troubled Era," is the product of 50 years of contemplation and engagement with his own Psyche and action with the world around us. It sparkles like the "*cauda pavonis,*" a peacock's tail, and illuminates many of the struggles of our time. It is a rich text, grounded in History, Psychology of Religion and Jungian Archetypal thinking. Its range is vast and draws on the work of Plato, Aristotle, Hildegard de Bingen right through to C.G. Jung, Avivah Zornberg, Tartovsky, and the author's own journals.

This is a living, breathing text. It will fire you up with its poems, its quotes, its dreams and images from photographs and movies. It will stir up many liminal experiences in you. You will hate it, love it and dream about it, which is of course the intention of Dr. Gibson. The book brings to the forefront the value of liminal experiences for the individual and the Collective, namely that these experiences can and do heal individuals and societies.

The crux of Dr. Gibson's book is that there is a split in both Human and Divine Psyches, that we are 'split' creatures and that the splitting is what drives us to war and incessant conflict with each other. We erroneously split mind from brain, male from female, white from black, science from spirituality, nature from humans. It is either/or rather than both/and. We are caught in a binary paradigm while the world really operates from a quantum perspective.

The liminal is a nondual event and offers a process of integration rather than a place of integration. It is where the rational and irrational, the mind and the body, the divine and the human, come "in" to an integrated repose with each other.

What are liminal experiences and what are the portals to them? The liminal is the space between us, our bodily selves, and the Gods or the Divine, between the profane and the sacred, between Body and Soul. One enters the space and experiences a different sense of time, not the time of the clock, Chronos, but time as everlasting, Kairos. When one enters a liminal space one is often infused with a feeling of the numinous-- the Ego temporarily moves aside and the Gods are here in our hearts and bodies. The liminal is a well that never dries up and informs us each night through our dreams. Dr. Gibson postulates that through liminal work the life force is awakened and that one can find one's true destiny. Liminal time is time spent with the Gods and it can have a powerful healing effect on both individual Psyches and the World.

The portals to the liminal are varied and can include experiences such as Beauty, Trauma, Comedy, Religious Practice, Birth and Death, Sunrise/Sunset, Image/Art, Poetry, Psychotherapy, and Synchronicity. Consciously entering these portals allows the individual to be touched by the Divine in both its beautiful and devastating aspects.

In this book Dr. Gibson looks at the liminal in Pilgrimage, Performing Arts, Politics, and Film. He is most concerned and disturbed by how contemporary society has become one sided, focusing on Patriarchal values such as competition, achievement, acquisition, dominance over Nature, resource extraction, and missing the essential attunement to Nature. Corporations, the military industrial complex and the world of politics have lost their Soul. Dr. Gibson points out that the economy should serve the people and not undermine them. Health care should be available to all and whistle blowers should be protected. Diversity provides a richness.

The challenge is to find a way to heal these intense splits so we do not end up killing ourselves or destroying the planet. Healing these splits is no easy task and can best be achieved by a number of successive contemplative liminal experiences. This means living in and acknowledging the tension of opposites--seeing both sides of the coin at the same time – and waiting until some new thoughts, emotions or images arise. Jung calls this the Transcendent Function. To heal, our profound suffering and sorrow needs to be acknowledged, felt, and transformed. An aspect of this journey needs to be a descent into the depth of our pain, into the "dissociated debris of childhood" and then to be able to return with a new understanding of where we stand and how to be. Dr. Gibson identifies Pilgrimage, "Spirit walking in physical form," and psychotherapy with an informed guide as two vehicles for this journey.

The Divine has both beautiful and devastating aspects. Darkness and Evil are real. Dr. Gibson sees Evil as a terrible reality and yet a necessary element to the fulfillment of individual and collective destinies. Everyone needs to see their own Shadow side and to own it, rather than projecting it into other people. Transformation occurs when one can look boldly into Darkness, enter it, feel the pain of it, and wait until a new feeling or image emerges.

The book concludes with thoughts about the end of the world as we know it. Dr. Gibson sees this ending, this disaster, as part of life "to live is to experience periodic collapse . . . this is true on the personal, collective, and cosmic levels". The reality is that the planet is dying because our civilization has and is destroying our lakes and rivers, seas and oceans, trees and farm lands. Our dominant Cosmology has been grounded in the Patriarchy: Man shall "have dominion over the fish of the sea, and over the birds of the heavens and over cattle and all the earth . . . "(Genesis 1:26). The Feminine, the Spirit of the World that animates Nature, Mother Earth, Gaia, has been raped, tortured and murdered. We are left with a Climate Crisis of catastrophic proportions.

Dr. Gibson tracks this pending apocalypse with an in-depth analysis of two films: Tartovsky's "The Sacrifice"(1986) and Peled's "Bitter Seed" (2011). He argues that while psychotherapy can help us transform on an individual level, the liminality of films enables us to move forward on a collective plane by making what is unconscious more conscious for the general public.

In closing, Dr. Gibson advocates for society to do a complete turnaround, what C. G. Jung calls " *Arbor Inversus*", the inverted tree of Alchemy. We need to recover the deep Feminine and our connection to family and friends (the Clan). We also need to extinguish the attitude of conquest and cultivate a loving relationship with Earth and Cosmos. Of particular importance is the development of a deeper sense of humility and compassion. In these times of devastating upheavals it will be the dual abilities to engage with the crises while at the same time disengaging from anxious and controlling effort that hold the hope for change.

This book will take you on a journey. To read it is to navigate a river with many tributaries, replete with golden nuggets, where the traveler may discover hidden treasures in this pilgrimage through liminal space.

JOHN ALLAN, PhD
Professor Emeritus
University of British Columbia
Vancouver, Canada

Preface

THIS BOOK COMES AS a time vault, a love letter to future seekers and practitioners of Care of Souls Craft. It is a legacy text as much as it's a life text. It's intended for future generations of ensouled living and healing practice as much as it is for contemporary ensouled living-in-beauty pursuit.

When I was a child, it was a popular community event to bury time capsules filled with all variety of thoughtful and whimsical tchotchkes that reflected a community's sense of what was most illuminating and important in their lives. All manner of children's organizations and civic groups festively designed, filled, and entombed these canisters of community care and hope. I'd like that same spirit to bless the launch into the world of this time capsule of humble ideas and visions.

For five decades I have loved my work. I stumbled into this vocation through a series of what I now perceive to be striking accidents and sychronisms. Those fated twists and turns of my young man's journey crossed the path of a brilliant pantheon of gifted mentors and soulful human beings who took the time and care to introduce me to and guide me through the sacred precincts of healing craft and care.

Frida Kahlo has a painting entitled *The Love Embrace of the Universe*. It shows her as a seated woman of world sorrow encircling the man face and child body of her gifted but often abusive husband. It stands for me as a striking image of the violent and ravaging patriarchy that is sucking all the juice out of our common compassion and humanity. But behind her, in an image of infinite embracing regress, are brooding Black Madonna, Black Goddess like figures that are containing and caring for this sorrowed but nurturing young artist as she suffers the travails of a painful marriage and a painful world. Behind my mentors, out of similar moments of *Weltschmerz*, I often experience seeing the infinite regress of shadowy ancestral guides all the way back to the Paleolithic caves-of-image from which the best of our human beauty and soul quest emerged. In many ways this book is an homage to their enduring and tender teaching mercies. I am hoping that this text is an honoring memoir to their graced wisdoms that will help provide respectful vessels for the survival of their central visions into an ongoing, essential sentient beingness.

TERRILL L. GIBSON
Steilacoom, Washington
August 2021

Acknowledgments

SINCE EVERYTHING TRUE AND AUTHENTIC is only experienced through the embodied liminal realms, everything I know and I have shared about this liminal phenomenon in this book came through close and loving relationships with soulful persons who have guided me to such portals of deeper liminal being. The cast of thousands of such ensouled Guardian Beings to so cross my life's path and destiny would be too numerous to list here but a few of special note I would like to mention. For the Halls of Grace that allowed so many gifted friends and mentors to cross my path and catch a glimpse of the soul in me that I was blind to—Eddie Burns, Everett Reese, Edith Wallace, Harrell Beck, Mary Drury, Judd Howard, Linda Leonard, Bill Gregory, Louise Bode, Merle Jordan, Bob Stuckey, Vera Buhrmann, Homer Jernigan, Mark Harvey, Harry Freeman, Ted Brackman, Katherine Dyckman, Mel Ritchey, Anne Devore, Duane Spires, Lofton Hudson, Clare Buckland, Ann Ulanov, Pam Gibson Bauer Nolan, Sally Parks, Russell Lockhart, Laura Dodson, Donald Williamson, Myriam Dardenne, John Allan. For all the patients and supervisees who have gifted me with the honor of witnessing their courageous, and generative testimonies of suffering and transformation. This manuscript owes much to the gracious dedication of my editor Elena Abbott. For my clinical peer group of nearly four decades who live in liminal realms so often and with such grace: Doug Anderson, Barbara Fischer, Jim Ingersoll, Carol Johnson, Don Smith, and Tess Taft. To my clinical men's group who generated a similar intense liminal guiding heat for me across those same decades: Will Dixon, Rick Gossett, Gene Harvey, Wayne McCleskey, and Jerry Smith. To the Third Trimester Tribe who has lovingly held my narratives of rant and grief and joy with faithfulness over a decade now. To my analytic, therapeutic, and clinical ministerial colleagues who have goaded and guided my evolving craft across my professional life. To all the various staff and board members of the nonprofits that have been my home of grace and light across four-and-a-half decades in both the Christian Counseling Service and Pastoral Therapy Associates, my deepest love, appreciation and blessings. To my caring, encouraging and enabling partner across the full spectrum of my clinical and personal life, Jerry Smith. And for the unceasingly generous vessel of confession, forgiveness, encouragement, solace and light, of my life partner over five decades, Rosa Beth Gibson.

TERRY GIBSON
Summer Solstice 2021

PRELUDE

The World of the Liminal

All life is bound to carriers who realize it, and it is simply inconceivable without them. But every carrier is charged with an individual destiny and destination, and the realization of these alone makes sense of life.

—C. G. JUNG[1]

WE LIVE IN A BADLY divided world. It always has been. Religion quarrels with science, alt-right with anarchist, Muslim with Jew, Hindu with Buddhist, Christian with everybody. economies and their rationalizing theories fight it out to the last cent—democratic socialist versus hard capitalist—as do the political handlers of economies: Republican versus Democrat, Tory versus Labor, Teabagger versus Progressive, populist versus socialist, alt-right versus Antifa, non-vaccinated versus vaccinated, masked versus unmasked, All Lives Matter versus Black Lives Matter. Even our brains are caught in seeming trench warfare between left and right hemispheres and their dueling neural integrities.

This is a badly divided world. Always has been. But recently there have been signs that this dualist tradition, this incessant struggle for philosophical hegemony, might be finding a more peaceful place of meeting and integration. In contemporary neurology and meditation practices, it is called the mindfulness movement; in the political realms, it is known as the Commons movement; in the environmental community, it is the Green

---

1. Jung, *Collected Works Vol. 12: Psychology and Alchemy*, 222.

movement. Among analytical therapies, this place of meeting and integration is called archetypal psychology.

Depth psychologists narrate this new kind of synthesis with a variety of descriptors, but this book will refer to it as the archetypal-liminal perspective, the liminal for short. There are many places to notice its more modern origins, such as William James's *Varieties of Religious Experience* (1900), Rudolf Otto's *The Idea of the Holy* (1918), or Joseph Campbell's *The Hero with a Thousand Faces* (1949). But within my Jungian-analytic school, lightning really hit the ground and broke things wide open when Carl Gustav Jung published *Answer to Job* in 1953.

Written in a fit of automatic, feverish writing, Jung's volume tore the veil off his flirtatious rejection of engaging in theological activity. Even while reproducing the same demurs in *Answer to Job*, the volume makes clear that his lifelong depth-psychoanalytical enterprise constituted psycho-theological work of the most profound significance. In the realm of divine-human dialogue, his work makes clear that the gods are as evolutionarily engaged as human beings; that creator and created are co-evolving together and that the whole enterprise depends on the co-extension of their being into wider and wider dimensions of conscious, compassionate lovingness. The widest container of the cosmos is not the gods, but compassion. In 1953, Jung demonstrated that the liminal is the place where this co-evolution most dramatically reveals itself.[2]

Then, in 1969, depth psychology cut another deep trench into understanding the thin places between personal and transpersonal experience with the publication of Joseph Henderson's *Threshold of Initiation*. For many in the Jungian world, this book's appearance heralded a deeper consideration of that fragile interface between human and archetypal, personal and numinal [from numen-divine nod]. Some consider it one of the biggest advancements of theoretical and clinical reflection made since Jung's *Answer to Job*. Gifted and complementary commentary has unfolded in its wake, from Jeffrey Raff, Clarissa Pincola Estes, Ann Belford Ulanov, John Dourley, Marion Woodman, Dyanne Sherwood, James Hillman, Murray Stein, Tom Singer, and many, many others.

The liminal buffer zone, this thin place between worlds or dimensions of being, is where the gods come to parley with our human angst. It is here where our Destiny—both collective and individual—is revealed. Many believe that this in-between liminal realm, this vast, ripe emptiness within

2. Raff, *Healing the Wounded God*; Raff, *Jung and the Alchemical Imagination*.

our understandings of conventional time and space, is where our primal wound is healed by the only ultimate balm there is—relationship and love, or what the alchemists called *relatio*. Many further believe that the gods and we humans are each afflicted by this primal wound; that this deep, authentic, liminal encountering and empathic relating and loving is the only hope for us all. It is by repeated and non-anxious depth repose in this liminal realm that both individuals and cultures can calm themselves and heal. So, it is necessary to find the doorway, the portal, into such depth chambers of the psyche in order for such repeated, transformative exposure to occur. It is through this portal that the depth psycho-spiritual journey begins.

> Because the psyche is a vehicle for the experience of the numinosum, and the personality is profoundly affected by archetypal processes, conscious development of the personality becomes a spiritual journey in its own right.[3]

Jungian psychology is a mystery psychology. Jungian analysis is a mystery religion. It initiates its celebrants into liminal realms, attempting to accompany them in their search for and submission to their authentic destiny. It is a genuine profession, a profession of service to the deepest essence, the core being-ness of those it serves. Of course, it uses pragmatic sciences to help frame and inform its protocols of engagement for companioned sojourns with suffering seekers. But tools are not telos, diagnoses are not destinies. Mystery inspires science, but science does not define mystery. At its best, science can only point the way. In the liminal Queendoms of Mystery, science discovers its true bride: the Soul. Only in the liminal can science complete its mission—the achievement of individual and collective consciousness and compassion.

This book explores ideas about where the portal—that Mystery Portal into the depth chambers of the psyche—might be more reliably located or, perhaps better stated, experienced. It turns its attention to wonderings about how, when, and if we might enter this liminal zone and receive its healing. We will imagine together what our world would look like if there were a depth numinal politics more broadly practiced in both our individual and communal lives. Through theory, cinematic example, depth cultural/political reveries, and input from depth therapists and philosophers, we will attempt to navigate a safe voyage and return across these liminal

---

3. Corbett, *The Sacred Cauldron*, 116.

seas of being with fresh clues and strategies for living less violent, more compassionate, and more meaningful lives both personally and collectively.

This book preaches a crusade—a crusade of recovery. It preaches for the recovery of soulful, public, communal, productive, creative, *liminal* space. This book offers hints about how we can broaden this peaceful place of co-habitation, civility, and even integration at both the personal and the cultural level. It is a book about Jungian analysis specifically and, more broadly, all psychotherapy. But most importantly it is about living life fully and well. The biggest hint this book provides is that we are in more than a human-to-human crisis; we are in a time of profound human-to-Divine crisis. The human and the Divine are co-evolving together. Anyone with a serious interest in psychospiritual wholeness and development should find a little aid, comfort, and direction within these covers.

The eye by which I see God is the eye by which [S]he sees me.

—MEISTER ECKHART[4]

Much written here comes from my experience as a North American, but my model intends to be a psyche [Jung's favored term for the integrating core of individual and collective being]-based polis model: one that births locally, applies universally, and then returns to its mother soil.[5] This book is intended to be both a classical and postmodern analysis delivered through a Jungian-archetypal-liminal lens. It is an adaptable model seeking to be worthy of broad application regardless of one's polis-of-origin.

This world never seems like a singularity. Life here never feels like it stands on its own. There is always the gnawing, distracting sense that this world is an in-between place. Not just in between birth and death, but between much broader dimensions of experience, meaning, and phenomena. We live in the often mean, desperate, and violent times that exist in between what we hope are the deeper, less cruel times and the space beyond our death. Jung said that this world is beautiful, but it is just as cruel. Why that is so, why such a compromised, imperfect, flawed dimension got so centrally designed into the place we live, is one of the main questions that has kept philosophers awake at night for millennia. We often hate our suffering in this place, this imposed affliction beyond our choice and control. But Jung audaciously suggests in *Answer to Job* that the Divine envies us for

4. Nichols, *Jung and Tarot*, 300.
5. Polis: an ancient Greek term for the locally-gathered democratic community.

4

what that suffering has made of the best of us: our soulful transformation into compassionate, loving, deeply related human beings. The gods want to be able to love like that, to feel that irrational, impassioned certainty. When standing before the unanswerably painful emptiness of death, they want the courage to grow quiet and speak the patient, non-anxious relational truth no matter the consequence—even if that consequence be extinction. That is the liminal: that urgent place of primordial truth-telling and envying, of human and divine standing naked and revealed before each other. It is the precious nursery of all creation. It is toward that place that this book turns all of its imagination and inquiry.

Jung's assertion that the gods are located right here in the center of things is as radical as Copernicus's view that the sun—not our earth—is at the center of our heavens, as Descartes's contemplative utterance, "I think therefore I am," and as Heidegger's eerily disorienting notions about emptiness and angst. The gods are not up there or down there; they are not over, around, or below. They are here, in the heart of our bodies and psyches. In us. Right here. Right now. We are gods; or, put another way, we are the Divine incarnating in our flesh, experience, and being.

And the location where this happens, as well as the event of its happening, is the liminal. The liminal is an evanescent, translucent place between worlds. It has its own special lighting and moods and memories and presences. It is the special effects of light and cloud and affect that hover around a conscious dawn or dusk. When I was boy in my prairie homelands, the atmosphere would turn a brooding and silent deep emerald right before a violent, awesome thunderstorm cracked down on the earth. The liminal, like these events, is a phantom between worlds and moments. It is in-between-ness: in between time, in between space.

Although the liminal is beyond space and time, we can still find special and temporal metaphors that help us locate the liminal portals. A frequently used spatial metaphor, for example, is a vertical one. In my office, I have an 1840 Bolonchen lithograph of a *cenote*, one of those deep limestone sinkholes common all across the Yucatan Peninsula. It was drawn by one of the first French artists to arrive in the area, who captured the scene at the majestic bottom of one of these deep freshwater wells. There is a huge wooden ladder with broad 20-foot-wide rungs rising over one hundred feet to the surface above. Native Mayans are backpacking pottery jugs of fresh water up precarious-looking steps to the thirsty community and fields above. The image calls to mind a Mayan Jacob's ladder, forming a healing connection between moist Earth Mother below and parched human lands above. It reminds me of Jacob's liminal dream as he lay on his stone pillow in Genesis 28: 11–19. His dream assured him there was a channel between this human world and the transforming worlds of the gods, and it promised him that there are always angelic agents hovering, ready to guide and return us to our pilgrim's true path.

My Jungian psycho-spirituality informs me that the liminal's dream emissaries are the living scripture in our body. Divinity comes to us through our dreams, and it is a well that never dries up if we draw regularly from it. That artesian well penetrates all theologies, all dogmas, all religions; it dives straight down to the source waters of the healing, numinal Other. Dreams are the moist lubricant behind all living prayer, vision, and trance.

Jacob's ladder is a model of the ascent to and from that well's source water; to and from earthly and heavenly realms. The ancient mystics called this rhythm *descensus* and *ascensus*, descending and ascending into the depth realms of soul that abide in every living being. They often teach that usually—not always, but usually—this rhythm begins with a suffering descent: a job loss, a divorce, an illness, a death, or a failure can throw us into abysmal depth almost instantaneously. It feels like we cannot breathe that pained fire and live a moment longer, but then hints of the ever-hovering Divine touches her compassionate hand across our brow and breathes her sweet incense upon our troubled hearts. Her presence is often signaled by a deep, vivid, healing dream of breathtaking beauty and release. It is then that we can begin the ascent back to our everyday lives, lives that seem normal, but which have been subtly chastened, humbled, and directed toward greater compassion for self and others.

Jacob's ladder. One set of rungs climbs up the *via positiva*, the *kataphatic*: the ladder of logos, patriarchy, science, technology, know-how. Another set of rungs climbs down the *via negativa*, the *apaphatic*: the ladder of eros, matriarchy, art, spirituality, soul-passion. And the reliable, guiding metronome is the dream, the special image-talk of the Divine coaching us gently forward through the steeplechase of life toward the realization of our full destiny and destination. We are destined to be the Pope, the King, the Queen of our unique soul-destiny.

Jewish mystics believe that the real text of the Torah is hidden between the lines. I generally feel this to be true about all things in life. The real juice is between the lines, between the walls. It is what anthropologist Victor Turner called the liminal realm of ritual, the space between ordinary and sacred time.[6] Before a community ritual is enacted, all is ordinary, everyday, uninitiated time. Everyone knows the right clothes to wear, the politically correct things to say, the right gestures of social decorum. Once the community enters the ritual space, however, liminal time takes over. Everyone is naked or ritually clothed. All talk is sacredly magnificent or mundanely burlesque. It is absolutely dark or blindingly light. The soul is provoked and transported to other realms of terror and beauty. The person emerges transformed. The old social decorum is reestablished, but the liminally affected see the subtle richness of things that they missed before. This liminal space is also often taboo space. It is dangerous to see the hidden, shadow side of things. It is nice when life is kept in strict, clear categories of male–female, light–dark, hot–cold, moist–dry, parent–child, eros–logos, good–evil. There is comfort in the boundaries even if there is a gnawing dualism to it all. We would like to have things be seamlessly whole, but we know that's not the way this messy world is, so instead we attempt to keep things stringently separated.

> *A patient arrives at early retirement feeling frozen, almost bereft. She despairs that she has no vision of what or where to move next in her life. An accomplished professional with years of exemplary clinical and academic service, she had engaged in a rigorous and contemplative training in the last several decades of her life. In a recent multi-day meditation event, she had a vision of a ceremonial teapot full of a special blend of sacramental tea. In her vision, she intentionally breaks the ancient pot and watches its rare and sacred tea spill out on the floor. She says to the stunned community witnesses: "I guess now we must fill each other's cups with love."*

In my early adolescence, I was once taken by my father to spend several weekends with one of his academic archeology friends to dig in ancient Amerindian burial grounds. On one such project, they had found the burial sites of people of high status. In the same quadrant of each grave, there had been a broken cup. Over simmering cups of vesper coffee served at the end of that cool fall day, the archeologist—a kind, professorial type—discussed his wonderings about their significance. He surmised that they might be symbols of this world, the container of this fretted life that needed to be broken in order to spill over into the broader richness of the worlds after death. Perhaps this could be a guiding image for my client— an indication that she needs to break the restraining container of her past

6. Turner, *Ritual Process.*

7

accomplishments and spill into the broader missions and destinies awaiting her life journey now.

Life is full of such destiny-inspired, vessel-breaking encounters. As a graduate student in Boston, I remember walking toward my homeward-bound bus stop on a back street of Harvard Square on a cold night in a driving Nor'easter rain. I clumsily bumped into an older man who was staring up at the rapidly clearing skies and the stunning constellations they revealed. "Do you know your astronomy?" he asked me cheerily. I had to admit I had next to no astronomy chops. He replied, "Well, we have to start remedying that right now." With that, he began an elegant, intriguing tale of spun science and myth about the part of the night sky gleaming most vividly down on us in that moment. The intimacy and intensity of this sudden encounter swept us both up into a rich stranger-Eros bonding. He asked if I had a partner, and I said I was married. He asked if I liked spaghetti; I said, "Yes." "Well then," he said, "you must come to my home this weekend to sup with me and my wife." He gave me the address, and the evening was mutually engaged.

We arrived at the appointed spot the next Saturday night. It was an elegant three-story brownstone. After ringing the bell and hearing the muffled steps descending a carpeted stairwell, a beautiful, round-faced crone woman beamed at us from the slowly opened door. She hugged us both, hung our coats on the door, and led us up the spiral stairs past images of a grinning, mischievous monkey that looked vaguely familiar. At the top was a framed Life Magazine-esque image of a man with the caption, "H. A. Rey, Creator of Curious George." That face belonged to my astronomer. I was having dinner with the noted children's book writer and his beloved partner.

The dinner was tastefully simple. My partner and I were enchanted by these two genial souls' ease, grace, intelligence, and lightness-of-being. Jewish, they had met in wartime Paris, right before the arrival of the Nazis. Friends had smuggled them south toward one of the last open ports in Europe. Enroute, their connection deepened. They told of making love in haystacks, watching bursts of almost celestial flame occasionally punctuate the deep, dark, sensual night. "God help us, it was so crystalline, so beautiful," my new friend said as both he and his partner blinked back tears. "Of course, we knew they were exploding planes, the last of the French Air Force, but we couldn't help ourselves. Death gave out such luster as we made love and got lost in our earthen reverie."

My partner and I moved to the middle of the country soon thereafter, and I never saw them again. But that night had changed something deep in me. It gave me a new myth by which to juggle my inner constellations of beauty and death whenever they appeared; it gave me a new register of soul, a new compass by which to guide my life. My youthful vessel lay broken on their floor, and my soul-tea spilled out into the wider embrace of their warm, elderly hospitality and consciousness. It was a liminal night to remember.

Liminality is like the portal of a Monet painting. It is *Impression Sunrise* [multiple images available with online web search]. The canvas on the wall eerily insinuates itself into the room and softens the edges on things, on reality, and, like damp fog, seeps into the marrow of your being and fills you in equal parts with dread and beauty, awe and soul.

Liminality is also the portal at the other end of our day: sunset. The poet Rilke correctly understood in a poem titled *Sunset* [multiple translations available with online web search] that such moments leave us between worlds, between heaven and earth, between the temporal and the eternal; lead us to another world that is unique, an authentic world of raw personal and collective essence.

Liminal space is collective space as urgently as it is private space; cosmic as much as psychic. It is *La Frontera*, the gringo-feared, guilt-saturated artificial "border" between the United States and Mexico. The terror of "illegal immigrants" flooding across the southern borders of the United States is as much a terror of surrendering to liminal flooding and the awakening of long-buried collective and individual terrors as it is an objective fear of actual "illegal aliens." It is the liminal alien "other" that is most feared and, yet, in the depressive Diaspora of our consumerist culture, most desired as our cook, our landscaper, our assembly-line worker, our fruit harvester. It is the alien other *within* as well, that unacknowledged other whom we repress and dissociate, and yet whose imprisoned resentment fuels our frantic—even frenzied—journey through life.

America is one of history's most gracious and democratic cultures. It is also one of history's most violent and oppressive cultures. The alien other is the long repressed and cruelly sold slave off the auction block in Savannah, the massacred Ghost Dancer at Wounded Knee, the slaughtered miner at Matawan, and the beheaded migrant at our border. Liminal zones awaken first the shadow of past and current crimes, psychic and physical, that plead for confession and remorse. Only then can the full peace and restoration of the liminal gods soothe our fretted brows and hearts. The liminal emerges in the fluid, post-institutional world we live in. It won't come from the past, from collective arousals of unconscious, anxious dogma turned into crusade or pogrom. It will come in authentically lived individual experience compassionately shared with others in similar authentic, soulful self-reception.

For liminality is a confessional zone. Jung suggests that the unconscious most often presents as a Shadow Portal, a doorway into un-recanted sin (any inauthentic, dissociated, being-wounding act). Like Dante's *Divine Comedy* journey, the way to the light is through the dark, through hell to the heavens. This axiom is as true for cultures as it is for individuals. Recall any global, liminal event in recent years and you can palpably recall the confessional aspect of it. John Kennedy's horse-drawn cortege somberly hoofing down Pennsylvania Avenue as we mutely grieved, fresh witnesses to the seemingly unending appetite in our national soul for collective and individual violence. We wept for him, we wept for us. Our tears stung confessional lips and tongues. Or the New York pilgrims in the endlessly falling Twin Towers of 9/11—silent refugees shuffling disconsolately across the George Washington and Brooklyn Bridges. For a while, we were a more sorrowfully accessible people, more soulfully pliant and extending of mercy. For a while. An abrupt and all-too-short while.

Analysis is a space and time confessional capsule hovering between worlds at such moments of urgent arousal. It is a capsule of reflection and witnessing, where we can regain lost bearings and reorient ourselves to lost polar stars and certainties. I have visited several monasteries that are only available at low tide. During high tide, they are surrounded and enclosed—contemplative wombs. They see the outer world but are untouched by it, unavailable to it, less exposed to its unbuffered, violent rawness. Analysis is such a tidal monastery, a liminal space approached only at the right, authentic moment.

The ancient Celts believed that the portals to the liminal isles were those very thin places that appear unexpectedly in our lives, like the collective traumas described above or that accompany the poetic moments of deep, sorrowful beauty—like a sunrise or sunset on a glowing Alpine mountain summit. The liminal is very thin, but it is also as wide as a cosmos. It is surface and depth. It is much more than skin deep, but it has the translucence of baby and elder skin. It is the soul under the surface.

The liminal is pure being itself. A state as much as it is a place or time. It is a state both dynamic and static; it flows and it pools. It is Presence. It embraces as much as it is embraced. And as many of the metaphoric references above indicate, it is the very earth itself. Our terrestrial home is the Liminal-One-and-the-Many; it is Self. The animated *essence* of Earth, its Gaia spirit, is the liminal "Other." Like the Ancestor-Crone Tree at the narrative climactic core of James Cameron's epic film *Avatar* (2010), the Earth-liminal channels us through Her rooted, molten being into the very root and core of the Cosmos Being itself.

And this Gaia spirit, this Earth-Other, highlights an essential aspect of liminal reality. The liminal is the motherboard, the master chip of the numinal Other. It is the vibrating media of numinality—that subtle membrane of exchange between human and divine experience. The liminal opens us up, sometimes tears us open, to the interior foundational resonance and registers of existence:

> Jung's theoretical understanding of religion makes of the analytic process a religious event. It recalls the Gods to their psychic origin and encourages unmediated conversation with them within the containment of the psyche. The analytic process thus understood is currently to be valued for a number of reasons. The internalization of divinity curtails enmity between religious communities bonded by external Gods. More than this, Jung's total myth contends that divinity can become conscious only in humanity. The education and redemption of God in history is an ongoing project. Currently it takes the form of an emerging myth of an extended compassion whose embrace supplants still reigning myths of lesser compass. The analytic process, though confined, in the first instance, to individuals, is a significant contributor to the now emerging societal myth.[7]

This book and the lifelong clinical enterprise from which it arises is not offered as a dilettante, scholarly hors d'oeuvre. It is a serious attempt at describing the essential element of the animating essence of consciousness—and therefore life itself—both personal and collective. Liminality locates the soul in each of us, in all living beings. And this soul is the locator beacon that receives and beams back communiques with the animating divinity of the universe. Seen this way, the soul in each of us and in all living cultural and collective endeavor is a part of the originary energy that

7. Dourley, "On the Recall of the Gods," 43.

launched the Big Bang that created the universe; it is part of the originary soul that imagined the universe into being:

> Hadewijch [a medieval mystic woman] is innovative in that her experience points to the pre-existence of the soul in eternity. It engages what McGinn describes as a form of Christian Platonic exemplarism in which the individual participates naturally and experientially within time in one's divinely grounded exemplar in eternity . . . .
>
> In this Platonic context, spiritual and psychological maturity come into coincidence. The telos of both is then to recover as a finite human in time, space and history one's native, eternal and essential truth as the ultimate meaning of one's life and contribution to history's advancement.[8]

When we sit in the liminal, when we awaken in the liminal and stay awake in the liminal, we participate in original time that is here and there and everywhere. The liminal is the ultimate factory that birthed relativity and quantum mechanics. In this effort, the liminal is both a dimension and an "exemplar," a Platonic Guide into the navigating and integrating of liminal realms.[9]

The liminal activates communication, connection, and cooperation between the human and Divine in creation's ongoing trajectory. That's why there has always been an urgent hunger in human experience for the mysterious and its sacramental constellations. In such places there is a ritual translator that shuttles key information back and forth about this core co-authored creation project. As Cicero so eloquently described it millennia ago:

> Much that is excellent and divine does Athens seem to me to have produced and added to our life, but nothing better than those Mysteries by which we are formed and molded from a rude and savage state of humanity; and, indeed, in the Mysteries we perceive the real principles of life, and learn not only to live happily, but to die with a fairer hope.[10]

Yes, these are mercurial, shape-shifting terms—as mercurial as the phenomena they attempt to describe for our frail human understandings. For me, the liminal is the container, the numinous, the content of

8. Dourley, *Jung and his Mystics*, 61.

9. Dourley, *Jung and his Mystics*, 61.

10. Cicero, *On the Laws*.

the Divine Other addressing human consciousness. Call it prayer, trance, vision, synchronicity—there is a place between our time and space where the gods do come to parley with us human critters.

And, yes, "numinal." I do like to coin words, play with words, give language plasticity like the unconscious it comes from. I also like the metaphor of the "fluid" matrix. It smacks of amniotic liquids and midwifery—therapy as a place where solids go into suspension. Or liquids become solid. It's the place where the substantial and the ethereal come into dialogue and recognize the world they co-create. Therapy seeks to heal this wounding duality in both the body and the psyche, the individual and the collective unconscious. It performs this alchemy in the numinal, liminal depths of the soul where the heavens are reclaimed and beauty restored.

> *A client dreams of heading out on a journey with her husband. It begins in a huge sailing ship. When they arrive at the pier, the ship is lying on its side in the water and has to be hoisted upright until the mast is erect. The mast is quite tall. They get on, eager for the sail, and go out to the open sea. It feels like the Atlantic Ocean. Suddenly, the ship becomes a space shuttle and launches upward toward the night sky, and soon they find themselves hovering there in the midst of the galaxy. The stars feel brilliant and close, and they just savor the stunning beauty of the experience.*

All true psychotherapies are liminal psychotherapies. This is true of all depth spiritual, sacramental, educational, artistic, travel, relational, or political events. Because all these events bore down into the psyche at the core of our individual and collective experience:

> Because the psyche is a vehicle for the experience of the numinosum, and the personality is profoundly affected by archetypal processes, conscious development of the personality becomes a spiritual journey in its own right.[11]

I once visited an archeological museum in Northern Greece. In their collection, they held what they reasonably thought to be the mummy of Phillip, father of Alexander the Great. His mummy had been discovered in a recent excavation of an unexplored mound, its interior found intact exactly as when he had been buried nearly three millennia ago.

One artifact was especially arresting: a giant bronze vase with two exquisitely carved handles. The handles were the two sides of the

---

11. Corbett, *Sacred Cauldron*, 116.

Ariadne-Theseus myth. This is the ancient story of the Athenian youth Theseus, one of the annual clutch of youth sent as never-to-return tribute to the
Cretan King. In an almost impossibly heroic act, Theseus slays the devouring minotaur residing at the core of an ominous underground labyrinth. It
would not have been possible but for the love of Ariadne, daughter of the
Cretan King, who had given Theseus her magic thread to unwind behind
him in the labyrinth to guide his return. Theseus returned Ariadne's loving
devotion with a marriage vow, but his vow only lasted part way through
the voyage back to Athens. He abandoned her on a lonely isle so that he
could continue broadcasting his young man's seed in the wide, wide world
beyond.

On one side of the burial urn, the tragically abandoned Ariadne sits
in abject grief on the remote island where her fickle husband deposited her
once his love blush dissipated. Although it was she who gave him the key
empowering intelligence (the secrets of the labyrinth) and the tools (the
unspooled thread to mark the way in and out) to slay the minotaur, his
patriarchal heart soon lost its ardor, gratitude, and integrity; she was set
adrift in tragically bereft circumstances. Her grinding, grieving abandonment moves the god Dionysos, who witnesses it from the handle of this
vase. Above and beyond Ariadne's human awareness, he is touched to his
numinal, divine core by this very human sorrow. It is a constellated sorrow that provokes an eros of profound depth. He loves this worthy woman
because of her worthy grief. She had loved with an authentic depth and
commitment and had not been met by a similar authentic depth and commitment. Her reaction is not an annihilating warrior rage, but a burrowing
earth-poet sorrow. She makes tears not wars; she weeps not warriors.

And her sorrow is received and responded to. Something happens
as the journey continues around the vase lid and to the other handle. For
there, she has heard or felt the stirring presence of the Other. She looks
up and into the eyes of her loving witness, and both are consumed in the
transforming fire of genuine love. Love born of the fragility of beauty, existence, truth, decency, and goodness. And they bask ecstatically in that fire.
This liminal, primal eros moment stood frozen in elegant bronze for three
thousand years at the foot of Phillip's mummy.

This book explores these liminal moments. It outlines three broad
terrains where spottings of such wild liminal beasts have been frequently
reported—pilgrimage, the arts, and politics. This book will explore, theo-
retically and clinically, personally and professionally, how to invite and

evoke liminal-numinal space. It will then discuss how to non-anxiously stay awake in its precincts and healingly interact with its archetypal energies. For liminal-numinal realms are dangerous realms. Liminality lies close to the core secrets of successful living and dying. The liminal is the All. And that All is abyss. It is enigma. It is empty. As much, perhaps more, the liminal-numinal-archetypal is beauty, meaning, vision.

> Liminality is pure potency, where anything can happen .... Where the elements, the basic building blocks of culture . . . are released from their customary configurations and recombined in often bizarre and terrifying imagery .... [12]

Although intensely personal, analysis and its potential individuations do not happen outside of the collective. This book assumes analysis is as much a public event (though a special, respectful, and contained form of public event) as a private one, and that analysis is a political event. It is a pilgrimage. It is an aesthetic experience. It is a sacrament. It is a child of communal, liminal reality, for pilgrimage, the arts, and sacrament are as much collective as individual moments. This book, then, will also explore these essential planetary dimensions of analytic enactments. As Thomas Moore writes, "There is no way to re-enchant our lives in a disenchanted culture except by becoming renegades from that culture and planting the seeds for a new one." [13]

SOME FLUID DEFINITIONS AND DESCRIPTIONS OF THE LIMINAL

Who looks outside, dreams. Who looks inside, awakens.

—C. G. JUNG [14]

A colleague once asked me where I learned about depth realms, about this "liminal stuff." My answer was swift and sure: over every hour, every moment of 16 years of personal analysis, a new revelation grabbed me, sucked me down, gnawed at my innards, and spit me back up into the conscious world of light and air. And after each harrowing descent, I felt cleaner,

---

12. Turner, "Myth and Symbol," 579.

13. Moore, *Re-Enchantment of Everyday Life*, 381.

14. Jung, "Spiritual Problem of Modern Man," 61.

leaner, and more certain upon my return. But analysis did not set me free until it put me through the wringer—the ontological soul wringer.

The liminal is ontological lubricant. It makes the moisture of a fully realized being possible. It can be imagined as the spatial-temporal realm between the worlds of conscious and unconscious, sacred and profane. It is the lubricating fluid between these realities, making it possible for them to be connected without grinding bone on bone so that they both can inhabit the same body of being. If there is an evolutionary trajectory, an arch of energetics moving through both the physical and existential cosmos toward a dynamic endpoint of penultimate meaning and fulfillment, then the liminal is the synthesis agent, the catalyzing psychic fluid that permits their moist cooperation. It is both the place and the moment where the oppositional tensions that drive the engines of the cosmos come to meaning-making repose and suspension.

There are two imagistic platforms that help us grasp the workings of this liminal integrator in our midst. On the individual level, it is the *Unus Mundus*, the *one world* of the medieval mystics, where we feel individually implicated in the inner workings of life and claimed by that same life force. When we are in communion with the *Unus Mundus*, we know we belong. Our existence is ratified. This belonging becomes a vividly felt sense at those synchronistic dream moments where the dangling morass of our life's jangled wirings seem suddenly to fire at the same ecstatic moment. It is the breakthrough moment in a protracted psychoanalysis. It is the deep serenity that infuses a moment of sacramental ritual.

On the collective level, it is the *Anima Mundi*, Plato's *world spirit*. It is those moments where we seem profoundly and peacefully engaged with the whole cosmos. It is one of the wordless moments of connective reverie that comes from a vesper sense of awe before a twilight mountain landscape or in the aching operatic aria of a soprano lost in the deep soul of her vocal rendering. It is the deep sorrow that a monumental collective trauma invokes in each of us after a 9/11 or the death of a beloved Martin Luther King, Jr.

In the West, a leading library of process, image, and memory regarding how to successfully enter and return from liminal realms is the *cura animarum* ("care of souls") tradition.[15] Probably, its archaic roots formed in the ancient paleolithic shrines of image, like Lascaux or Altimira. Of

---

15. Clebsch and Jaekle, *Pastoral Care in Historical Perspective*; Woods, *Mysterion: An Approach to Mystical Spirituality*.

shamanic origins, this soul care tradition was birthed by the psycho-spiritual creatives of intuitive genius who forged the first image-frames painted and carved on cave walls through which to perceive and then recognize the numinal worlds and the guiding divinities of the liminal.

These cave-journaled experiences of the liminal ignited the human imagination. No one can ever be certain about the significance of these paleolithic icons, but I have an increasingly certain, feeling-informed presumption about these precious masterpieces. The images at Lascaux were the first theological reflections in image. They recorded and amplified this initial experience in stone-engraved intaglios of haunting beauty and resonating fascination. Encounter with the Primal Awe at the heart of the cosmos incited an urgency to create, to repeat, to reflect, and to preserve such destiny-marked moments. The process of this effort to record revelatory events became the originating technology at the core of the *cura animarum*, the first healing ceremonies and sacraments designed for the living experience of deep healing and the profound widening of psycho-spiritual horizons that was produced through first-contact with the enveloping liminal otherness.

Near the beginning of Stanley Kubrick's classic film, *2001: A Space Odyssey*, two Neanderthal giants battle to the death with broken jawbone weapons. Their annihilatory, all-consuming violence shrouds the screen in horror until a moment of stillness fills the frame, a hushed sense of the arrival of the uncanny fills cinema surface and audience breath. A gunmetal grey monolith emerges out of the earth accompanied by electronic, roaring monotone. The liminal has arrived. Nothing to do but drop your weapons and retreat to the clan cave to sketch the moment in earth-toned ochre and mineral-based pastels. Sketch until the spell is broken and embodied wordlessly into the soul depths that receive all such events in individual and collective human experience. The *cura animarum* was birthed in myriad episodes of original contact; glimpses into the mystery of the *Tremendum*. Such moments abound all around our carefully ordered contemporary gardens of denial and refuge.

The liminal zone of being is as old as the visionary paleolithic caves of Lascaux. It is anywhere and anytime the life force awakens and is aware that there is the reality of this moment; what the ancient Greeks called Chronos time (the origin of our chronological, clock time), and its unsettling dissociation or disjuncture from a wider horizon of being, Kairos time (numinous time, time of the gods). Liminal time resides as a portal in the ruptured Great Empty Space of Kairos.

This book wants to reside as a witness and chronicler of this liminal portal. Its narrative observations will be part clinical, part philosophical, part theological, part aesthetic. But, hopefully, all poesy. All heart. It has an urgent tone. Time is precious. Both as individuals and as a species, we are going somewhere important. And we are in real danger of missing our train and not getting where we were supposed to be. Yes, this book assumes that there is a place we are supposed to get to, both individually and collectively as a species. It assumes that there is an individual and corporate destiny; the achievement of that destiny is the central fueling engine of existence for us as persons and as a species.

> It has been said that animals "live in the present" and don't fret about the future. But all these exertions and strivings and migrations are about getting somewhere you will need to be. Mating and raising young are future-focused. DNA itself is blueprint for something that will be built. All life recognizes time. And that *this* moment—is already gone . . . . The philosophers whose thinking is imprinted in our thinking largely rejected the future. Future people posed no concern because of their "remoteness," "incapacity," "non-actuality," and "indeterminacy." Easy for those philosophers to say, but from where we sit now—local, capacitated, actual and determined—they appear wrong on all points. Yet we indulge the same fallacy, granting ourselves the same clemencies. And that's the problem, because the future—and all those people—arrives daily.[16]

Liminality is always a portal between worlds, between different experiential realities. There are many sacramental portals, some active, many passive, into these liminal places. Take, for example, this whimsical partial list of what can trigger a liminal doorway:

---

16. Safina, *View from Lazy Point*, 47–48.

- Beauty
- Trauma
- Politics
- Pilgrimage
- Seasons
- The moon
- Sunset/sunrise
- National parks
- Jazz
- Blues
- Love
- Hate
- War
- Birth
- Violence
- Comedy
- Tosca
- Death
- Tragedy

While this list is whimsical, the reality is deadly serious. Without regular individual and collective commerce across such portals, human—and maybe *all*—existence would be threatened with extinction. Only when ordinary and extraordinary, immanent and transcendent are devotedly served and placed in dialogue with each other is the urgent, primally necessary yeasting of creation fulfilled. This flat, limited, deterministic human world meets an eternally plastic, open, numinal world. In the liminal realm, the immanent and transcendent are both within and beyond.

This alchemy of process is most profoundly activated in human suffering, the suffering that necessitates depth psycho-spiritual methodologies like Jungian psychology for its healing uncoverings and wonderings. It is a paradoxical enterprise that defies rational understandings—a painful paradoxical truth that only the mysteries of liminality can anneal. This is what many of the ancients discovered and relayed to us about their personal experiences of consolation and consolidation at the breast of such mystical experiences as could be found at an Eleusis or Delphi. This is the paradox of the unconscious, of this world, of depth, transformative suffering: our "Immanent . . . godhead achieving realization in actual experience." The deterministic "ontic" becomes the mystical "ontological." As James Grotstein wrote, "relativism, intersubjectivity, and the ineffable" become the authentic rhetoric of authentic being.[17]

And these portals all evolve from certain central phenomena that seem to contain and constellate the liminal event and experience itself. The liminal requires numinal portals. It needs places of access to and from our world. Bottom line: No liminal, no numinous. No numinous, no transformation.

The Korean multimedia artist Do Ho Suh created a piece for the Seattle Art Museum's 2011 exhibition, *Luminous: The Art of Asia*. It depicts a portal in a garden wall recreated from his parent's home in Seoul. The sky changes color and tone with the sun's daytime arc across the sky and the moon's nighttime glimmer. The gate seems to be made of marble at one moment, parchment paper the next. Then, a fluttering and flocking flush of crows swoops and preens in cacophonous medley; they rush in a dense pack through the portal. Beyond, all is silence. Then they come rushing back as I cover my eyes to avoid their jabbing claws and wings. Silence again. Little patters. Hooves. Deer hooves clattering as they race back and forth against and on the garden wall. Silence. Plum blossoms on stark moonlit stems. Flocking crows again and then little Asian angel Putti carrying cryptic Kangi banners across twilight skies. Silence. A broad palette of affective pastels from crying crow dread to plum orchid ecstasy. Thus, the liminal frames the empty, pregnant place between worlds.

> *Our notion of emptiness is quite different in the East. The void is not empty or bleak, but charged with meaning.*

—Do Ho Suh (2011)

Luminous indeed. Liminal. This is the portal between East and West, conscious and unconscious, human and nature, human and Divine. It is such portals, their discovery and their traversing, that fulfill a life—or empty and destroy it. Memory and anticipation, ancestor and descendent,

---

17. Grotstein, *Beam of Intense Darkness*, 122–23.

past and future meet and engage each other, fulfill each other, transform each other.

Liminality escapes specificity, it is perceived in the traces of mood, reverie, and memory with which it scents everyday Chronos consciousness. So, let's explore some of these evocative fragrances.

A. THE LIMINAL PORTAL AS A NUMINAL PORTAL

The intimacy Jungian psychology establishes between theory and therapy is particularly prominent in matters religious. Jung's greatly extended sense of religion rests on the unmediated experience of the numinous working ever more intense patterns of personal integration and universal relatedness. The experience of the numinous also lies at the heart of Jungian therapeutic practice . . . . In effect the analysis becomes a personal revelation of the individual's unique myth, originating, in Jung's view, from the same source that gives rise to all religions, namely, the archetypal dimension of the psyche.[18]

This book respects a classic recipe for effective and influential psychology, a recipe whose primary ingredients are artful theory and artful application. But they should be theories and applications that are not reductionist or positivist, but pragmatically mystical. They should advocate a mystical liminality that is core to a fully engaged psychology—both as individual therapy and healing and as cultural therapy and healing. This book believes the liminal reality is all around us, though it is often invisible to the manifest world. It is anywhere that numinally charged experiences touch us and/or the collective. I agree with Wolfgang Giergerich in believing that the "soul" is a phenomenon beyond the defining embrasure of science or logos—it is a mood canvas that absorbs all the affective and cognitive colors of being into an affective-imagistic wholeness.[19]

Immauel Kant initially discoursed these paradoxical yet overlapping realms of phenomenal and numinal experience in our human perceptions. He clearly enunciated the Enlightenment era dualist dilemma, the splitting of knowledge. Science and religion were cut apart. Scientists live in the phenomenal world and mystics live in the numinal. Jungian psychology arrived a century ago as a discipline of an accelerating variety of creative endeavors. It attempts a meaningful re-connection of these split-asunder

18. Dourley, "Jung and the Recall of the Gods," 43–53.
19. Giergerich, "Disenchantment Complex: C.G. Jung and the Modern World."

realities. Science and religion can once again be cooperative handmaidens of creation. The liminal is their place of meeting, engagement, and love making. A Jungian understanding of the liminal sees that science and religion both live in the same world of interactive and co-participatory phenomena and noumena. As Susan Rowland puts it, "Phenomena are those objects existing in time and space, while noumena can only be objects of belief."[20] Our whole inner and outer lives are bathed and informed by both calculuses of experience.

But of late there has been a disheartening movement in analytical psychology to split them apart again, even to ban the mystical from its official discourse of method and practice. Such thinking forgets that, at heart, analytical psychology is a poetic discipline serving liminal deities. The liminal is very thin, but it is also as wide as a cosmos. It is surface and depth. It is the soul under the skin. We contact and connect with this poetic essence or we die—individually and collectively, metaphorically and, ultimately, literally. Extinction is the price exacted for abandonment of our liminal core.

Therefore, liminality is really a process of psycho-theology:

> Throughout the whole philosophy of Ideas there is a certain conception of duration, as also of the relation of time to eternity. [S]he who installs [her]himself in becoming sees in duration the very life of things, the fundamental reality. The Forms, which the mind isolates and stores up in concepts, are then only snapshots of the changing reality. They are moments gathered along the course of time; and, just because we have cut the thread that binds them to time, they no longer endure. They tend to withdraw into their own definition, that is to say, into the artificial reconstruction and symbolical expression which is their intellectual equivalent. They enter into eternity, if you will; but what is eternal in them is just what is unreal. On the contrary, if we treat becoming by the cinematographical method, the Forms are no longer snapshots taken of the change, they are its constitutive elements, they represent all that is positive in Becoming. Eternity no longer hovers over time, as an abstraction; it underlies time, as a reality. Such is exactly, on this point, the attitude of the philosophy of Forms or Ideas. It establishes between eternity and time the same relation as between a piece of gold and the small change—change so small that payment goes on forever without the debt being paid off. The debt could be paid at once with the piece of gold. It is this that Plato expresses in his magnificent language when he says that

20. Rowland, *Jung: A Feminist Revision*, 6.

God, unable to make the world eternal, gave it Time, "a moving image of eternity."[21]

The nineteenth century re-discovered this liminal garden in their birthing of modern anthropological sciences. In this budding discipline, there was an almost romantic fascination with "primitivity" and its ritual, ceremonial collapsing of the tensions of ordinary and extraordinary time. In his hallmark *Rites of Passage* (1909), the French ethnologist Arnold Van Gennep discerned a pattern to the ritual data from the growing hoard of anthropological field research emerging out of the study of indigenous peoples in Europe's vast and often oppressed colonial holdings. In all instances, he noted a process of liminal movement in ceremonial orchestrations. There were three distinct stages: pre-liminal, liminal (*liminaire*), and post-liminal. It was in the liminal phase that the artificial disengagement of sacred and profane time is merged and integrated, the impact lasting for both the ceremonially transformed individual and their surrounding society. Van Gennep had a biased hierarchical assumption to his model, scaling Western society at the more secular-time-dominated top end of the continuum and the "semi-civilized" primitive society at the bottom end, as more sacred-time dominated.[22] But in his work there is palpable, almost romantic yearning for the bottom's more embedded relationship to sacred time, despite a parallel pride and arrogance at being enfolded in the Victorian Enlightenment's secular, omniscient perspective. Jung shared a similar yearning:

> You are quite right; the main interest of my work is not concerned with the treatment of neuroses but rather with the approach to the numinous. But the fact is that the approach to the numinous is the real therapy and inasmuch as you attain to the numinous experiences you are released from the curse of pathology. Even the very disease takes on a numinous character.[23]

A central aspect of the turn-of-the-last-century era of social science was its secularist fascination with esoteric spiritual experience. In a highly rationalist, Victorian academic culture increasingly denuded of overt religious affirmation, there was an almost chic undercurrent of absorption

21. Bergson, *Creative Evolution*, 317–18.

22. Van Gennep, *Rites of Passage*.

23. Jung [selected and edited by Gerhard Adler], *Letters of C. G. Jung: Volume I, 1906–1950*, 377.

with things psychic and other worldly. There were parlor psychic readers, as well as group visitations to tarot readers and mistresses of the Ouija board. William James published his classic and still eminently readable *Varieties of Religious Experience* in the same turn-of-the-century corridor that Freud published his seminal *The Interpretation of Dreams*—a richly cadenced exploration of the mysteries of dream and the night in both personal and collective realms (his quality prose-work ultimately garnered him the Goethe prize in literature). The new hybrid discipline—psychology of religion—exploded across Europe and North America.

The ligamental bond of this undercurrent was a fascination with the numinal worlds—with the realm of animated experience beyond the everyday and the ordinary. With institutional religion increasingly held in suspicion, there was broad recognition that something else beyond conscious event and moment did exist, and that it had a charged impact and interaction with our phenomenal time and space. The infant social sciences of anthropology, ethnology, and psychology provided just the legitimizing lens through which to safely pursue this numinal fascination without it being invalidated as an activity of discredited and outdated religious devotion. Jung increasingly plunged into the deepest thicket of this burgeoning cross discipline of the numinous.

And the numinous is about the mystery and centrality of the Other, whatever or whoever this Other may be. A current and growing consensus of the philosophical bedrock underlying psychotherapeutic process (the foundational psycho-theology of humanness if you will) is the primordial importance of the Other where the "the responsibility for, and obligation to, the Other are absolute."[24]

I had a patient who built and used a chicken tractor. It was a chicken shed on wheels that could be moved from one part of the garden to the other, leaving its soil-building, fecal gifts behind. Each piece of accomplished individuation, internal and relational, is a piece of our inner psychic pasture, whose soil is enriched by the droppings of released, cathartic affects closely held for too long. The liminal, numinal Other comes to us from our accumulated efforts after consciousness and the wisdom of our ancestors. That is why anthropology is so deeply appealing; we are attracted to the living traces of this effort after consciousness in the ritual artifacts, artwork, and daily survival objects the ancestors left us. Jung lived through this anthropological heyday. It was the very air of the helping professions in his

24. Marcus, *In Search of the Good Life*, xv.

era. Comparative religion, psychology of religion, mythology, linguistics, semiotics—all these disciplines exerted a companionate renaissance of craft that fueled each other's frenzy of discovery.

There was an imperial tone to this literature, as though it were written from the heights of an academic Olympus. Its condescending bias infected even Jung's early narratives. But, even within this paternalistic frame, there was a genuine soul-stirring fascination with the mysterion of indigenous ritual and transformations in Jung and in this bourgeoning *fin de siècle* social science literature. And as both Jung and that literature aged and matured through the twentieth century, the tone became humbler and appropriately tentative.

In the second half of the twentieth century, it was an American couple, Edith and Victor Turner, who returned liminal studies to the indigenous ground from which the fertile notion sprang. They revived Van Gennep's earlier framework and grounded it in breathtaking field research of vanishing primal rituals in central Africa. Concurrent with their anthropological field research, a generation of Jungian analysts were deepening their intrigue into the liminal dimensions of the analytic craft. Joseph Henderson wrote his classic initiatory text, *Thresholds of Initiation*, in 1969. Donald Sandner, always and essentially interested in "the workings of the soul," studied with Navajo Beauty Way Shamans and Balinese trance dancers, aware of the soul's propensity to fully constellate only in the temenos of liminal ceremonial practice—like analysis at its best.[25] These analysts soon discovered the Turners's work, and the field of Jungian analysis was set on fire.

The contemporary liminal conversation circles around all things postmodern. Theorists of the postmodern talk of the "more real thing": the real non-essentialist, non-patriarchal, non-universal thing showing up in the gap between modern and postmodern. This postmodern epistemology is both a novel way of explaining and navigating the western world's dualist divide and a reinvention of an ancient understanding about the ultimate insufficiency of everyday, pedestrian ways of organizing our ordinary and extraordinary experience. It seeks to provide a meaningful connection to our overall sense of meaning and destiny within our lives and being. The liminal hides in the closet of both modern and postmodern philosophies of being; it suffuses and energizes these different phenomenological ways of organizing experience.

25. Sandner, personal sharing, 1991.

I once had a graduate school professor who said you could walk down any humanities or divinities department faculty hallway, stick your head in any door, and ask, "Plato or Aristotle?" You'd get a quick reply. Plato's ideal, eternal forms or Aristotle's secular, sensory taxonomies; Plato's essential contents or Aristotle's fundamental structures. Ask, and you'd get a clear preference. The academy has been organized by this dialogue for nearly three millennia.

We all gravitate to one end of this schema or the other. I am a Plato-forms person myself—the magic of the implicit, animate structure of being is there from the beginning. Our experiments and experiences after consciousness are the filled-out content. Take, for example, the core American democratic notion of fulfilling the will of the people. The will is obviously an abstract visionary construct that only becomes tangibly and percepti-bly recognized and realized in often maddeningly cross-purposeful acts of enacted willing. In true Jungian fashion, I value the opposite pole's con-tribution to the full, rounded, whole truth of things, as well. But we must humbly respect the shadow of our bias. With me, this means a life-long and gentle expansion of Aristotelian concreteness into my originally grand-but-shallow understandings that were filled with an intuitive and often quite sloppy, giddy expansiveness. As Jung wrote, "spiritually the Western world is in a precarious situation, and the danger is greater the more we blind ourselves to the merciless truth with illusions about the beauty of soul."[26]

Both sides of this core philosophical-operational opposition in our dualist culture contribute to the liminal's essence. But alone, either pole is lifeless, devoid of the imagination-triggering animation of the liminal:

> There is a kind of truth in Descartes's claim that God arranges the interaction between the two sources of knowledge, because the phenomena of religious consciousness are known by means of a third source of knowledge that does mediate between the other two. We have primary access to spiritual and religious phenom-ena, neither through conceptual reason nor through sense data, but rather by means of a third source of knowledge. Between the sense perceptions and the intuitions or categories of the intellect there has remained a void. That which ought to have taken its place between the two, and which in other times and places did occupy this intermediate space, that is to say the Active Imagination, has been left to the poets.[27]

26. Jung, "Spiritual Problem of Modern Man," 89.
27. Cheetham, *All the World an Icon*, 17.

Hegel talks of *Aufheben,* the facility to lift up beyond the apparent contradictions and negations we encounter in this world. This is an excellent description of the paradox-resolving capacity of emersion in liminal time. Whether achieved by individuating analysis or mystical practice, one is transported beyond the maya, beyond the illusions of this world, to the true organic wholeness of seamless psychic Being that undergirds all existence. The kundalini snake has risen up the spiritual spine and burst through the crown chakra where heavens are merged with earths, the ground with the sky, the human with the Divine. At this liminal place and moment, as Echart says, God sees with our eyes, we with Hers.

> *A client dreams of tending to her wounded, eerily hard-headed baby. Then, holding the baby up in front of her, the child becomes a snake with a flowered head. We bask in the lovely Crown Chakra image effulgence. Her hard psychic work is moving deep individuating energy up her Destiny Spine.*

I once had a patient who came in with a numinal wheel dream. He was ascending a gentle mountain stream trail below a verdant slope. Just ahead of him, the wheel of a road bike whirled comfortably along. Suddenly, to his left, he noticed that the slope above was incredibly saturated with moisture. It was pouring unnervingly out from the rocks, trees, and tufts of grass. He became quite concerned that the slope could give way into an avalanche—burying him in its muddy mass.

Then, the scene shifted. He was descending from the mountains along another path. This time, his focus was not on the wheel still rolling gently ahead of him, but on the hub—an elegant silver marvel of graceful, simple, almost genius technology. The hub: a still center at the heart of a spokey, wondrous chorus of elegant round motion.

In a final scene, he was on a mountain ledge, inching forward despite an abysmal drop off to his left. A brash young man brushed thoughtlessly past him as his two buddies nonchalantly brought up the rear, chattering carelessly. He balked at the brazen young interloper and felt suddenly arrested in an attempt to correct his off-balance posture. "Oh, it's my backpack," he exclaimed to himself in the dream. "I'm out of here . . . " And he woke up.

It is all spheres, planetary wheels within wheels, a whole cosmos wheeling on to its planetary eschatology, its endpoint into another round of the Great Round. It is focusing on this endpoint that we keep our inner and outer balance in a precarious world that constantly threatens to bury us alive or hurl us into the abyss.

> *A client comes in with a screensaver picture of a three-year-old child in a thick Irish sweater. It is a picture of himself at the family home. He is holding a ukulele and his head is thrown back almost ecstatically as he strums out his soundless little tune. In a gentle, Dada-esque twist, a framed picture of him—smiling—at about the same age sits to the right of him on a 50s-era lampstand. There is a high-back sedan chair behind him, another lampstand to the left, an elegant little sugar bowl, and, most curious of all, in the right front field of the carpet, is a spool upended at a rakish angle. All five key inanimate objects in the dream—picture, sweater, sugar bowl, ukulele, spool—are punched out in lustrous white in the old black and white snapshot. As I deep-noticed these soulful details and their combined compositional ambience, the client was brought to immediate tears. He exclaimed in a broken voice, "Only here would someone notice that—we miss so much in everyday living."*

The liminal is that noticed, unacknowledged ancient beauty of sorrow and the dimensionality of existence. It is what therapy can do best if the frame is quietly and respectfully held. Liminality lives in between things. It warps and woofs two strands into a woven ontological tapestry that grounds and embodies meaning and essence. The Middle Ages would chart this oppositional divide as an apophatic (without speech, to deny, the negative way) and kataphatic (to speak, to affirm, the positive way) chasm through which the liminal would inhere, express, and guide. The list below outlines the way different contemporary therapy and healing models might find their efforts predominating on one side of this liminal chasm or the other; e.g., evidence-based interventions (kataphatic) seek science-informed procedures and medications (exoteric) to mindfully empty out behavior blocks or early psycho-sexual developmental barriers to growth. By contrast, depth-analytic treatments favor contemplative psycho-spiritual processes (apaphatic-esoteric) that enhance transformational connection to one's full-life destiny and meaning:

Kataphatic	Apophatic
Regressive	Progressive
Symptom	Symbol
Sexual	Spiritual
Stoic	Platonic
Sealed	Permeous
Empty Contents	Fill Contents
Malevolent	Benevolent
Deception	Revelation
Reduction	Amplification
Adjustment	Transformation
Brief Therapy	Long-term Therapy
Unconscious	Conscious
Behavior	Insight
Exoteric	Esoteric
Via Positiva	Via Negativa

As already mentioned, the liminal portal is actually a bridge between humanity and the gods. Liminality lives between worlds—human and divine—and balances and harmonizes these worlds. Jungian psychology calls this the compensatory function, and it is a central pillar of analytic craft. A forceful regressive consciousness is balanced by an often savagely blunt unconscious intrusion of equally forceful progressive energy; it demands that the offending conscious world pay attention and pull its share of the burden of cosmic harmony. So, divinity and humanity share a common divide of ethical responsibility to balance and calm their respective houses of being:

> In effect, we get the Gods, saviors, and religions we deserve and need. For Jung's myth moves from a trinitarian paradigm of a self-sufficient divinity only contingently involved in the human historical drama to a quaternitarian paradigm. In this paradigm, divinity and humanity are codependents in processes of reciprocal fulfillment in time.[28]

Such a blueprint of living requires that one live not automatically, but consciously. One must lean into living, not hold back from it in a constant search for the comfort and safe harbor of distracted, mindless hedonism:

28. Dourley, *On Behalf of the Mystic Fool*, 49.

I believe that the psychological task does not consist in a search for remedies, but in making conscious the kind of archetypal fantasies that always already underlies our automatic approaches, values, and aims, and conversely the new archetypal perspectives that impress themselves on us in dream images, in pathology, and other experiences. What matters therapeutically is not how to get out of a distressing situation, but, on the contrary, how to get properly into it, so that we are no longer simply its passive victims but allow ourselves to be gripped and transformed by it.[29]

The liminal realm is a holistic realm, a realm that reunites rational to irrational, masculine to feminine, mystical to scientific, human to divine.

A colleague described meeting with the famous hypnotherapist psychiatrist Milton Erickson late in Erickson's life. Erickson would greet such pilgrims in his office garage by being wheeled in, clad in a bright purple gown as he sat in his polio-victim wheelchair. He would meet with them for an hour or two and, after listening to their narration of purpose regarding their visit, he would often gently launch into a string of stories. He told my colleague the story of being a young man in the upper Midwest, thrashing hay and bailing it with the other young men of their farm community. At the end of the day, those men would be exhausted from having thrown the hay up onto the hay rack with just one hand from dawn to dusk.

Milton Erickson studied their efforts and fashioned an alternative technique. He would work with one hand until tired, and then he would switch hands and work with the other. He developed a gentle cadence through the workday so that, unlike his exhausted companions, he found himself energized and enlivened at night. To live in liminal time is to be psychically ambidextrous; to be able to switch hands, switch sides of the brain, sides of the heart, and sides of being in a gentle symphony of cadenced living. It is then, at that balanced, awake moment between left and right hands, head and heart, that the portal into numinally alive, liminal worlds is discovered and entered.

B. THE LIMINAL AS MYSTERY

The liminal weaves itself with the scraps off everyone's factory floor. In a rational, consumerist, material world, the liminal lives on the side of mystery. This is not a contemptuous placement for the liminal. It has deep affection

29. Giergerich, *Soul-Violence: Collected English Papers*, 47.

for this real, though partially blighted world of ours. Yet the wide horizon of cosmos and meaning can only be fully grasped from the panoramic precincts of mystery, what the ancient mystics of the West called the Mysterion.

Back to the scrap weaving. The liminal always seeks to lure this partial reality back to the grandeur of its full psycho-spiritual inheritance. That grandeur insists that everything in this existence be used, integrated, metabolized, claimed. It may not all be explained, but it all must be claimed.

Jung was a scrap weaver. He hated to waste anything. In an Enlightenment-dominated professional world of hard science, he increasingly—across the six decades of his clinical practice and scholarly research—sought to add the dimensional counterpoints of mystery, spirit, and depth to healing psychological craft.

This fit in well with the era's widening theoretical appetites and intellectual palates. Darwinian, pragmatic, exoteric, scientific skepticism was met with a growing chorus of theo-philosophical, expansive, esoteric essentialisms and vitalisms. The tried-and-true rational simplicities securely buttressing Victorian certainty were being buffeted by these new psycho-spiritual complexities. And now, our post-millennial world is having to gear up and fight a new and equally vigorous reappearance of evidence-based and bio-fundamentalist scientism.

But whatever you call it, however you define it, any which way you frame it, it is liminal space that houses the scrap weavers and harmonizers. Liminal space is the vessel for emergence, for supervenience, for archetypally charged strange attractors, for complex dynamic systems theory. But it is much more even than these recent Large Theories. At its most vivid, liminal space simply whacks the center of my being with awe and whispers with reverie. It is numinous feeling, it is the song of creation itself. It is beyond a theory. It is essential mystery.

I am actually a kind of liminal GP—a family psychic doctor of sorts. I have accompanied many people across decades of clinical work. I have also often seen their extended families. I see the grandkids of people I first saw when I arrived in my little city forty years ago. Mine is a kind of systemic, intergenerational liminal practice. I see them from major liminal event to major liminal event across their lives as they attempt to digest and absorb each liminal lightning bolt as it pounds the ground at unpredictable but unforgettable moments. These moments awaken them to the true fate and destiny lying just under the surface of the mundane and ordinary.

One is fated to act as one does because how one acts is what one is. Human beings are pieces of fate. Thus, to love one's fate is to love one's life, to affirm the relationship of the self and the world .... However, in the same way that we talk about the character of a person, we also talk about the character of a culture, of humanity and of the world. Indeed, the piece of fate that I am is a part of the piece of fate that my culture is, which is part of the piece of fate that is humanity, which is, in turn, part of the fate of the world.[30]

We are a pregnant species. Each of us births the cosmos. The death and emptiness of this world is an illusion that a grounded liminal consciousness can penetrate and transform. We are a pregnant species, but most of us deliver stillborns. We lose faith. We lose face. We lose heart. And we die full of the burst remains of our dead fetus of soul. We miss the pilgrimage of our lives, the depth and true politic of our being.

> A middle-aged, high-level corporate woman comes to a session after a bone-crushing several weeks of multi-continent business travel. She feels exhausted and "a bit jaded." The trip included a high-end corporate junket into a wildlife park, where she had the first of two dreams. She is in a hockey rink converted into a drab mass business area, like a cubicled trade fair. The mood of the place is depressive, which she realizes she feels about many of the work environments that attend her daily professional journey. A favorite young intern comes to her and movingly presents her with his martial arts black belt. A slighter younger, very likeable work peer, recently pregnant, then comes up to her and announces she has successfully completed a mile-long run.
>
> Then, in a dream on the thirty-hour return flight, she is in a small enclosed area where male attendants strap "gadgets" on to her left leg—binoculars, pens, calculators, etc. But finally, and most curiously, they double over a charming little snake, which my client awkwardly buckles to the leg, as well. Near journey's end and worried, she lifts up her pant leg and notices that the little snake friend is in agony; it is withering.
>
> We sit for a moment, moved by these dreams. Then, gently, we wonder at their initiatory power, at the inner youthful pregnant warrior resources at hand, enabling her to do important leadership-destiny work if the core Goddess snake eros is more gently and soulfully attended to amid the rounds of crushing professional tasks undertaken in their bland, often dehumanizing décor.

30. Hauke, *Jung and the Postmodern*, 174.

The liminal world rarely seeks to extinguish, but to expand; not to disengage, but engage—if we cherish and nurture the little soul-snake-eros strapped to our precious being.

C. THE LIMINAL AS A SANCTUARY OF SILENCE

The twin of emptiness is silence. Silence knows the language of the vacated place at the core of all existence— "the *challal ha-panui*—the vacated space, which God leaves when [S]he creates the world."[31]

Analysis is a mystery process. It is a mystery process seeking to integrate and tame these wild, violent energies of inner and outer creation. Being a mystery process, it is inherently a secrecy process. Not a cauldron of toxic secrecy, but a protected, sacred, creative secrecy. Since the surface of the public space is often a shallow surface, artificially smoothed and contoured to deny the threatening gargoyles of violent being on all sides, one has to be judicious about revealing the fragile, nascent whiffs and whims of new soul nativities. If one is too naïve, the public curs of the violent marketplace will eat their young kits. Innocence terrifies and insults unconscious violent brutes by threatening to expose their inner sense of shame and insubstantiality. I, and many of my liberal friends and neighbors, had the strong feeling that we had to be very careful and often silent in the Bush-Cheney dominated post-9/11 days of military-industrial madness that swept our planet. One wrong naïve quip in that aroused public marketplace of opinion might result in a sudden, merciless social banishment. Or worse. Plato wrote in allegorical disguise for this wise reason:

> If Plato had undertaken to write about the theology of the Athenians, and then in bitterness had accused it of containing mutual discords of the divinities, and their incests, and devouring of their own children, and of deeds of vengeance of fathers and brothers— if Plato had brought up all this in open and unreserved accusations, then according to my opinion he would have given them an occasion to commit another wrong, and to kill him, like Socrates.[32]

The silent and the secret are close allies. Both, well executed, protect and enhance the sacred:

---

31. Zornberg, *The Murmuring Deep*, xvii.
32. Brisson, *How Philosophers Saved Myths*, 73.

If indeed, while myths have deliberately chosen the apparatus they put in the foreground rather than the truth that dwells in secrecy, and if they use visible screens to hide notions that are invisible and unknowable to common people—and this is where the most remarkable quality of myths resides, that is, not to reveal to the profane any of the true realities but only to present dim traces of the entire mystagogy to people naturally capable of being led by those initiated.[33]

D. THE LIMINAL AS DAIMON CONSCIOUSNESS

Plato believed that each of us had a numinous witness, a divine guardian. He called it his Daimon. He believed it was an animate, embodied presence, a voice of connection to the numinal world that embraces all of our existence.

This Daimon resides in the liminal realm. It is the translator between the experience of the gods and our human experience. It is the presence that fuels depth therapy, that coaches our birth and will guide our death. It manifests and reminds us of our destiny.

Recent research in brain plasticity confirms that our style of living and its neural imprint impacts brain behavior and transformations through time.[34] We make our brain as we make soul. In fact, our brains may be the material side of soul, with the Daimon residing in the synapse juncture. That juncture is the liminal realm, the twixt-and-between space and time that is neither fully material nor wholly psyche. It is both.

The twixt-and-between liminal space is core to both theory and practice in Jungian depth therapy. This "mytho-poetic-matrix between the worlds" is where consciousness expands both horizontally and vertically, spatially and temporarily. It is the resonant "indwelling" space where the gods and their interlocutor, Daimon, reveal our destiny to us.[35] It has been visited and appreciated by a variety of contemporary therapists: it inspired D.W. Winnicott's "transitional space," where playful healing interaction can transform development trauma; it is mysticism-appreciating analyst Michael Eigen's "area of faith," where one experiences the full undiluted dimensions of being-ness; it is the essence of Thomas Ogden's "analytic

33. Brisson, *How Philosophers Saved Myths*, 102.

34. Wilkinson, *Changing Minds in Therapy*.

35. Kalsched, *Trauma and the Soul*.

third"; it is the nameless wellspring of Wilfred Bion's ineffable tremendum "O";[36] and it is Jung's *tertiam non dator*, the third not given, which gives rise to the pan-psychic synthesis of the Transcendent Function.[37]

The liminal embraces the truth. It is the truth which like all authentic truth is fashioned of complexity and complication. It's the truth that is paradoxical in that it relies on the necessity of elements of both light and dark, good and evil, right and wrong, masculine and feminine, earth and sky. In the COVID-era tragedy of left versus right and pro-vaccination versus anti-vaccination, this question of how to find it, reside in it, and repose in enlivening liminal truth becomes all the more urgent.

The liminal requires welcoming and suffering this unwanted paradoxical Shadow into our embodied Soul-marrow. Individuated beings cannot find their way Home through a Disneyland weekend pass or any other kind of revival service. The flatness and desperation-of-being always returns as the American founding psychologist once observed:

> In his essay "What Makes Life Significant," [William] James told a personal story during his talk to students about a happy week he'd spent during a summer at the famous assembly grounds on the borders of Chautauqua Lake. There, he says, he got "a foretaste of what human society might be, were it all in the light, with no suffering and no dark corners." He realized while he was there on sabbatical that "all of the ideals for which our civilization has been striving: security, intelligence, humanity, and order," all of these goals, had been superficially attained in a sort of superficial Utopia. He meditated on the fact that at "Chautauqua there was no potentiality of death in sight anywhere, and no point of the compass visible from which danger might possibly appear." He went on: "What our human emotions seem to require is the sight of the struggle going on." In Chautauqua there was no struggle to be seen. James then concluded: "An irremediable flatness is coming over the world." Flatness suggests no vertical dimension to connect us to our Higher Self, only the objects of our lower instincts, passions, and emotions, which can easily lead us astray.[38]

An individuated, authentic pathed way Home only comes in the humble, daily toils of our ceaseless and earnest efforts after a sustained, conscious loving-kindness as James further noted:

36. Grotstein, *Beam of Intense Darkness*, 77.

37. Jung, "Transcendent Function."

38. Herrmann, *William James and C. G. Jung*, 116.

He'd never noticed the great fields of heroism lying roundabout him. He thought of the heroism of the innumerable democratic individuals that make up our vast nation, who pick up a scythe, an ax, a pick, or a shovel every day, and sweat and toil with powers of patient endurance for hours upon hours of strain. All of this heroic life all about him and the toils of untold masses of humanity doing their daily jobs woke him up suddenly from his Chautauqua illusion, and the scales fell from his eyes. Suddenly, "a wave of sympathy greater than anything I had ever before felt with the common life of common men began to fill my soul."[39]

Only such daily sufferings-after-truth can produce a genuine democracy, an achieved personal and collective healing-network of compassion and generativity.

The liminal is the apparent channel for the unique individual and cultural destinations to appear. It is destiny that lures us toward the Telos, the achieved fullness and meaning of our individual and collective lives. Telos is an ancient Greek word meaning direction or point. Telos seems to be the direction-of-matter formation and movement deep-baked into the Big Bang that created the Cosmos and the apparent dynamis of the next round of cosmic expansion and contraction.

From the deepest wisdom synthesized from the most mature of world religions, psychology and sciences, it seems that a key component of this guiding Telos is relational compassion, an embodied and interactive compassion that blends in all the apparent dualities of the Cosmos into the kinetic and seamless One World, Jung's Unus Mundus. It is destiny that makes friends of energy and matter, space and time, science and religion, human and divine, all the essential ingredients that are Cosmic-oven-baked into this ultimate cuisine of Oneness. If Destiny is the key energizer of this One World Matrix-of-Meaning behind the Cosmos, then only the successful achievement of Destiny in our individual lives and in our shared cultural and political lives achieves and assures this final One World compassionate End-to-Things.

Destiny is the code of the Self hidden deep inside the liminal matrix. Destiny is the structural, chrysalis-core of the liminal DNA. It imprints our flesh with a locator beacon so we can find the gods and they us. Amid the almost blinding light of the liminal realms, it charts a soft pastel path, a

---

39. Herrmann, *William James and C. G. Jung*, 117.

via destine, toward our true path of beinghood. It shows us the embodied, prospective way-of-soul forward:

> Behind the horizontal dimension of the parental complexes in the personal unconscious are what Jung later called the mother and the father archetypes, and these two archetypes sink their deepest roots into the subsoil of the collective psyche, while extending into the higher realms of the Spiritual Self (a term coined in 1890 by [William] James), which grounds the individual in a more-than-personal-destiny. These powerful twin dynamisms, mother and father archetypes, operate out of an instinctive and spiritual foundation, transcendent of any causal determining factors, or personal complexes, that may influence a child's fate...
>
> Behind the mother and father complexes and their helpful, or hindering, influence is a mightier hand, a destiny-principle, that emanates from the Self, from above and below.[40]

The liminal seems to be the nursery for the archetypal. It is a nursery that lives beyond science, flourishes outside time. Genetic arguments for the archetypal are ruled out by current science, as there is no genetic, DNA, human-genome evidence of universal archetypal forms. And emergence theories cannot explain the complexity of archetypal templates, as original shared elements can produce novel expressions out of random interactions, but "saying that archetypes are emergent properties does not really explain how these properties came into existence in any detail."[41] Therefore, the trans-rational, non-dual, transpersonal realm of the liminal provides an appealing place to look for the budding plants of archetypal realities in our lives.

There is no real movement of soul without liminal emersion. What otherwise passes for movement is faux movement. It is like the film *The Matrix*, a depth dissociation that produces the implanted suggestion of growth and movement while the actual physical body and psyche shrivel and die—the anaerobic darkness of unmediated Chronos time eating them both alive. Real breakthrough to repose in dynamic, transformative soul time—Kairos time—requires submission to a depth mediated light:

> *A patient dreams of a figure of light approaching her. She is given a stone inscribed with the simple word "breakthrough."*

40. Herrmann, *William James and C. G. Jung*, 15–17.
41. Roesler, "Are Archetypes Transmitted More by Culture than Biology?", 239.

The liminal reminds us that we are all Argonauts, heroic voyageurs on a journey of transformation for ourselves and for our earth tribe. True Argonauts do not choose the time of their journey, they simply accept, humbly, the call when it arrives. It is an initiatory venture. Initiatory ventures seek to embrace and surrender, consciously, to the core mystery that enfolds our individual and collective lives. When we have rowed the true seas of our intended voyage toward our destiny, we can plant our "shapely oar" of ordeal into the ground as a symbol and talisman of what we have accomplished. We can then return peacefully home to abide with loved ones in the beauty of this world. As the blind seer Tiresias prophesizes to Odysseus:

> "Let this be your sign, you cannot miss it: that meeting another traveler he will say you carry a winnowing-fan on your broad shoulder. There you must plant your shapely oar in the ground, and make rich sacrifice to Lord Poseidon, a ram, a bull, and a breeding-boar. Then leave for home, and make sacred offerings there to the deathless gods who hold the wide heavens, to all of them, and in their due order. And death will come to you far from the sea, the gentlest of deaths, taking you when you are bowed with comfortable old age, and your people prosperous about you. This that I speak to you is the truth."[42]

Such soul-journeying requires an initiatory community of mentoring elders and associate novices. Although the central trials and ordeals of the journey are often solitary, the journeying pilgrim is never alone, never uncontained. The best of conscious human and divine community always accompanies the voyager—archetypal Daimons who escort us into liminal realms and keep us awake in profane lands. Odysseus was never alone for a second of his perilous sojourn. The blind mentor Tiresias, his crew, his beloved wife Penelope, his gifted and endearing son Telemachus, and his goddess sponsor, Athena, all watched over his every move, heartbeat, and dream, encouraging him on to his singular heroic achievement. At the end, he arrived home an aged, humbled [Wo]Man, cleansed of youthful ego and arrogance, ready to be a wise, steadying ballast for the next generations of questers.

42. Homer, *The Odyssey*, Book XI, 90–149.

E. THE LIMINAL AS AXIAL AND RENUNCIATORY EVOLUTIONARY CONSCIOUSNESS

Liminality both requires and reflects two essentially new forms of evolutionary consciousness: axial consciousness and renunciatory consciousness.

Liminality cleanses history, restoring time and its personal and cultural trajectories to their eternal visions. Individual and cultural complexes can create massive despairs and disconnecting traumas. Some discordant events can be so severe that people—even whole civilizations—become lost to time, to a sense of any meaningful thread in one's life or a culture's destiny. These are often moments provoking the collective barbarities of genocides and wars of extermination. The collective soul becomes so numbed by despair that the limbic brain takes over in its automatic aggressions and rages, in mad seizures searching for any relief-bringing sense of agency and power. Finding a collective scapegoat that bears full accountability for the anguish of a meaning-drained universe becomes the all-too-easy and tragic solution.

Recent musings in particle physics wonder if the master media of cosmic change and evolution is time itself. Time is mercurial. Like Hermes, it is fleet of foot, cunning and capricious. It seems to want both to be caught and to remain elusive—the ultimate cosmic hide and seek. Image and its reflective register, history, seem to be several of the cleverest human inventions to capture time. With those first grazing mastodons painted with herb dye on a paleolithic cave wall, a vivid day-memory was captured in animated form. The first book was deposited in our species' Smithsonian Library of Image. History was born. Time, at least a holon-fragment of it, was caught in an image bottle and still glistens when light is applied thirty-five thousand years later.

> We and the present in which we live are situated in the midst of history. This present of ours becomes null and void if it loses itself within the narrow horizon of the day and degenerates into a mere present . . . the present reaches fulfillment through the historical ground which we bring to effective activity within ourselves . . . .On the other hand, the present reaches fulfillment through the future latent within it, whose tendencies we make into our own, either by rejecting or accepting them . . . .A present that has attained fulfillment allows us to cast anchor in the eternal origin. Guided by history to pass beyond all history into the Comprehensive—that is

the ultimate goal which, though thought can never reach it, it can nonetheless be approached.[43]

In 1949, the psychiatrist and philosopher Karl Jaspers proposed a simple but profound notion. In his survey of ancient world meta-philosophies, he noticed a global trend settling on our species. In the millennium before the common era (~800 BCE to 200 BCE) a new voice and presence appeared in human experience and consciousness. He described this as a liminal "breather" moment wedged between frenetic epochs of empire-building. In this moment, "lucid consciousness" appeared, fresh and new. It was a consciousness that was moist, reflective, philosophical, grounded, and regenerative [44] Individual thinkers spontaneously and almost simultaneously constellated across the planet, sounding a psycho-spiritual clarion call for a deeper personal and social justice, a deeper ethic and ethos of personal and collective responsibility for our common culture of being. Confucius, Lao Tse, Mo Ti, Hebrew Prophets Elijah and Isaiah, the Buddha, and Greek thinkers Homer, Parmenides, Plato, Jains, Gurus, and Zarathustra all seeded vibrantly in this synchronistic new earth. History, the idea of destiny-imbued being-ness, was born:

> The future is undecided, a boundless realm of possibilities . . . This history cannot be limited in either direction, cannot be conceived of as a rounded form, a self-contained and completed structure.[45]

The first axial age ripped open the liminal realm walled up in the ancient Neolithic caverns. But the heat of their surge of consciousness drove them, in their new aesthetic rise of philosophy, science, and governance, to split the energy into theoretical and practical, light and dark, good and evil. Dualism and its tragic ongoing dissociation were fully unleashed in human experience.

> What is new about this age, in all three areas of the world, is that [wo]man becomes conscious of Being as a whole, of [her]himself and [her]his limitations. [S]he experiences the terror of the world and [her]his own powerlessness. [S]he asks radical questions. Face to face with the void [s]he strives for liberation and redemption. By consciously recognizing [her]his limits [s]he sets [her]himself

---

43. Jaspers, *Origin and Goal of History*, v.

44. Jaspers, *Origin and Goal of History*, 51–56.

45. Jaspers, *Origin and Goal of History*, v.

the highest goals. [S]he experiences absoluteness in the depths of selfhood and in the lucidity of transcendence.

All this took place in reflection. Consciousness became once more conscious of itself, thinking became its own object. Spiritual conflicts arose, accompanied by attempts to convince others through the communication of thoughts, reasons and experiences. The most contradictory possibilities were essayed. Discussion, the formation of parties and the division of the spiritual realm into opposites which nonetheless remained related to one another, created unrest and movement to the very brink of spiritual chaos.

In this age were born the fundamental categories within which we still think today, and the beginnings of the world religions, by which human beings still live, were created. The step into universality was taken in every sense.[46]

If we are living at the cusp of a Second Axial Age, as this book on contemporary experiences of the liminal both suggests and yearns for, perhaps a depth re-visiting of liminal realms will help us endure the fierce fire of the opposites without being driven to precipitate anxious sutures that attempt to deaden and tame the very fire we seek for our renewal—and for our individual and collective transformations.

Carriers of the first axial consciousness were what Robert Bellah calls "Renunciators."[47] Renunciation and the axial seem as bound realities. Axial realities are liminal realities, and they are always experienced as a profound threat to status quo comforts no matter how artificial, distorted, and contrived. As the alien liminal is always felt at the far frontiers of the status quo— above, below, or beyond—so, too, do those sensitive renunciating souls inspired and embedded by axial graces speak to their times in the threatening, strange accents and undercurrents of the liminal Otherness. Since they speak from this Otherness and at the margins of the ordinary status quo, they are frequently ascribed to be speaking in heretical, adversarial (to the status quo credos) cadences. They are seen as declaimers, denouncers, renunciators of the safeties afforded by status quo comfort. They become blasphemers, dangerous intellectual pagans.

But, actually, this renouncing is more an annunciation than a renunciation. It is heralding a new, deeper, unsplit cosmos time and space; an undivided, real-time living liminal, an animated symbol of evolving being welcomed into a fully lucid and inhabited moment of undivided clarity.

46. Jaspers, *Origin and Goal of History*, 1–2.
47. Bellah, *Religion in Human Evolution*.

Renunciators attempt to reside in the liminal, the self, to repose in liminal selfness as long as possible. Because liminal time is seamless time, fully congruent time, it is impossible for any living creature to reside there full time. We are chronically flawed by our dualistic fate. Dissociated, suffering consciousness is endemic to our species and probably all sentient life. Though often seeming to be a chronic design flaw, dissociated time and its requisite suffering is the necessary structure for producing the alchemy of compassionate transformation. And only compassion can recognize compassion, liminal self in the liminal Other.

So, renunciators all seem to have practiced a thorough, contemplative process capable of achieving and then enduring sustained periods of non-dissociated, compassionate presence. This axial grounding is necessary for renunciating's marginalizing vocation. Renunciators always live on the permanent fringe of their times and their cultures. To stay awake is to live in truth. And truth always confronts and affronts accommodated, compromised, dulled-and-often-deadened consciousness. Truth constellates the depth shame and guilt of habitual submission to the compassion-vanquishing behaviors that saturate ordinary time—defensive self-righteousness, projective scapegoating, class and clan-inflated exceptionalisms, raw, fear-engendered emotional and physical hoarding, unending false-self-protecting warfare, sexual violence, genocides, pogroms, ethnic cleansings. These are all behaviors that individuals and cultures default to as a way of evacuating and exterminating the intolerable introjected pain that resides in all of us and our socio-political entities. They are emergency procedures to survive the aching angst of living in a seemingly endless dissociated and violent world.

Renunciators reject this regimen. They reflect the often-unwanted news that there can be compassionate light at the end of suffering's long, long tunnel. But the suffering must be acknowledged, confessed, contained, owned, and transformed, not projected and then hunted down in the victim Other. So, when confronted by such an initially unappetizing and monumental task, it is often just easier to hunt down the renunciator. Little wonder that renunciators often live in inaccessible monasteries, wilderness forests, or on remote islands.

> My outline is based on an article of faith: that [wo]mankind has
> a single origin and one goal. Origin and goal are unknown to us,
> utterly unknowable by any kind of knowledge. They can be felt in
> the glimmer of ambiguous symbols. Our actual existence moves

42

between these two poles. In philosophical reflection we may endeavor to draw closer to both origin and goal . . . In the beginning
was the manifestness of being in a present without consciousness.
The fall set us on a path leading to knowledge and finite practical
activity with temporal objectives, to the lucidity of the consciously
manifest.

With the consummation of the end we shall attain concord of
souls, shall view one another in a loving present and in boundless
understanding, members of a single realm of everlasting spirits.[48]

So, to reprise, cultural evolution was an imaginative enterprise that
began with ancient Greek philosophers beginning with Parmenides, but
it really gained cultural mainstream traction in the mid-to-late nineteenth
century. Although Darwin stands at the prow of this vessel of conceptu-
alization, all the psychology of religionists, mythographers, cultural an-
thropologists, and social justice evolutionary Darwinists stood stoutly and
closely behind him. Jung linked arms with the best of all of these. Every
hour of analysis is an event of evolutionary accomplishment.

Jung arose in the middle of this evolutionary pack of thinkers and
influencers. A contemporary was Henri Bergson, mentioned above, who
felt that something core had escaped the space-time continuum. He called
it "duration," the moving merger of the One and the All that is the absolute
vortex of the cosmos, a reality which can only be grasped by the moving dy-
namism of intuitive knowledge flashing through time. This mobile concept
was fueled by the alchemical *élan vital*, the vital element, the animating
spark-impetus that drove all post-Big Bang forces from the least microcosmic to the most macrocosmic.

Pierre Teilhard de Chardin followed closely on Bergson's heels. His
notion was that the evolving universe was driven by its unquenchable thirst
for culmination; a dynamic relation of all-to-all, oogenesis, a fluid consummation of an animated absolute Omega Consciousness that could best be
described as a comprehensive love or compassion.

The chrysalis for this invisible, black-hole, essential vitalness is the
liminal. The liminal is the stew pot of creation from which the animating
matrix of cosmic being emerges:

Since there is no independent origination of anything, the vision
is emergence out of a fecund nothingness, a seeming paradox
that sounds curiously like some discussions of the singularity

48. Bellah, *Religion in Human Evolution*, xv.

envisioned as the point of origin in modern cosmology . . . To conclude: cosmology has now identified a pervasive force permeating the entire universe previously unrecognized, until the mapping sectors of darkness revealed regions of voidness and their evolution in time. The results point to a new, unknown force, "Dark Energy" generating increasing regions of relative "no-thing-ness" and producing the intricate patterns of the Cosmic Web.[49]

F. THE LIMINAL AS ANIMA NATURA: RECOVERING THE LIVING DEEP FEMININE

Analysis is planetary work. This declaration comes without sentiment. It is a sober truth. Depth work disconnected from the living energies of the Earth and its cosmic surround is a hopeless task, for any authentic hope we have is grounded in our planetary home:

An individual's harmony with his or her own deep self requires not merely a journey to the interior but a harmonizing with the environmental world.

—JAMES HILLMAN[50]

Landscape is the primal liminal. The ancient world saw it littered with doorways into numinal lands—*locus genii*: the locations, the exact earth-spots, of the guiding spirits. It was during the Renaissance and Romantic periods that this essential liminal embeddedness of landscape was rediscovered.

"LINES COMPOSED A FEW MILES ABOVE TINTERN ABBEY, ON REVISITING THE BANKS OF THE WYE DURING A TOUR, JULY 13, 1798"

. . . For I have learned
To look on nature, not as in the hour
Of thoughtless youth, but hearing oftentimes
The still, sad music of humanity,
Nor harsh nor grating, though of ample power
To chasten and subdue. And I have felt

49. Cambray, "Ecological Metaphor in Jung's Thought," xvii.
50. Hillman, "Psyche the Size of the Earth," xxii.

A presence that disturbs me with the joy
Of elevated thoughts; a sense sublime
Of something far more deeply interfused,
Whose dwelling is the light of setting suns,
And the round ocean, and the living air,
And the blue sky, and in the mind of [wo]man,
A motion and a spirit, that impels
All thinking things, all objects of all thought,
And rolls through all things. Therefore am I still
A lover of the meadows and the woods,
And mountains; and of all that we behold
From this green earth; of all the mighty world
Of eye and ear, both what they half-create,
And what perceive; well pleased to recognize
In nature and the language of the sense,
The anchor of my purest thoughts, the nurse,
The guide, the guardian of my heart, and soul
Of all my moral being.

~ William Wordsworth

Contemporary existential philosophies parse the urgency of authentic indwelling in soul-saturated landscape, as well:

> Let us think for a while of a farmhouse in the Black Forest, which was built some two hundred years ago by the dwelling of peasants. Here the self-sufficiency of the power to let earth and heaven, divinities and mortals enter in simple oneness into things, ordered the house. It placed the farm on the wind-sheltered mountain slope looking south, among the meadows close to the spring. It gave it the wide overhanging shingle roof whose proper slope bears up under the burden of snow, and which, reaching deep down, shields the chambers against the storms of the long winter nights. It did not forget the altar corner behind the community table; it made room in its chamber for the hallowed places of childbed and the "tree of the dead--for that is what they call a coffin there: the Totenbaum--and in this way it designed for the different generations under one roof the character of their journey through time. A craft which, itself sprung from dwelling, still uses its tools and frames as things, built the farmhouse . . . .
>
> The real dwelling plight lies in this, that mortals ever search anew for the nature of dwelling, that they must ever learn to dwell. What if [wo]man's homelessness consisted in this, that [wo]man still does not even think of the real plight of dwelling as the plight?

Yet as soon as [wo]man gives thought to [her]his homelessness, it
is a misery no longer. Rightly considered and kept well in mind, it
is the sole summons that calls mortals into their dwelling.[51]

For the ancients, Gaia—divinity—infuses landscape. And the craft
that Gaia performs is inherently a Deep Feminine task. If the skies bow to
Zeus and Thor, the Earth bows to Gaia. The next chapter talks of literal and
metaphoric pilgrimage as a liminal delivery vehicle. Pilgrimage demands
landscape for its actualization; no earth to wander, no pilgrimage. Pilgrimage burns landscape into the flesh. It travels up from the feet in a cellular
memory that etches every muscle, every breath, every heartbeat.

Jungian psychology is a nature-based psychology. It is a craft-grounded
pantheism, or, drawing on Mathew Fox's felicitous correction to the notion
that gods are not a stone but rather that the goddess-numinal is the energy
experienced *through* the stone: panentheism.[52] It is nature that grounds sacred and secular, primordial and historical, universal and particular.

As hinted above, analysis is evolutionary. Its liminal core is an evolutionary dynamis. It is currently one of the best epochal tools for locating the
liminal sweet spot that moves consciousness forward. Unfortunately, it has
mainly been an individual tool, focused on the liberation of lost individual
destinies. It has not focused equally on collective evolutionary destinies.
That is one of the great process reformations of this generation of craft.

The goal of evolution might be the non-anxious, neo-permanent
conscious dwelling within liminal time.[53] This seems a likely possibility for
both our personal, individual evolution through the life cycle from birth to
death and for our species as a whole. Maybe even all cosmic sentience seeks
this ultimate non-anxious, conscious co-communion in being:

> *A patient in profound relational, vocational, intergenerational stress
> dreams of an Earth Mother, a celestial earth mother bathed in a
> starry garment opening her arms, offering a welcoming hearthside
> embrace of maternal soul.*

The liminal is a portal to the creative cyclicity at the heart of Mother
Nature's being. The clinical experience does not cure, it commences. The
process of descent into the liminal's often terrifying, empty realms is cycli-
cally recurrent in both individual and collective encounters. No one can

---

51. Heidegger, *Poetry, Language, and Thought*, 148.

52. Fox, *Illuminations of Hildegard of Bingen*.

53. Kerr and Bowen, *Family Evaluation*.

dwell in such spacious emptiness forever. Everyone gets anxious, lonely, and starved. They must return. But the dwelling can be broader and deeper upon each return to the liminal realms; it can imprint memories of a much wider horizon that can calm and comfort in the turbulence of our frenzied world.

The liminal is fertile nothingness, an animate Deep Feminine place where the fullness of our being is experienced in its complete emptiness, its absolute apophasis:

> Marguerite Porete . . . was to write of her soul, "Without such nothingness she cannot be the all" . . . A Jungian translation might read, "My embrace of the world will never be more inclusive than the depth of my entrance into the mother of the all." In a period when a terrorized humanity looks for salvation from its saviors to avoid its extinction, Jung's myth points to a moment of dissolution in the mother of the all as the ultimate resource to the lethal squabbles between her children fatally possessed by mere fragments of her always surpassing and redeeming wisdom. This is the wisdom which seeks to become conscious in every analysis moving through the individual into society.[54]

The empty Deep Feminine is the abysmal chalice of transformation.

> I was working for a while with a middle-aged woman. But I had a hard time with her; her symptom would not change. I did not suggest sandplay for her, because I thought she would resist "just playing." But one day I pushed myself to see if she would respond. She began to work at the sandtray with much more involvement than I had expected. I did not say anything about her tray at that time. However, seeing how and what she did, I felt: "Great! Now I can cure her!" At the next session I invited her to do sandplay. She refused, to my amazement. "Why?" I asked. "I don't want to be cured," she said. "I'm not coming here to be cured." "Then why are you here?" I asked. "I come here just to come here."[55]

Analysis should always be about resonant emptiness. The world we have created all round us is too full; it is full nigh to bursting. When people arrive for therapy they might not even know it when they first arrive, but they want to empty out, to deflate, to exhale. The analytic space should be a place to empty out time and space, rush and bother, *Sturm und Drang*.

---

54. Dourley, *On Behalf of the Mystic Fool*, 52.

55. Kawai, *Buddhism and the Art of Psychotherapy*, 30.

Jerome Bernstein, an innovative contemporary analyst who has worked for decades with Native American traditions, believes that many of those we deem as borderline personalities, mentally-ill personalities, may actually be gifted "borderland personalities"—personalities with a special redemptive connection to and anchor in the natural world; a connection that harbingers what all of us must find in ourselves individually and collectively if we are to survive and heal this violence-ravaged planet and culture of ours. He believes "the great need of Borderland personalities is to have their connection to nature and transrational reality validated, not analyzed, not interpreted—simply witnessed."

> . . . It seems to me that what I have identified as Borderland consciousness is the most evident manifestation of that mystery in the liminal realm between the collective unconscious and the collective consciousness.[56]

And it is this natural link, Bernstein suggests, that is our conduit to the transpersonal, numinal Other. "The problem is that we inflate and idealize consciousness," he writes. "We don't see its shadow side which is not unconsciousness, but hubris—consciousness split off from ethics, split off from an informing transpersonal link."[57]

> The cosmic meaning of consciousness became clear to me . . . .
> [Wo]Man, I, in an invisible act of creation put the stamp of perfection on the world by giving it objective existence.[58]

For such Earth–work, such Gaia-work, there are four assumptions we can make:

1. The liminal is an essential element of being and soul making, not a peripheral one. Debate rages in Jungian circles about the primacy of Logos (word/thought) over Eidos/imaginatio (image) in our craft. Consensus theory says it is an integration of both—and I agree. We also debate whether we are talking about an empirical and clinical event or a numinal and archetypal one. (I strongly hold the latter perspective.) But there is no questioning the unique role image plays in personal and cultural-collective individuation.[59]

---

56. Bernstein, *Living in the Borderlands*, 142, 69.

57. Bernstein, *Living in the Borderlands*, 62.

58. Jung, *Memories, Dreams, and Reflections*, 255–56.

59. Kugler, *Raids on the Unthinkable*; Marlan, *Black Sun*.

2. In our era, the liminal image is voiced in a profoundly feminine register. We are deeply enmeshed in a dangerous time, a time when patriarchal animus is aroused in a disproportionate fury. As a colleague warned nearly twenty years ago, "The reign of the Patriarchal ego is still quite entrenched in the Western psyche and it leaves little room for 'causes' of human behavior that do not emanate from itself."[60]

3. It may also be that our species will only survive by a calculated and committed return to a depth experience of nature and her wildness. In 1921, Jung wrote, "True to my nature-loving bias, I have followed the call of the wild, the age-old trail through secluded wilderness, where a primitive human community may be found."[61]

   The most essential accent in the post-modern reassessment of our collective fate is the recall of the depth feminine to its shared cultural home:

   > In the beginning the Goddess created consciousness to become self-conscious in her child. Though from the outset she already dwelt in her child, she had to recall her child to a moment of immersion in herself to become more fully incarnate in the child then reborn from her womb. For the child reborn was now aware of the turbulent, conflicted life of the Goddess and, so, painfully conscious that her self-contradictions could only be perceived and redeemed in suffering toward their resolution in the life of humanity.[62]

   Jung believed that the Western world is in a precarious situation. "The danger," he wrote, "is greater the more we blind ourselves to the merciless truth with illusions about the beauty of soul."[63]

4. And, finally, we can assume that the liminal Gaia-force has a special affection for the body and the spirit that animates its core. "The spirit is the life of the body seen from within, and the body the outward manifestation of the life of the spirit—the two being really one."[64]

---

60. Bernstein, *Power and Politics*, xvii.

61. Jung, *Collected Works Vol. 6: Psychological Types*, 418.

62. Jung, as quote in Dourley, *On Behalf of the Mystic Fool*, 53.

63. Jung, "Spiritual Problem of Modern Man," 89.

64. Jung, "Spiritual Problem of Modern Man," 195.

G. THE LIMINAL AS DESTINY WORK

Foundationally, liminal-realm work is destiny work. Let me repeat the salient quotation that began this chapter and book:

> All life is bound to carriers who realize it, and it is simply inconceivable without them. But every carrier is charged with an individual destiny and destination, and the realization of these alone makes sense of life.[65]

I had a patient, a professional performance artist, who reported in early treatment a dream she had while sleeping in the hospice room of her dying father. This man had been an often underpowered and absent presence in her early life, but years of intensively focused personal therapy and courageous interpersonal encounter had blunted the invasive growth of that father-wound. Now, she slept on a chaise in his death room, one of several family members accompanying his last days. In the dream-vision, she observed a cloud or damask of light enter from the room's west side. Though agnostic, she associated the animated shape emerging out of the center of the amoebic light field as a Christoform image. It seemed to call to her magnetically pulling her up from the chaise and into the light until she suddenly felt it necessary to energetically resist and cry out, "No . . .

. . . Not now.

. . . Not yet.

. . . Not me."

She had felt that this light had come for her father and that it must redirect its attention his way. Her destiny, her unique destiny, lay fully before her even as her father ended his.

Everyone enters analysis with a spiritual question. Many just don't know it consciously when they arrive. They often think they come for their symptom; that they *are* the symptom. They don't know that their symptom is a doorway into resolving their alienation from their destiny, from the pure lure of meaning-making that they came blazing into this world long ago to manifest and fulfill.

Our corporatized, consumerist culture trains people into this confusion, for if what they feel is a symptom, it is a commodity that can be sold to remedy rather than claimed as a doorway to transformation. As Ann Belford Ulanov posits, "Whatever spirituality is, we know from our

---

65. Jung, *Psychology and Alchemy*, 222.

glimpses along the frontier with the transcendent that it wants to step over into living."[66]

A dream deferred is often a dream denied. A destiny deferred, is often a destiny lost. Analysis is inherently destiny work. It is mainly destiny retrieval work. Retrieval work because our destiny dreams us from the womb onwards, but we often become accomplished saboteurs of its urgent witness to our lives. The opportunities for fulfilling our destiny never abandon us. Although, if we are not very careful, a particularly harsh and violent quelling of that voice can kill the dream and the soul animating it long before we physically die.

Winifred Bion suggests that, when conducting an analysis, "one must cast a *beam of intense darkness* so that something which has hitherto been obscured by the glare of the illumination can glitter all the more in that darkness."[67] My analytic office has broad, high windows that devour strong northern light. This is the light artists prefer. It is steady, even. While not the "intense darkness" Bion conceptualized, it is just the right light to hold on to clear vision in liminal realms. Northern light is tempered light; it is not strident, bold light. The liminal eschews bright light. It prefers luminescent light. It adores backlighting. The suggestive silhouette is preferred over the bold profile. It is psyche's Photoshop, constantly imposing its preference for luminescent darkness and shadowed light. Psychotherapy—deep psychotherapy—opens its true heart in such lighting. In soft, soothing light. In the illumination of early dawn and late dusk.

The liminal is where both humans and the gods find their home. It helps us all find our true direction:

- Our place on the earth
- Our craft for the earth
- Our love from the earth

Liminal places are also where everyone discovers their truth:

---

66. Ulanov, *Religion and Spirituality in Carl Jung*, 302.
67. Grotstein, *Beam of Intense Darkness*, 1.

- True destiny
- True vocation
- True place on the earth
- True loves
- True home

These places exist for everyone. Sadly, however, many people never discover them. The achievement of this destiny—the discovery of these places—requires consistent, life-long discipline. It is the engine of individuation. Terry Tempest Williams best summarizes the rigor required to walk this path of destiny discipline:

"CHOOSE ONE'S TRAVELING COMPANIONS WELL"

Choose one's traveling companions well.
Physical strength and prudence are necessary.
Imagination and ingenuity are our finest traits.
Expect anything.
You can change your mind like the weather.
Patience is more powerful than anger.
Humor is more attractive than fear.
Pay attention.
Listen.
We are most alive when discovering.
Humility is the capacity to see.
Suffering comes—we do not have to create it.
We are meant to live simply.
We are meant to be joyful.
Life continues with and without us.
Beauty is another word for God.[68]

SUMMARY OUTLINE OF THE LIMINAL'S CONTRIBUTIONS TO LIFE AND BEING

The meaning of events is the supreme meaning, that is not in events, and not in the soul, but is the God standing

68. Williams, *Open Space of Democracy*, 56–57.

*between events and soul, the mediator of life, the way, the
bridge, and the going across.*

—C. G. JUNG[69]

In its essence, Jungian psychology is a liminal psychology because it affirms
the mystical traditions of Western and Eastern thought:

- The psyche is inherently gnostic, alchemical, and mystical in its pragmatic functioning.

- The psyche is inherently gnostic, alchemical, and mystical in working out its prospective destiny. The psyche leads—it lures—us toward
wholeness.

- The psyche teaches and provokes through experience, not dogma or
creed.

- The psyche reveals its archetypal core through image.

- The psyche counsels a paradoxical attitude, a "hermeneutic," of both
suspicion and affirmation regarding the "real" world and its organizing institutions.[70]

- Individuation (activating the ego–self axis) is the central, ethical imperative for each person.

- The self is the divine splinter in each person—the living *imago Dei* in
each of us.

- Opposites are the essential engine of spiritual transformation across
the life cycle—consciously interacting with their tensions is the only
way to realize the *mystica unio.*

- The self is the divine splinter in each person—the living *imago Dei* in
each of us.

Once, after an event of professional shame (I felt I had failed in my
personal expectations during an important public lecture), I had a dream
that I was a major-league slugger, a man who had just eclipsed all the leg-
ends before him in a triumphal World Series. The following day (still in my
dream), I was next in line at a famous neighborhood take-out burger joint.
As I gently and humbly kibitzed with the window attendant, I saw young
couples nudging each other behind me in awed recognition that I was the

69. Jung, *Red Book*, 239.

70. Homans, *Jung in Context.*

heroic hitter in the flesh. I graciously and almost shyly acknowledged their honorific greetings and, feeling blessed and at peace in my home town, began jogging home through a sudden evening shower, up a twilight boulevard to my simple urban apartment.

Jung believed that the most important function of dreams is that they are compensatory. My primal shame complex had been punctured. Disappointment with self had flooded in. But the unconscious had restored gentle balance by reminding me of the humble slugger within, the man who persistently slugged and slogged his way through the rough trenches of life in a heroic and often self-effacing way. But not *too* self-effacing. I needed to be reminded that the hometown folks of the psyche recognized, remembered, and valued what I offered as my fair share of the human community contribution. The gods enjoyed my accomplishment and blessed them with a vesper shower. The psyche's fraught balance was restored and calmed.

At times in our lives, we are all required to bear an agonizing, almost unimaginable suffering—the suffering not only of our abandonments and annihilations, but, even worse, the abandonments and annihilations experienced by the divine:

> Jung confronts contemporary humanity with the question of whether it is up to suffering divinely based conflict in the immediate precinct of human interiority, the matrix of all the Gods, without breaking containment and destroying itself in destroying the evil other.[71]

And the only salve we have, the archetypal herbal that fate has placed to grow within reach of every suffering being, is compassion—the compassion of our fellow beings for our pitiable plight, we for theirs, and both of ours together for the suffering gods. It is solely by this compassion, *sola compassio*, that we survive:

> To the extent any analysis births the self in consciousness, it also births God in humanity and in the process redeems both. The effect of such redemption always has wider societal import.[72]

This book attempts to essay how liminal presence can be found and experienced at the bottom, above, and all around this catalytic suffering. It is redemptive suffering that fuels liminality—not sadistic suffering. It is a suffering that has numinal grace and compassion at its core—not grinding

71. Dourley, *On Behalf of the Mystic Fool*, 180.
72. Dourley, *On Behalf of the Mystic Fool*.

inner annihilation and nihilism. In fact, liminal, redemptive suffering is the only known antidote for sadistic suffering. Numinal suffering redeems nihilist suffering. The world has experienced far too much mindless and being-less suffering for its own good.

This book reflects on both the individual and collective experience and expression of liminality. It assumes that liminal space is sacred space, where the numinous meets the human. It starts by suggesting pilgrimage as a metaphor for the core reality of life, an intentional journey toward being. It then follows with reflections of liminality as performance art—that the aesthetic is an essential handmaiden of the liminal. It moves on to a discussion of politics as a collective liminal craft that needs to be practiced with much more consciousness and dedication if we are to survive as a species. The book concludes with a chapter meditation on how to restore the *Anima Mundi*, the precious soul of the world that seems under unusual duress in the current era.

In an age threatened by professional agnostic scientism, this book affirms depth clinical craft as an inherently numinal, religious, sacramental craft. In the face of the blowing gale of data-possessed factory psychology, depth therapy offers the treasure of the respectfully received, sacramentally honored, and personally experienced event. William James once famously remarked that psychology needs to "bracket off" philosophy; that if the choice be between "seraphic insight" or cure, one must take the more mundane cure.[73] This book takes a different approach, suggesting that both these poles of experience—philosophical-spiritual vision and pragmatic, curing technology—need each other, and that suffering happens if either is absent.

May the pilgrimage begin . . .

73. Shamdusani, *Jung and the Making of Modern Psychology*, 26, 203.

Pilgrimage

Sit as little as possible; do not believe any idea that was not born in the open air and of free movement—in which the muscles do not also revel. All prejudices emanate from the bowels.—Sitting still (I said it once already)—is the real sin against the holy ghost.

—Nietzsche, *Ecce Homo*[1]

It began as a relaxed amble into one of the truly beautiful cities of northern Europe: Bruges. I was quietly wandering, focused on a contemplative quest. The day was threatening with low clouds and patterned cloudbursts, but, in sporadic moments of breakthrough, the sun-bathed greens greened, cheered songbirds sang, and a pastel light sparkled in ancient waterways that poured past orchid-festooned brick and marble walls. I had chosen to follow the circuitous canal towpaths rather than the cobblestoned main thoroughfare into the hubbub of the central market.

As I walked, I marveled that this gracious city, so recurrently aesthetic and consistently alive, was birthed out of an originally generative capitalism. How did it continue to survive into our era's rapacious brand of dark, hard capitalism?

On one of the abandoned side-lanes I happened across was an enchanting yellow-frescoed wall complete with an exquisite devotional inset honoring Madonna and Child. At the far end, the open top half of an ageless Dutch door beckoned. Peering over it revealed a garden fantasia, and my breath seemed sucked away by fairies. A balanced, orchestrated

---

1. Gros, *A Philosophy of Walking*, 11.

riot of color, sculpture, and blossom charmed within. There was an icon of St. Christopher on a white bricked wall, a Buddha under a flowering hyacinth, an old potter's wheel elegantly upended by the edge of a small pond. Whoever created this sculptural, botanical paradise and left its door open to surprise discovery did so out of love and delight. I had a sudden impulse to find the creator (probably the owner of an art shop fronting the hidden grotto), but I hesitated, not wanting to be embarrassingly gauche or intrusive. I started on my way, but had gotten no further than three steps when suddenly I was at the shop threshold where a man stood vacuuming the entry way. He gently opened the door, "Would you like to come in?"

There was nothing urgent or entrepreneurial about his invitation. I could demur or enter. But there was meaning to his portal presence. I sensed a current of encounter running both ways, through us both, from whichever gods govern such meetings.

A flyer on the door held a picture of an artist and a lovely abstract triptych of his provenance. A quick scan made clear that the cleaning man and the artist were one and the same. Stimulated by the richness and thoughtful collisions of image and form in his studio shop, our conversation quickly strayed into those other worlds that are inevitably addressed in destined meetings. Why was I here? (*The archetype of capitalism birthed in Bruges*, I answered.) What motivated his painting of animate but shy-souled apparitions of pastel wonder? (*They paint me to announce that which will follow capitalism*, he replied. *They calm me; reassure me that something quite wonderful is coming. Next year would not be dark.*)

What constellated his non-pressured optimism when I increasingly felt—and continue to feel—a silent dread of what might be emerging from the dark bowels of modern global capitalism? (*I don't know*, he declared. *I just feel grateful. I feel that is what I am here to do: to feel grateful and paint it. It may be wrong. It may not work. But I just trust it. Yes, like your Jung, whom I have read and enjoy, I believe that religions must leave. Let go. Yes, we are god. We must be god in a light, un-prepossessed way.*)

Where did his calm knowledge come from? Did he dream? Or have visions? (*I dream every night*, he responded. *The dreams tell me that this world is a playground. That I must play and urge others to play. Last night I dreamed of "them" telling me over and over again, "Accept, just accept and accept and accept." I paint my dreams. These Guides ask me to invite you to dream right now . . . go to the basement chapel of the Basilica of the Holy Blood here*—he points to a town map—*and then go here*—again, the map—*where capitalism was born. You were there a thousand years ago. You had a major role in things then. You came back. You are here right now to help in the necessary change. A key role. You will return to Bruges. Why don't you stay here, come back soon? But, first, go to the Holy Blood chapel and be there for a while.*)

What about suffering, sorrow? This plane of being is not always joyous. (*If I were to lose my granddaughter, I cannot imagine what that would be like. It would seem unbearable, but They would have a way for me. They always have. Maybe not this time, but I think so. It has been my experience so far. It's in the painting. I'd paint my way through.*) I echoed a similar experience in my life. (*Yes, my wife and I lost several fetuses. The oldest one dreams me through—she comes back at the age she would be if she had hatched into this world, recurrently dreaming me through.*)

By now, we two early-elder men were in silent tears while a heavy summer shower fell on the fairy garden behind us. The wind came up and I could smell jasmine. The liminal seems always to be there, dreaming us through.

Walking away from this dramatic, synchronistic encounter, I mused about capitalism and the soul. Possession drives hard capitalism. Hard capitalism craves possessions. There is never enough. And possession disposes the soul.[2]

Possessions possess. They introject. Or, more correctly, they extroject. They are false attempts—ultimately empty attempts—to organize our anxiety. Control it, vent it, heal it, even. But such possessive consumerism ultimately addicts, absorbs, and eventually psycho-spiritually annihilates its victims. If introjects are the walled-off toxic dump sites of early life (often very early-life traumata), possessions are extrojects: shiny new objects literally riddled with the projections of past traumatic pain. We hand our pain over to these glistening consumer jewels in the hope that they will transform and disappear from our lives. It works for a while, but the existential angst and dread always return—deeper and more dulling than before. There is no genuine retail therapy.

I found this Bruges man on what, over the past dozen years, has become an annual walkabout. I go wherever the ancient paths call—Japan, Spain, Norway, Italy, Ireland. There has been a renaissance of interest in these ancestral paths, most of which are connected to healing mysteries. I am revived and refreshed every time I take one of my pilgrimage

2. Soelle, *Silent Cry*, 233–58.

constitutionals. I have less weight. I tread more lightly. I have more hope. My soul deepens and is more assured.

And the light of liminal encounter usually falls across my path some-where along the way—mystery like this Bruges art shop event. It happened. It stirs up acausal sense, it makes the heart more curious and open, the deep sorrow of common compassion more molten and ready to geyser to the surface. In short, I feel more healed and whole after I go wild and walk about the urban and back way wildernesses of the planet.

In recent years, I have increasingly seen everything through a pilgrim-age lens, a journey lens—including my vocational-analytic work and my avocational-photography work. In my office, in a kayak, on the Iceland Ring Road, on a round-trip Caribbean cruise with my 92-year-old mother, I increasingly see all things as part of the Great Round.

> Life migrates. It is dynamic. It moves from the south pole to the north pole and back again in a single season. It is turbulent. It has its own inner gyro. It flies, as do the great migratory flocks through the sky at night, fixing on its own constellation, its own guide star, its own polar star. And unlike ocean surfing Grebes, we are not flock fliers. We fly individually. We may feed with others and make love to one another, but we are born and die alone; we migrate alone to the drum of our own hearts and our own desti-nies. But, we must move or we perish. Our creative fires disappear without the fluttering of our soul wings. The liminal self is a flier. The liminal nestles close to beauty, especially beauty's primal ves-sel, the earth. The liminal always walks the earth, it always finds its opening through a crack in the earth whether that be literal earth or inner psycho-spiritual terrain. Therefore, all liminal work is walking earth work. It is pilgrimage work.[3]

Pilgrimage is pattern recognition. Deep pattern recognition. The reveries, silences, and abstentions of the path scour through the noisy per-turbations of this world to deeper realms of archetypal mystery and reso-nance. The distractions, addictions, soul-signal-jamming buzzes and hums of the temporal world—the Chronos-clock world—become distilled and transformed into the soothing tranquilities of the being world, the psyche-Kairos world.

Pilgrimage is a journey, a ritual, a commemoration, a search for something, perhaps something the pilgrim cannot express in words, per-haps even something the pilgrim does not fully perceive. Pilgrimages are

3. Gibson, *Journal*.

connected with the spirit, but it is difficult to say precisely how. A term in such constant use is inevitably used for many different kinds of activity.[4] Active pilgrim shrines of many faiths provide archetypal validation for liminal reality. I once took an elder to visit the Shrine of Montserrat near Barcelona. She is an anxious traveler, her Bible Belt vigilance on alert for anything that might terrify her, anything that is beyond the secure precincts of a Protestant, sanitized worldview. Knowing I traveled frequently to Europe, she asked that I accompany her, though she wished to see no "pagan" sites, just Christian heritage ones. I negotiated an alternative—a half-Orthodox itinerary, a half-"pagan" one. She hesitantly agreed.

We traveled through Greece and Spain. I took her to the ancient mystery temple at Eleusis and arranged a private entry into the Paleolithic cave at Altamira. She was surprisingly open and effected by these "pagan" eccentricities.

Emboldened by these successes, I urged, after a lovely day in Barcelona, that we plan for the following day a visit to the famous and nearby Black Madonna shrine at Montserrat. I explained that such sanctuaries existed all over Europe, all with miracle stories about a Madonna and child statue that miraculously survived multiple fires and mayhem across the centuries, the wood's originally light surfaces blackened by tragedy and soot. This survival became attached to reportings of profound physical and psycho-spiritual healings in the presence of the venerable ebony divines, and they soon became pilgrimage sites. I further explained that many, if not most, of these statues were in sanctuaries built upon or in close proximity to ancient pre-Christian Goddess healing shrines. Having sufficiently aroused her anticipatory anxiety, we retired for the night.

The next day, we drove the lovely 30-odd kilometers up into Our Lady of Montserrat's mountain stronghold. Entering the hushed precincts, we saw the Madonna high above the altar, the pilgrim's access stairway spiraling up to the right. She had visiting hours, and She was thankfully open to receiving callers. My elder apprehensively looked at me and asked, "What do I do?" I told her to do whatever felt comfortable and explained that I would stand before the Madonna and touch the orb in her outstretched hand, imagining healing energy coming from it. I told her I would then go out into the sanctuary and meditate for twenty minutes. Instruction offered, we silently walked up the staircase for our visit.

---

4. Clift and Clift, *Archetype of Pilgrimage*, 9.

Afterward, she re-joined me in the garden atrium, tears swelling from her softened eyes. "I touched her hand and she spoke to me. So much light. I feel so peaceful."

These active sites exude transformative "presence-ing." There is something about the serene Deep Feminine compassionately holding her vulnerable, divine child that evokes profound affect, touching both the traumatized inner child in all of us and, I believe, the culturally traumatized child:

> And this sacred dimension often comes to presence during the suffering of the individuation process in the image of the child . . . a part-divine innocent child whose life is the preoccupation of mythology the world over. The human/divine child, in other words, does not belong entirely to "this world." And neither do we.[5]

Pilgrimage is an ambling art, a wandering aesthetic. And so it becomes in Joan Miró's late-life painting, *Passage* [images of this painting and the ones below are easily discoverable via a Google image search]. We join him as pilgrims on a barren white canvas landscape. We are a red splash of Holy Grail blood looking up at a beacon-star sun and a distant blue and black figure above the blank line of horizon. Are we heading toward them? Are they heading toward us? We are on this canvas, not standing before it. On this vertical canvas, are we walking up the wall of the universe, scaling our way like Jacob to that distant star home? Here, in *Passage*, we are part of the silent soul and its "immobile movement."

"What I am looking for," Miró tells us, "is an immobile movement, something which would be the equivalent of what is called the eloquence of silence, or what St. John of the Cross, I think it was, described with the term 'mute music.'"[6]

Miró was not the only one to know that the skein of landscape is the liminal interface between worlds. In my own region of the world, the mystical painter Morris Graves knew that. Active in the middle of the last century, he used "white writing," a unique graphic arts technique that looks like flowing calligraphic terrain, to capture the effect. In his *Spring with Machine Age Noise*, we find a soulful landscape put in motion—left to right in increasingly vibratory dislocation and agony as agitated patterns swirl in wider and wider arcs of disturbing intensity. In his world-war-saturated,

5. Kalsched, *Trauma and the Soul*, 15.

6. Miro, *Miró: The Experience of Seeing.*

61

mid-century life space, he clearly envisioned profound disturbances to love, compassion, and peace, and he yearned for healing his whole career.

Similarly, Camille Patha's *Yella Thrilla*, painted in 2008, is a landscape that oozes and undulates with bottled, boiling dynamisms that surge and slog and leap ahead from birth to death. There is a linear field bubbling through the middle of the whole frame, while all around are ghostly and sometimes even ghastly images. They seem almost like witnessing Archons to me—the liminal divinities that do, indeed, ghost every nomad's step as we negotiate the difficult landscapes of our lives.

"Look at how one passage weaves into another," Patha encourages us. "How it's really, really powerful. You read it left to right. I'm talking about the journey, the journey of life . . . it's intricate, it's beautiful, it's sad, it's exhilarating. It's all the things we are in our lives."[7]

The cave dwellers of Lascaux painted on the landscape interface itself. They knew that rock is enfleshed with living charisms of being and light that emit charged messages back and forth between distressed humans and gods, each seeking the other in a more lasting state of *e pluribus unum*—the many becoming the one of lasting love, compassion, and peace.

Our lives are as enigmatic as these various paintings. Just a star there, some black on the horizon there, our red feet beneath us. All else is empty and abstract, often just a line in the in-between. The plane is three dimensional, all dimensional, and no dimensional all at once. And it feels as if we move through this landscape all a-kilter. Disoriented, lost, we still pilgrimage on in an alien landscape, seeking our true home.

And what synchronistically comes to us out of this often disorienting, barren landscape are outer images of our inner soul process. I was once hiking with friends in the magnificently animated desert of Arches National Park. We were heading to chant and meditate in one of the fantastical rock formations that dot this terrain. I had gotten ahead of the group in my reverie-driven march when I noticed a thin, dark blur of motion on the southwestern horizon. It began to zigzag toward me in wide, lazy patterns. It was a small animal moving at a casual trot. But it was not the wary trot that often marks a wild animal's approach. It was purposeful and assured. Closer and closer it came until I could clearly recognize it as a desert fox. I was breathless at the oddity of this encounter and the beauty of the fox's sun-glimmered fur livery.

---

7. Pathe, *Punch of Color.*

Eventually the fox came to a full stop, barely one yard in front of me. I slowly sat in my tracks on the path. We gazed upon each other—animal on human, wild on domesticated, soul on soul. I would tilt my head. She would tilt hers. I would lean forward slowly, she would lean forward slowly. In her eyes I saw clear, high desert waterfalls where we both swam and played, naked and assured in the mid-day sun, her soft fur rubbing up against and releasing the tension from my skin. It was one of the purest cross-species encounters of my lifetime. We were not different. We were one conscious-ness and being on a common landscape of aching minimal beauty. We both ordained something deeper in each other that we would remember the rest of our lives. When my party approached (nearly an hour after first meeting the fox, I later discovered), the visitor rose gently and retraced its path, crisscrossing back to its horizon home.

Pilgrimage burns landscape into the flesh. It travels up from the feet in a cellular memory that etches every muscle, every breath, every heartbeat. Landscape is divine. Deep landscape, deep earth is where the gods live. We see this in Black Elk's youthful vision:

> It was when I was five years old that my Grandfather made me a bow and some arrows. The grass was young and I was on horseback. A thunderstorm was coming from where the sun goes down, and just as I was riding into the woods along a creek, there was a kingbird sitting on a limb. This was not a dream, it happened. And I was going to shoot at the kingbird with the bow my Grandfather made, when the bird spoke and said, "The clouds all over are one-sided." Perhaps it meant that all the clouds were looking at me. And then it said: "Listen! A voice is calling you!" Then I looked up at the clouds, and two men were coming there, headfirst like arrows slanting down; as they came they sang a sacred song and the thunder was like drumming. I will sing it for you. The song and the drumming were like this:
> "Behold, a sacred voice is calling you;
> All over the sky a sacred voice is calling."[8]

Traditional culture—ancient, original culture—knew this. Our culture is "orphaned" from this profound awareness. Dorothee Soelle en-courages those of us who are white, non-native, and "orphan-like in rela-tion to nature" to ask several important questions: "Which culture works with such experiences? And which culture destroys them?" She suggests that native culture not only has a high regard for dreams, the regard grows

---

8. Soelle, *Silent Cry*, 9.

through an educational process for taking dreams seriously. "Among the first questions a native mother asks her child in the morning," Soelle writes, "is what did you dream?"[9]

As C.S. Lewis tellingly captured in his autobiography, even a simple walk back from a local tavern can have one falling down Alice's rabbit hole into deeply stirring liminal realms.

> On the way back, suddenly, without warning, I felt I was in Heaven—an inward state of peace and joy and assurance indescribably intense, accompanied with a sense of being bathed in a warm glow of light . . . a feeling of having passed beyond the body though the scene around me stood out more clearly and as if nearer to me than before, by reason of the illumination in the midst of which I seemed to be placed. This deep emotion lasted, though with decreasing strength, until I reached home, and for some time after, only gradually passing away.[10]

And only the unifying simplicity of such liminal encounters can calm the brazen, clashing noisiness and frequent violence of this fallen world all around us. Martin Buber's reflections capture the daily whirlwind of our lives:

> The commotion of our human life, which lets in everything, all the light and all the music, all the mad tricks of thought and all the variations of pain, the fullness of memory and the fullness of expectation, is closed only to one thing: unity. Every gaze is secretly crowded with a thousand blinking glances that do not want to be its siblings; every pure, beautiful astonishment is confused by a thousand memories; and even the quietest suffering is mixed with the hissing of a thousand questions. This commotion is sumptuous and stingy, it heaps up abundance and refuses encompassment; it builds a vortex of objects and a vortex of feelings, from whirl-wall to whirl-wall, things flying at each other and over each other, and lets us pass through, all the length of this way of ours, without unity.[11]

It is union, simplicity, and emptiness that the pilgrim seeks. And we are all searching pilgrims.

Pilgrimage walking is walking into the void. It is a conscious bi-pedaling into transformative silence. Pilgrimage is deep repetition. Each

9. Soelle, *Silent Cry*, 11.

10. Lewis, as quoted in Soelle, *Silent Cry*, 29.

11. Buber, as quoted in Soelle, *Silent Cry*, 31.

day seeks the same elegant rhythm, a rhythm designed to constellate maximum physical and psychic receptivity. Pilgrimage is a moving alpha state, a dynamic bipedal repose. Pilgrimage is awake trance, pedestrian prayer. Bipedal locomotion is in itself a wondrous experience. From when our species first climbed down from trees and discovered this fearsome world from an erect bipedal stance, walking has been a mystery religion all in itself. Observe any infant in the first lustrous moment of rising from a crawl or a toddler swaggering atop their wobbly legs and you witness this sacrament. Why are our ancestors' earliest painted and inscribed images on cave and rock walls spirals, whorls, meanders, and labyrinths? Is this a visual representation of the physical ecstasy experienced in the first terrestrial strolls? Was it that nascent thought blended with physical accomplishment—*modi intelligendi* (modes of understanding) bonded with *modi essendi* (modes of being) to forge our first encounter with numinous wisdom?[12]

Pilgrimage walking is all of these forms—mysterious walking, spiraling, whirling, meandering, labyrinthing—rolled into one extended experience. For on any pilgrimage, no matter how linear the path seems at the start, no matter how thorough the guidebook, the path gets lost. It bends back on itself. And, on some days, it circles back to its beginning.

From the disoriented trial and tribulation of such meander-walking—on the days that seem full of nothing but endless suffering and deprivations—the terrain suddenly becomes lustrous. One's dreams become especially vivid. The atmosphere itself vibrates. Only then, there at that moment, does one realize they are not alone; that the earth itself is alive and has been an ever-faithful companion and witness. And only then does one realize that they have other undiscerned core companions of being who have watched over our collective plight from the beginning, always luring us through our pain to the destiny and destination that is ours to claim. Pilgrimage can reveal to us our earthly and inner angels, our better angels of destiny.

Life is repetition. Some philosophies and spiritualities see it as a repetition of two cycles: synthesis and antithesis. Some perceive it as a triplicity: birth, death, rebirth; mother, child, holy spirit. Some discern a quaternal circulation: masculine, feminine, shadow, evil. But whatever cycle one perceives, it is a cycle of repetition, of return. The Great Return; the Great Round.

---

12. Cheetham, *All the World an Icon*, 65.

PILGRIMAGE AS INDIVIDUAL AND COLLECTIVE LIMINAL INITIATION

Solvitur ambulatio
(It is solved by walking)

According to Viktor Frankl, there is a space between stimulus and response for our own power and freedom.[13] I suggest that pilgrimage is that freedom-opening—that liminal niche between the incessant stimulus and response of our existence.

We live most of our lives out of sync, asynchronous, against time. Pilgrimage restores us to the synchronous, vibrant, authentically animated space described by Frankl. Part of our existence is reality-based. We cannot ignore or put off that aspect of living. But just as essential—not more or less, but *as* essential—is our numinal life. Philosophers call this ontic time: time with the gods. A point beyond time and space—without time and space, really. Neither container of essence (reality-based or numinal) is better than the other, they are simply twined dimensions that need each other. They are lovers, really; lovers who only get in trouble when they live apart. They are the twins Chronos and Kairos discussed in Chapter One.

> *He dreamed of being in the atrium of the French Quarter, in a five-star-like hotel in his hometown of New Orleans. He worked there as a high schooler doing odd jobs, from pool cleaning to bar serving. He deepened his already bourgeoning drinking addiction there, fed illegal drinks by sympathetic bar managers. "Eventually, for carding reasons," he shares, "they asked me to pour my own."*
>
> *In the dream, he is his current age. He is sitting at a round table in the hotel. To his left is his good friend L., a state representative and the wife of a woman chief justice. Also to his right is a state senator—another powerful woman. Both women are progressive forces in the state for gay and other minority rights. L. had asked him to endorse a gay marriage legislative initiative when he first moved to the state. He had demurred, having just arrived in his new Big Eight CEO position. He had sensed she was disappointed in him.*
>
> *To his right are his two young adult children, sitting up expectantly and waiting to see if this time he will step forward and be his fully, authentically voiced self.*
>
> *"Is this an atrium of initiation?" I ask.*

---

13. Yalom et al., "Many Faces Of Wisdom," 31.

I wondered if my patient was in analysis now, in that moment, to fully and authentically step forward into his unique, embodied destiny. Would this be the substance of our work together? His unconscious was inviting him to analytic pilgrimage. Fortunately, he consciously assented. Many do not, often to their great suffering and detriment. If one walks through their journey awake and calm, the gods might, just might, embrace them as one of their own and help them cherish their destiny in this world.

Because its numinous precincts are so startling in their space and time disorientation, the liminal requires initiatory preparation. The soul is stripped naked in such encounters, the heart opened up fully. The beauty of opening is so vivid and profound that it can feel almost like agony. To enter the liminal is to be introduced to and ultimately wed to deeper, long-vanquished parts of our precious soul-selves. It is a sacrament, a wedding of deepest being to deepest being, of core human to core divine.

> A woman dreams of being in a round, airy room with many close friends and assorted friendly souls. There are windows on all sides, floor to ceiling. Full-pane French windows with views of an endless procession of breathtaking forests, desert moonscapes, and seas through which the room is voyaging. Then, in the midst of this journey, the woman is being mantled in a green foundational garment by a close friend who is a talented tapestry maker. A white surplice is put on top. She feels as though she is being prepared for an anointing, a baptism, a marriage that will occur soon—after her traveling mandala room lands and she steps onto her deep-greening earth home.

The woman having this dream was in significant transition. She had recently moved intercontinentally. She had left behind childhood homes and was now coming to rest in an enchanted Celtic isle, her destined true Home.

The liminal and the synchronous are one and the same. They share a-Chronos time, a non-Chronos time. They inhabit and envelop Kairos time. In analysis, the synchronistic always paces the process and announces. It accompanies the major transitions, the crucial moments of transformation in the analytic orchestrations.

To enter safely and return, we must be mentored, guided through the labyrinth of this new world of vivid being we find when we fall down Alice's rabbit hole. Usually, the initial visits are short, presumably so ego can slowly absorb a bit of the immensity it is confronting. Very often, there are careful, coded instructions about what to puzzle over upon our return to ordinary time.

> *A patient dreams of going to a retirement celebration for a 75-year-old colleague. A professional scholar and one never to miss a reflective moment, he arrives with his writing pad and pen to record his observations of the event. While there, in a large impersonal hotel ballroom qua conference room, he finds himself in a darkened corner. He is facing an old mentor, but their face seems strangely different.*
> *"Is that you, S.?" The mentor asks.*
> *"Yes."*
> *"Then I will be in relationship with you if you can find and disclose your true, sorrow-connected self."*
> *The dreamer returns to the retirement fête only to discover he has lost his seat, his pen, and his writing pad. He feels disoriented. Are these the mentors and Sachems ahead on his vocational path if he stays awake and calm? To find out, he must observe—not write about or analyze. He must observe and deeply experience.*

The language of the dream seems coded because it is so packed tightly with ancient, time-engrained, soul-saturated wisdom that ego has to take its contemplative time in order to ponder the immensities. And the images and words and experiences of this rich, dense realm can be dangerous if not mindfully approached and respected. The mercurial fluids of deep-soul processes are so volatile they must not flow into consciousness too briskly or too slowly. Speed, temperature, valence must all be just right:

> *A patient dreams of seeing a rough, circular hole in a nondescript inner-room wall. A fluid is flowing out—a "trichloroethylene" fluid. An inner voice tells him, "It is going way too fast. I must slow it down so people, the community, the world are not hurt."*

Liminal, initiatory lands are wild lands.

> *A woman dreams of being at Ghost Ranch, a famous New Mexico wilderness retreat, with a beloved couple of friends. They are up late at night and notice her left arm lifted high in sleep at a very awkward angle. They awaken her to make sure she is alright. Then she is at an Oregon coast restaurant, taking the chef's famous cooking-and-then-eating class. An old, hapless co-teacher of music is there. He is saying he has to talk to her urgently, though she is engrossed in the lovely class and not much interested in attending to his latest, anxious crisis.*

Then she is moving into her lovely, open-frame, Sunset maga-
zine home. On the new lawn is a white sweater which she picks up
only to discover slugs and a dirty starfish unpleasantly mottled on
the underside. She espies her former husband dating the nice woman
next door. She attempts to be discrete, unnoticed, though she can
see this woman can look right back into her home's interior—some-
thing that will have to be quickly resolved in her new residency. The
dreamer steps out into the breathtaking backyard—Bryce Canyon
with a lovely light snow dusting. Two adolescent girls suddenly next
to her enthuse over the fun they'll have exploring the canyon's an-
cient Anasazi ruins.

The most precious element in us is wildness. Rawness. Primitiveness. Without wildness, we become flat, desiccated, and empty. The wild is the window to the soul. It is the portal by which the soul fuels our ongoing animations after our own true destiny. The wild re-animates deadened, hapless parts of our creative soul. It reminds us that under the most ordinary persona sweater the forgotten instinctual underworld of slugs and starfish thrives. Wildness tears us open, makes everything dangerously transparent. It is the renewing lobo and canyon of our being.

A client dreams of going to a colleague's house for a twilight dinner
gathering to work and have some leisure time together. As she treads
up the front walk, she sees a large dog drinking from a big silver
bowl. Then she realizes, with a rush of terrified fascination, that it is
a large vesper wolf peacefully drinking and gazing.

The liminal is the sanctuary of the wild, filled with the protective canyons of beauty where the primal wolf roams and hunts. If we enter these liminal realms with an attitude of respectful reverence—a welcoming, devotional openness to its empowering presence—they can honor our humility with the tonsure of mature, individuated wisdom:

A patient dreams of entering an old growth cedar forest late at night.
She heads south, down a path under a broad, black, starry sky. Then
she turns right to walk up a platform with water standing straight
up before her—air on one side and water magically on the other.
She wades into the water and keeps walking west. Then along the
L-shaped water course, the path turns north a short way toward a
giant, sacred mountain. She turns around, facing south and is given
a sacred tonsure by two or three wise crones.

Apparently, the liminal is an initiatory incubator for the gods as well as for us. The gods are no better than humans or vice versa. The gods and humans are lovers, really—needing each other, completing each other, fulfilling the mission of the cosmos that is lost forever if they irreparably disjoin. Jung knew this when he wrote a controversial little volume in the middle of the twentieth century. He had discovered a central part of what was missing in modern and post-modern life, what was driving many of his patients to a tortured and often disastrous distraction. In *Answer to Job* (1953), he wrote what was almost a psychoanalytic romance thriller about how the numinal and the phenomenal, the human and divine, had so needlessly and persistently betrayed each other with disastrous and often violent results. Pilgrimage can restore repose between these painfully parted lovers. Everyday reality and cosmic reality can once again co-inhere and find their rightful place in each other's arms.

Every therapy visit is a pilgrimage journey. It is an accompanied descent into liminal realms of both unexplored promise and pain. Most of the promise is the discovery of unknown gifts and capacities of being. Most of the pain is the psychoactive, dissociated debris of childhood trauma and adult situational trauma.

But the multiple visits are intense journeys charged with numinal power. If one stays the course and keeps to their unique pilgrim's path, the path of their true, basically unexplored destiny, it can result in an often significantly enhanced sense of personal vitality and meaning. But the visits must be accompanied for it to work. Transference really does happen. The process provokes archetypal energies that are held by the experienced therapist and the suffering client in their relationship. At first, when these deep wells of energy become unleashed from behind their trauma walls, a surge of uncomfortable feeling and even terror is created. It is projected back onto and into the therapist's being and body for containment until re-exposure. And re-encounter helps one grow accustomed to the material, lose one's fear of it, and develop mastery with these primal energies. This process allows primal, dissociated pain to be remembered, understood, and reclaimed. Once this slow, cyclical process spirals deep enough, one can acquire a new, integrity-based, soul-grounded capacity for the deployment of non-anxious, destiny-connected consciousness instead of destiny-avoidant unconsciousness and falsely soothing addictions.

As with individuals, cultures are always on pilgrimage. Individuals need initiation into deeper wisdoms. Cultures need initiation into deeper wisdoms. Culture's highest repository of pilgrim presence and memory is the art it produces and leaves behind on its outer and inner journeys. What we witness repetitively in that repository are primal geometries of form that infer journey and pilgrimage. The spiral is the most universally recurring image, but it is closely ghosted by labyrinths, whirls, mandalas, quaternities—all icons of the way the human spirit circumambulates the core essences of being, losing the way and wandering in the wasteland but always finding the way home in the end. Pilgrimage is always about getting home. That is why psychotherapy is inherently pilgrimage craft—because it is home craft, a depth narrating of our way back home from all our desperate wanderings.[14] And our widest, deepest, and truest home is the cosmos herself.

Cultures are always on pilgrimage because culture is the public forum where we commence our most profound conversations about who we are as a species, where we come from, and where we are going. Culture asks, "What is destiny?" and, "What role does the individual and her societal surround play in constellating and achieving authentic destiny?" This is why the highest repository of presence and memory is a culture's artistic output.

We all want to get home.[15] Home is the place of innocent repose and transformation we all seek from the first breath of life we draw. We can never know this home directly, only through the inference of all our senses. Projection is the indirect way that we know the world. Like submerged submarines pinging radar into the surrounding depths, listening for an echoing rebound ping, we project out into the world and look for a hard reflection of meaning and synthesis. As James Grotstein says, we have a homing instinct that is behind all our normal and anxious projections.[16] Liminality is both the zone of origin and consummation for such homing desires.

The gods, too, want to get home. We are not alone in this urgent desire. All creation, it seems, wishes to find this consummative place of repose in beauty, truth, and meaning. So, we meet not just one another, but also the gods and their emissaries in this liminal place, in the common, pilgrimage-accomplished meeting place. Home-pining, home-desiring, and home-projecting. Recent Jungian thought is the cutting edge for engaging

---

14. Gibson, "Process and Politics in Pastoral Psychology."

15. Hill, *At Home in the World.*

16. Grotstein, *Beam of Intense Darkness,* 181.

contemporary metaphysics and epistemology into such transcendent and transpersonal things.[17]

Pilgrimage is really spirit walking in a physical form. It is a healing of the mind-body split. It is body-moving prayer. The mythic cycle of the Grail quest, the quest for the vessel of true soul, is perhaps the most central saga narration of our restless pilgrim wanderlust in search of our true core of being, our true home of spirit. Indeed, Jean Shinoda Bolen identifies the three essential elements of the Grail quest as the features of its three most prominent questing knights:

- Galahad—Pure-Spirit
- Perceval—Heart-Dedication
- Bors—Contemplative Mind[18]

The liminal realms constellate pure, visionary spirit, heart-true dedication, and a contemplative, calm mind. Pilgrimage, our individuating journey through life, is the constant vehicle for the realization of individuation or its loss, depending on how pure our spirits, how dedicated our hearts, how quiet our minds become.

In our various pilgrimages, we re-weave the trauma-torn fabric of our being and experience anew the underlying, ineffable unified tapestry of things. The cosmos is animate, it is creaturely, it sings, it speaks, it dreams. And each one of us is an essential chord in that choir of creation. As James Hollis suggests, "We resonate to such images because they are the carriers of such energy as it courses through us even as it animates the cosmos. We are moved only by like to like. What beckons from the other side, and to whose mythic motions all of us move, is, in ways we could never comprehend, like us, of us, about us."[19]

Pilgrimage is "afterwards walking," what German depth therapy calls *Nachträglichkeit*. It is not reductive to look at what happened before—say, in our childhood—to determine what happens later in adulthood, especially by primally organizing traumatic events. Rather, it is a hermeneutic process, the core dynamic of depth therapy, where we "project retroactively"

17. See, for example, Corbett, *Religious Function of the Psyche*; Edinger, *Mysterium Lectures*; Heisig, *Imago Dei*; Sandner and Wong, *Sacred Heritage*; Raff, *Healing the Wounded God*; Raff, *Jung and the Alchemical Imagination*; Ulanov, *Religion and Spirituality in Carl Jung*.

18. Bolen, *Crossing to Avalon*, 40.

19. Hollis, *Archetypal Imagination*, 84.

into the past in a present living moment to review, relive, and rearrange a delaying/detouring/disturbing moment in our lives.[20] Pilgrimage is a dynamic individual and collective way of walking ancient paths in the company of ancestors for the purpose of rearranging traumatic constellations of being. *Nachträglichkeit.*

So, we are all minefields of complexity. Pilgrimage and therapy safely explode our minefields. Depth therapy, soul therapy, seeks the opening of these complexes into something more whole, meaningful, and useful for our individual and for collective existence. An often stagnant collective consciousness fears these unnerving openings and meaningful pryings, for therapy is inherently an act of revolution, not accommodation. It is an act of prying open lost and forgotten chambers of soul treasure.

Pilgrimage walking is thus revolutionary walking. Pilgrimage walking is holographic walking. It is an intentional walking that spirals down into the avoided, uncomfortable truths of being. It is liminal ambulating. It walks around things and then penetrates them to their core. Pilgrimage walks between time and space. It fills the interstices between time and space with numinal presence. The ancestors, the gods, the guardian spirits of all our collective species' history abide in pilgrimage-mediated time.

Aboriginal people historically lived in liminal time. They walked in a state of almost incessant pilgrimage. They inscribed themselves in the terrain within which they lived. The terrain inscribed itself within their flesh. They ceremonially tattooed images of the encounter with sacred earth and sky upon their bodies. Both body and earth were sacred, as was the liminal ether within which they co-abided. This was the *illud tempore*, the eternal original time. It was the on-going creation myth. Creation was not historical and static. It was contemporaneous and dynamic.

Pilgrimage is a descent into the Mithraeum—underground, Mithraic cult chambers later adopted by Christians for secret performances of their most sacred paschal rites. Embraced by intensified darkness, pilgrimage seeks transformation in chaotic nocturnal raptures. As was the case with Parmenides, the founder of esoteric Western philosophies and mystery traditions who studied and embodied shamanic craft, pilgrimage is an act of shamanic auto-entombment.[21] Parmenides buried his students in tombs for three days so they could die and be reborn into their full meaning and destiny. Pilgrimage walking is just such a dying and rebirthing, a journey

20. Caruth, interview with Jean Laplanche.
21. Kingsley, *In the Dark Places of Wisdom.*

to the gates of death and beyond, seeking intimations of a next incarnation. If we are lucky in the intensified darkness of our pilgrim's tomb, the gods incarnate at their most elemental and raw. They are right before us, speaking clearly and movingly about our unique gifts and missions in this world and beyond.

Pilgrimage is a descent into the Mithraeum of life. It is a continuing incarnation journey burrowing deeper and deeper into the mysterious flesh of this ambivalent world. The darkness embraces and intensifies the journey, which can lead to nocturnal raptures of transformation. It is shamanic entombment and possibly enactment. It is a journey unto the gates of death, beyond which we might catch a glimpse of future incarnations and travels of spirit and body.

Journeying into liminal realms is risky business. Such soul-work is dangerous work. It is ordeal work. It will take one into the very bowels of personal and collective experience, there to encounter the energetic beasts that fuel all creation:

> A long-term patient in mid process, caught in the doldrums that often occur mid voyage in an analytic passage, dreams of being violently raped and tossed into a cave-like cell guarded only by a rickety bamboo gate/door. Her dream ravisher joins her in her grieving, traumatized prison chamber, violently kissing her upper neck.
>
> Then the scene shifts dramatically, and she accompanies an old friend to two rooms in a massive vertical mesa shelf. She discovers her husband in her room. It is a simple, modern, bare room such as one finds in a low-end budget motel chain. Restless, she wanders around the surrounding terrain to discover the entrance of a massive cave that thrusts steeply down into a chasm-like depth. Timidly easing into the cavernous darkness, she espies three white grizzly bears—a mother and two cubs. They glisten eerily in the dank darkness. The mother stands suddenly and glares her way. Terrified, the woman eases back out of the cavern and runs to her room. Desperately, asks her husband, "Will they find us in here?"

Pilgrimage is ordeal. It is the hero's journey and the crone's due. Ordeal is soulful suffering in response to the restless call of existential angst. We set out on unknown paths because the known has become unbearable and empty. We seek respectful inquiry of and protection from the great mother bear as we seek the truest path of our ordained destiny along this life-way.

The 2010 film *Scott Pilgrim vs. the World* captures a sense of the angst-driven developmental ordeal that is behind all authentic pilgrimage. It is a quintessential American tale of a darkly romantic pilgrimage: a high school rock musician must win a dream-prophesied new love interest by defeating her seven other suitors—an outer quest overlaying the more essential interior anima development necessary for any young man to gain a heroic and successful foothold in the world. The eternally young puer-man must find a more substantial, soul-based relationship to his life and destiny; an initiation into the deeper, true mythos of Self that will lead to a vibrant, initiated life of cultural and relational contribution—a life that is lived well to die well—and to end life as conscious, achieved, calm, and awake as possible.

There is a clear trend of such puerish and puellaish behavior (a Jungian clinical term for immaturely frozen narcissistic personalities[22]) throughout all of American history. It begins with the romantically esoteric Thomas Jefferson himself, an angst-driven youth who set out to recover his Rousseauian noble savage agrarian roots atop his isolated Monticello Shangri-La.[23] His fiery puer declarations are burned deep into our founding national documents even as we too often overlook the violent, slave-raping shadow behind this puer brilliance. Genuine pilgrimage would confess, atone, and transform that shadow as the most essential task of passage, a task few human journeyers fully accomplish.

Pilgrimage addresses the same symptom constants as therapy. It processes in similar ways. Pilgrimage penetrates traditional, often childhood-generated defenses against introjected pain. This penetration is created by the inevitable moments of time-space disorientation that pilgrimage produces. No matter how comprehensive the personal or written guide, one gets lost on the way, lost many times over and over again. One is in strange terrain, often where residents speak in strange languages and observe foreign customs. This lostness in the moment triggers the Global Lostness we all feel. It is the fear at our psychic core—the person and species terror—of absolute abandonment and annihilation of being.

Once this penetration has been affected, core shadow issues of personality flood out. Shadow appearances always come coated in expressions of primal rage and sorrow—the secondary defenses against the most primitive terror of all for most in our species—being swallowed up in the

22. von Franz, *Puer Aeternus*.

23. Ellis, *American Sphinx*, 30.

immense undigested sea of sorrow that we have reservoired at the pit of our existential and spiritual being.

Henri Corbin and the ancient Persian philosophers from whom he caringly borrowed believed that careful attention to this trajectory of re-alized imagination-induced meaning across our lifetimes brings us to the great bridge (what the ancient Persians called Cinvat Bridge). This great bridge spans the chasm between life and death. If we have lived well and consciously, the bridge leads us to where our angel of destiny, our soul-Daena, lovingly awaits us. Only then, after a lifetime of staying awake amid the turbulent darkness and despair of this existence, do we find wholeness. "Up to the moment when the earthly soul meets its Angel on the bridge," Tom Cheetham reminds us, "the earthly soul is lacking its eternal half—it is "lagging behind itself," incomplete and confined within the limited time of the combat of daily living. The earthly soul lives in nostalgia and anticipa-tion, in exiled incompleteness, in longing and hope.[24]

Pilgrimage is a practice in conscious living and conscious dying. It is a rehearsal of our mortality and its full consequences. Is death just the com-puter turning off? A surrender to the primal nothing? A blank screen? Am I just gone, a forgotten now-empty space? Or is it a doorway, a portal into something more vast—the next stage in an evolving sequence of personal and collective Being? Pilgrimage doubles down on the latter.

Perhaps the liminal and its pilgrimage consort serve as a midwife di-mension to both birth and death. Perhaps liminality is the amniotic fluid containing both processes, both dimensions sequentially or maybe even simultaneously.

PILGRIMAGE AS EARTH, AS COSMOS CRAFT

Psyche is not mind but a landscape in which things are alive with meaning and mystery.[25]

Pilgrimage reminds us that we are contiguous with the all the cosmos. Cit-ing Holderlin, Pascal, and Plato, James Hollis reflects this notion of con-tiguousness in *The Archetypical Imagination*. "We frequently find strangers in our dreams who seem to know us," he explains, "so there is something

---

24. Cheetham, *All the World an Icon*, 46,
25. Brooke, "Self, the Psyche and the World," 603.

which is familiar in all of us, for we are of this contiguous cosmos—plant, animal, and soul, and only ego splits us off."[26]

In pilgrimage, we reawaken to our unity with the All, our embeddedness in foundational creation. Pilgrimage, like a good course of analysis or a big dream, can restore repose between the painfully parted lovers: everyday reality and cosmic reality. It can create space for these realities to once again co-inhere and find their rightful place in each other's arms.

What can initiate a pilgrim's desire to begin the mindful wander? Many times, it is the cumulative impact of decades of needling—little nudges of dissatisfaction, an underlying angst to make more of life, a desire to feel more deeply in life. The tipping motivation might be found in such urges as:

- To come see where something historically or culturally key happened
- To draw near something sacred
- To achieve pardon
- To hope and ask for a miracle
- To give thanks
- To express thanks for love of the gods
- To answer a sense of inner call
- To assuage curiosity about why others went
- To jumpstart a stagnant everyday reality
- To reclaim lost, abandoned, forgotten parts of self
- To admire something beautiful
- To make a vacation more interesting
- To honor a vow made in an extreme circumstance
- To prepare for death
- To "keep up with the Joneses"
- To find and penetrate sacred portals/thresholds (limen)[27]

Pilgrimage restores the centrality of the mystic earth to human progress and procession. Neither individuals nor cultures fare well when exiled

---

26. Hollis, *Archetypal Imagination*, 84.

27. This list has been adapted from Clift and Clift, *Archetype of Pilgrimage*.

from the earth. As Tom Cheetham puts it, "No one has seen the soul with the eyes with which we normally perceive the things of this world. Only the lament of the mystic flute cut from the source, from the Earth of Light, can give some premonition of it. All that grows from that Earth and is separated from it, the story of exile and return, this it is that haunts."[28]

Pilgrimage walks between worlds, between things. It is Henry Corbin's *Ta'wil*—the spiritual nature within all things. It is *tohu va vohu*—waste and void.[29] It is *challal ha-panui*—the vacated space.[30] And it is animate and relentless, pursuing us *lo dumiyah*—with no respite.[31]

Pilgrimage is a panentheistic process (divinity is in everything, not that everything is divine). It is a walking through a world infused with the numinous. The longer one walks, the more one generally realizes that all is touched by *all* the transforming radiances *all* around us *all* the time—earth, sky, fire, water, being. All being is fired and animated.

There is cosmological conjecture in some theological circles that there was a noisy void before the Big Bang that generated creation. This void was filled with a murmuring, an incessant thrumming hum. The moment of creation brought this hum to a halt. Silence was born. Here, noise is an eternal given. It is silence that is the novel creation.[32]

Pilgrimage discovers original wildness and wilderness under the most urban of terrains. The most liminal spots in a city are its sanctuaries, its civic buildings, and its graveyards—all places cherished by the numinal ancestors. *Spoon River Anthology* and *Our Town* are liminal classics which get the burial-ground, ancestral stones to speak.[33] Homer and the ancient Greeks would never set out on or return from an epic journey without the visionary ancestral consults achieved by a visit to the earth openings into the underworld.

My travels, all travel really, is created, executed, and remembered in liminal space. Ordinarily blinded by the defenses of our everyday security systems, we travel in an attempt to leap to other nodes of experience.

When I was an undergraduate, I used to go out from my university town into an adjacent wild prairie grass area called the Flint Hills. This is

---

28. Cheetham, *All the World an Icon*, 38.

29. Zornberg, *Murmuring Deep*, xx.

30. Zornberg, *Murmuring Deep*, xviii.

31. Zornberg, *Murmuring Deep*, xxii.

32. Zornberg, *Murmuring Deep*, xvii–xviii.

33. Masters, *Spoon River Anthology*; Wilder, *Our Town*.

a wide-horizon part of Kansas State; hundreds of square miles of craggy limestone outcroppings covered with a thin cling of bluestem grasses, the only organic that can find root traction in such gritty, en-stoned undersoil. I'd go with a student-ghetto apartment chum who lived in Emporia, a town bordering this serene expanse of grazing cattle, post-stone ranch homes, and incessant, melancholy wind moan. We'd go out at the beginning of the burn season when, like the aboriginal stewards they displaced, ranchers would set the early and late season grass ablaze to release a new round of super-charged nitrogen grass-growth enhancer—nature's all-organic fertil-izer. We'd just lie on the prairie grass atop one of those flint hilltops and watch the world burn from horizon to horizon.

The fires were set at dusk, igniters poured like windrows around their corn and wheat fields. The fires would flare right up and hiss along the earth like aroused serpents snaking lazily along the contours of those ancient limestone outcroppings. From our vantage point, the fires made fanciful images like clouds puffing up rapidly in the supercharged thunderhead skies of a hot summer twilight. Thinking of them now I imagine close par-allels between the cryptic lines carved in Peru's Nazca plains—archaic fire-breathing creatures awakened and bellowing into the vast cosmic night of things. Ley lines. The gods marking the sacred flanks of the earth, caressing hidden tender points of access into her soft, vulnerable underbelly. Ley line beacons along earth runways inviting lost souls down from their frenzied aerial disorientations into furrowed safe havens.

Liminality leaves its footprint in our psyches. We can find its fresh tracks. We know it is has made a visit. Most often these inspections are nocturnal, like dreams, so as not to spook a too-vigilant ego, ever wary of anything uncanny and unsettling—two commodities the liminal trades in heavily.

Pilgrimage allows a more conscious tracking of these footprints. There is currently a revival of ancient pilgrimage paths all over the planet. The Camino Santiago had tens of thousands of pilgrim walkers over the millen-nia but had died down to just a straggling handful of faithful sojourners by the mid 1980s. Since then, there has been a renaissance of interest, from the Orthodox devout to the New Age seekers. Now there are nearly a million *peregrinos* (pilgrims) annually walking some part of the Camino. And the embodied intenseness seems similar for all. There is deep healing to be had in walking the stones that so many of our suffering forebears have tread. Whether a Christian on the Camino or a Buddhist on Japan's Shikkoku

Island, the earth remembers the gentle pilgrim's footsteps and willingly offers up its compassionate, merciful alms of calming peace.

Some say these paths were "discovered" by ancient seers and mystics. They say crone shamans were given Earth's third-eye sight, that a lighted path opened up under their feet and guided them on. Some say the ancient Polynesian navigator mystics saw a similar lighted path in the phosphorescent seas, a path that led them to outer blessed isles, sea paths that ultimately revealed to these sage navigators the Hawaiian archipelago. Some contemporary Western mystics even say that the Camino does not end at the tomb of St. James in the Cathedral of Santiago (a building thrown up to a Christian war machine fantasy that served as a useful piece of theological propaganda in the bloody Reconquista against the Spanish Saracens). They say, rather, that it ends at Finnistera, "Land's End," a promontory fifty miles due west of Santiago and the last dagger of mainland Europe jutting out into the empty Atlantic. It is here, many say, that the Druid crones led their faithful to annual rites of marrying, anointing, initiating, and burying, all performed on giant flat stones. The grooved outlines of human devotees are still visible under their gorse underbrush mantle.

Ley lines are real. Charged god lines. Angel paths. The ancients found their ways home on them. Some say ley line power has receded into the deep earth, the deep psyche, the deep imagination. But in northwestern Spain, I know they live for sure.

Ley line detection requires special equipment and special perception. I once co-led a regional Jung Society group on the last hundred kilometers of the renowned Camino in northwest Spain. The journey was designed as a nomadic, on-site seminar. The group engaged a local guide to handle housing and transportation logistics so that I and my co-presenter could attend solely to content and group process responsibilities.

My colleague and I spent considerable time carefully preparing for the pilgrimage. We wanted the participants to have a true experience of the Camino, not a drive-by titillation that would be over at the Cathedral in Santiago. We began each day's walk with a trailhead chant (drawing from many different global spiritual traditions) and a strong encouragement for each participant to walk alone in silence for at least the first half of each day. We'd end the day in silence, whenever possible, with respectful group debriefing of their depth experience along the way. Often, the sharings were moving and visceral.

About one-third of the way into the event, the delightful Spanish guide came to me. A bright, world-wise Galician, he had been unexpectedly moved by our pilgrimage design. He told me he had led many jaded, wealthy tourist groups on this path. But he felt that the archetypal sensitivity our group brought to the Camino honored his homeland and its globally known historical asset. He felt he had spiritually grown through the experience with us and wondered if he could return the favor by adding some visits to locked templar guardian churches along the way. I readily assented to his largesse.

The next day, he and the bus met us at trail's end. But instead of driving us to our local housing, he took us to our first ancient templar chapel, one of a number of chapels built by the venerable secret Templar Order a millennium ago to protect and house pilgrims on their sacred way. A friend next door gave him the giant skeleton key for access, and, in short order, we were in a musty, dim, stone emptiness that greeted us with solemn silence. We wandered amid templar crypts and paused before a somber altar to Mary and Child.

Then I heard a gentle, rapid clanking of metal on metal. A psychologist participant from Australia had two metal rods bent at a 90 degree angle hanging from her upper palms as she walked back and forth across the main axis aisles of the chapel. She noticed that I was watching her quizzically and explained that she was using divining wands given her by aboriginal dowsers near Alice Springs. She was experiencing something quite extraordinary. She gave me the rods, showed me how to let them dangle from my upper palms so no muscle could influence their movement. She backed me away from the center aisle several feet and told me to walk transversely across it again. Every time I walked over this center line, at about 18 inches from dead center, the rods would turn 90 degrees out. They would remain in this position until I was about 18 inches on the other side, when they would close again. A ley line detected, enacted, activated, aroused—here where it lay dormant and unsuspected in a shrouded space of protected soul. Ninety percent of the group experienced the same phenomenon.

The excited guide rushed with us back to the bus. He pulled out Camino maps. The group hastily conceived a research project. We'd see how long this rarity lasted. We ley-line-dowser-proofed every day all the way up to the casket of St. James himself in the Cathedral in Santiago. If the Christian myth was correct, the rods very movement should cease there. If the ancient Celtic myth was correct, then the Camino was really a Christian,

Reconquista hijacking of a much older Druid healing path. If the Celtic history of Solstice ceremonies at the stunning cliffs above Finnesterra were true, then the rods should "open the door" to the way—all the way to the Western Sea. The rods opened from the casket 10 kilometers beyond Santiago's walls. Apparently, the Druids were the original shaman seers of this precious ley-line journey.

These pilgrim paths are telluric tell-lines, song-lines in the service of reviving an emergent mono-myth that pays homage to a depth recovery and amplification of the ancient goddess-earth-body sacred Oneness. Depth psychotherapy is an exact intra-psychic replication of outer pilgrimage. It is helping people find and navigate by these illuminated inner ley lines of destiny guidance, these inner song lines of the soul.

It seems that in these pilgrim travels the liminal always visits the collective. But, strangely, the access seems mainly across and through personal psychic lands. It is like the collective/social/cultural sphere is surrounded by the moat of personal psychic protections. They form a web of barrier for these precious, fragile domains. As the vulnerable beauty of our national parks is surrounded by vast interstices of private land, so the vulnerable beauty of our shared collective culture is surrounded by private psychic estates.

Terry Tempest Williams captures this sentiment perfectly in her reminiscences and reflections on time spent in America's outdoors:

> "The purpose of life is to see," the writer Jack Turner said to me on a late summer walk at the base of the Tetons. I understand this to be a matter of paying attention. The nature of our national parks is bound to the nature of our own humility, our capacity to stay open and curious in a world that instead beckons closure through fear. For me, humility begins as a deep recognition of all I do not know.
>
> Our national parks are blood. They are more than scenery, they are portals and thresholds of wonder, an open door that swings back and forth from our past to our future. "This something we call America lives not so much in political institutions as in its rocks and skies and seas," wrote the photographer Paul Strand.[34]

As the ceaseless onslaught of an often rapacious and subdividing consciousness subdued this seemingly eternal immensity into slayed forests and brutally tilled land, so the collective unconscious sometimes seems

---

34. Williams, *Hour of Land*, 13.

enclosed and subdued with national park cameos of quaint irrational moods and spirit-possessions left as whispers of once primeval domain. Maybe the way to heal the collective wilderness wound is first to heal badly-ravaged personal, inner-wilderness terrains?

Trade centers in the ancient world were generally violence-free zones because trade meant exchange, which meant survival. And these trade centers became cosmopolitan with Celtoi, Roman, Jew, and *pagani* [pagan] intermixing, sharing ideas, discussing cultural aspirations, and revealing personal and collective dreams for improvement and enhancement. Holy people, too, often navigated to and practiced within and along the trade routes connecting these centers.

The liminal is the spirit of that wildness and not the location. It is as uncanny, omnipresent, and irreducible as ever. And the bridge of its shaping presencing—from individual to collective and probably back again—is myth, both personal and collective. Myth is the source of the *urground*, the primal birth land of all life's shared being, its origins and its ends. Myth is the narrative of cosmic purpose written in dynamic, evolving pentameters of meaning-making that underscore every Big Dream.

The individual's growing into one's personal myth in the analytic process is never a solipsistic event. Such growth is a significant social resource because it provides society with individuals endowed with the critical perspective that only living out of their personal myth affords. This side of the religious role of the analytic process is peculiarly pressing in a time of epochal change. Jung thought his time and ours was a moment of such epochal change. He refers to "the end of the Christian aeon" and to "the invalidation of Christ," describing himself as a modern Joachim di Fiore ushering in a new age of the Spirit.[35]

"In this context," writes John Dourley, "the analytic endeavor can be revisioned not only on a personal level as an occasion for the surfacing of individual mythologies. The analytic endeavor becomes, through the individuals it touches, a major contributor to the emergence of a more encompassing collective myth or now-dawning revelation which Jung anticipated but understandably could not describe in more than general terms."[36]

And the collective, the mythic realm that is channeled by the liminal, is not an inauthentic, anxious, fearful collective but a grounded, broad-visioned collective:

35. Jung, *Two Essays in Analytical Psychology*, 138.
36. Dourley, *On Behalf of the Mystic Fool*, 44.

> With the departure of those with a native religious sensitivity and/
> or developed mind, collective religion is largely abandoned to
> various forms and degrees of fundamentalism in both West and
> East. The numerical surge of institutional fundamentalism bears
> stark witness to the baser lusts of humanity collective religion so
> often serves, namely, the need for instant certitude collectively
> reinforced in the face of the anxiety and fear of living with doubt.[37]

Pilgrimage and its sacrifices and rigors make it increasingly easy to surrender ego. And with a relaxed, healthy ego, it is easier to be absorbed into the All that is beyond our petty desires and ambitions. Liminal literature from all depth psycho-spiritual traditions seems to confirm the importance of not just penetrating liminal realms, not just reposing there for longer and longer moments of being, but eventually seeking merger with the All that is waiting in this garden of coalesced divine human love. As Dourley points out, "Recent scholarship confirms that though they be continuous, the experience of the birth of God in the soul and the experience of the breakthrough are distinct though related. It is as if the birth of the Son in the soul demands of its very dynamic the deeper ingression into the preceding Godhead as the culmination of the soul's spiritual life."[38]

It also seems that this merger dynamic is required of the divine with the created, that divinity goes beyond just visiting liminal realms—it seeks to become an incarnated, merged resident. This dynamic merger, this emptying of self to fill with Self, might be dynamically awaiting all sentient life as it passes through the black holes of this transitory world into the dynamic, compassionate stasis of the beyond. Henri Corbin, scholar friend of Jung who often came and lectured at the famous Eranos Seminars in Anscona, Italy, was the modern world's most knowledgeable advocate of the angelic. For Corbin, the repetitions of pilgrimage—the daily repeated path of process and devotion, the sharing of the tales of life's true path both recent and ancient—were critical. In these pilgrim repetitions and recitals, angelic presences—real, liminal beings bearing divine intimacies—become constellated in our conscious awareness. For Corbin (as for Jung), Tom Cheetham suggests, "this dawning consciousness is an opening onto the profound mystery that envelopes the human person."[39] It is through such daily pilgrim devotionals that divine presence, animate divine presence

---

37. Dourley, *On Behalf of the Mystic Fool*, 44.

38. Dourley, *Jung and his Mystics*, 93.

39. Cheetham, *All the World an Icon*, 68–69.

and companionship, becomes manifest and embodied. It is then that we become most fully human . . . and divine.

It is then, indeed, that the true wisdom at the core of our being, the true Gnosis of inner and outer worlds, becomes pilgrimage transduced into our awareness.

> *My guide and I entered by that hidden path, to make our*
> *way back to the shining world: and, not caring to rest, we*
> *climbed up, he first, and I second, until, through a round*
> *opening, I saw those things of beauty that the sky holds:*
> *and we issued out, from there, to see, again, the stars.*

—DANTE, *INFERNO*, CANTO 34[40]

40. Dante, *The Divine Comedy, Inferno Canto XXXIV.*

PERFORMANCE

Art is not made to decorate rooms.
It is an offensive weapon in the defense against the enemy.
—PABLO PICASSO[1]

EVERY NIGHT, EVERY BEING ON the planet—and maybe even every life form—dreams new scriptures, new stories about where to find the meaning, the gods, and the destinies in their lives. Every night, all cultures do the same thing.

The liminal is where all that is whole, complete, and transformed resides. It is where all the dynamic knowledge of ultimate wisdom is stored. It is the library of soul. And this library is the central room in the Home of Soul. It exists at the farthest reaches of both interstellar and intra-stellar space. It is the Matrix Home, dynamically equipoised at the core of authentic relationship and connection between humanity and mystery.

In the 2014 film *Interstellar*, Christopher Nolan cinematically explores this home. The film's inception moment is our world, just a few clicks ahead into the future. It begins on a dustbowl farm—only this dustbowl is not set in the 1930s. It is set on our planet, a planet robbed (presumably by profit-driven corporate chicanery) of nutrient soil. It has withered. It now aimlessly and maliciously blows in grimy, desperation-cloaked misery, coating bookshelves and toy models of long-ago space shuttles. It is the motherless farm of a cranky, caring maternal grandfather, a puerish, formerly gifted astronaut, his dutiful mid-teen son, and a perky pre-adolescent daughter.

---

1. Picasso, *Picasso: Masterpieces from the Musée National Picasso.*

The mother died because the post-millennial, dustbowl-collapsed medical system could not afford early cancer-monitoring equipment.

It is a doomed farm, home to a doomed species, in the middle of a doomed planet. As we learn during the plot's well-gaited unraveling, the organic light on Mother Earth is about to be irreparably extinguished. As a result, the vocation-crushed farmer astronaut is re-knighted into his beloved captain's chair. He is to lead a Hail Mary pass through a suddenly manifested black hole orbiting Saturn's rings. (Yes, that mythic Saturn, patron home of benched, saturnine-brooding, patriarchal puer-heroes.)

What is most relevant here is the central room of that dusty farmhouse—an almost magisterially provisioned wall-to-ceiling shelved library. It is the bedroom of the daughter, Murphy, who is named after a positively reframed Murphy's Law: if something is meant to happen, it will happen. This gifted daughter has been disturbed by ghosting visitations—a phenomenon which the skeptical father reframes through the lens of science—until, one day, a dust storm leaves gravity anomaly Morse Code patterns ridge-etched on the bedroom floor. This code is discovered to be coordinates, coordinates that lead the father—that vanquished argonaut Don Quixote—back to his silver-phallused orbital rocket-steed.

It is also in this room that he bids adieu to his beloved daughter on the eve of his species-saving ordeal to see if one of three newly-revealed planets near the Saturn-adjacent black hole might be a workable new home for refugee earthings. His daughter keeps her back resolutely turned, understandably enraged that this second and now only parent is leaving her, too, and probably forever. Flatfooted by his daughter's anguish—as puers almost inevitably are—he leaves her his watch, his Chronos-logos parting gift. He places it on the bookshelf next to the shuttle model, where it ticks out its sad patriarchal tattoo.

Meanwhile, the gifted expedition scientist, Dr. Brand, has left her earth-bound, expedition-director father in order to be a member of the fated crew. It is an inverted father-daughter mirroring within the film, and in this iteration, she discovers that her father had abandoned her in a carefully kept, fatal lie.

Flash forward across much empty, black-hole space, through high Grail-Planet-Quest adventure, through human betrayal, near death encounters, and bourgeoning love. Now, with all new-home, near-planet options exhausted but one, the whirling mandala-wheel of space is on the edge of being fully sucked into the Gargantua black hole. But just before this absorption, the Heroic Argonaut flings Dr. Brand's escape pod toward that last planetary hope, thus surrendering his own fuel-meager vessel into the primal gravity-maw of the black hole.

There, he calmly awaits his Samurai-sacrifice fate. He dutifully records his experience as he travels through a 2001: *A Space Odyssey*/Stanley Kubrick-esque wormhole of special effects and awe. And in the midst of that terror-gripped immersion, he is ordered by his faithful onboard robot (a cinematic counterpoint to 2001's cyber-evil Hal) to eject into the raw core of the black hole's mysterious singularity. And there, the rushing of adrenaline and space and image and memory becomes the deep calm and padded comfort of a multi-dimensional cosmic library room. But, unlike 2001's glass-and-steel cosmic Scan-design, this living space does not have an aging old man in the new dimension. It has glimpses and peaks into that farmhouse in the old earth dimension—glimpses and peaks from between the books neatly shelved in his daughter's chamber.

Murphy herself fades in and out, both young and in her current mid-thirties. She appears hopeless and hopeful as he frantically dives up and down five dimensional slats, experiencing peaks and glimpses of his beloved daughter. This new dimensional space is multi-layered, multi-formed, multi-fabricated—like the models of time-warped space his physicist friend had shown him to provide a graphic of the black hole's mysterious architecture.

Frantically, he wills his head-thought and heart-thought to find his daughter. First, he does so through the gravity-ridged coordinate coding. He sees himself as the young father, recognizing and believing his daughter's gravity ghosts and deciphering their message—his message ghosted from the future. Then, he tries to connect by willing the watch he gave her to move backward in Morse Code sequences. These relay the new black hole-derived quantum data, which will help solve the space-time-gravity formula and thus allow the surviving human billions to escape their doomed planet and find new homes within interstellar colonies. And he accomplishes this all through a strange dance across time, space, gravity, and (central ingredient) father-daughter love.

Murphy "gets" the message. She has an *eureka* moment. The species is saved. Daddy wakes up on a new colony circling Saturn's rings. He is told he is one hundred and twenty—though he looks middle-aged. And, more incredibly, he is told his centenarian daughter has, against stern medical advice, traveled to greet him. They meet; he fulfilling his promise to return, she remembering her sardonic thought that she'd be as old as he when he warp returned through the black hole. She says that no parent should see his child die, that she is fulfilled now, surrounded by thirty or more of her— and his—extended family. He should now go find his beloved Dr. Brand, waiting alone on the last planet, a verdant world filled with water, plants, and light. Lancelot has found his Guinevere, father has redeemed daughter, daughter has transformed father. The cosmic alchemy of love has spiraled one full turn closer to its destined home.

This is liminal space rendered as pure and whole as humanly possible. This is the therapy room on the best of days—a cosmic library where generations of both fulfilled and frayed love can find their love-completion in one another. Fathers and daughters, mothers and sons, beloved and beloved, divine and human. The ultimate singularity is love. As Luke Hockley writes, " . . . we are discovering that one of the reasons we enjoy films lies in the way that they use images that have a psychological relevance for us."[2]

This book possesses a theoretical and philosophical/theological bias— a Jungian psycho-spirituality. Unlike many psychological theories (which start with experience, breaking them down into their insular units of meaning), a Jungian perspective begins with the insular moment of experience and builds it up toward wider vessels of possible meaning—what Jung called the archetypes.[3]

And the vessel of experience par excellence is image. Not flat, shopping-mall image but whole-bodied, well-rounded image—what this book calls soul-image. Image here is what the twentieth-century philosopher Immanuel Levinas would call "image as optics"—a deep way of seeing that is beyond the flat, hard surface of things, beyond event, beyond the unconscious and anxious projection of our inner turmoils and desires onto the world.[4] It is a deep optics that sees these things as they truly are, sees the real essence of the world and the Other. It sees the soul of the world.[5]

The essential fuel of society is art and soul. The essential fuel of therapy is art and soul. No psychotherapy, and especially no depth psychotherapy, is just technology or methodology. For the arts "offer us a way through our predicaments with the tempered light of imagination instead

---

2. Hockley, *Cinematic Projections*, 165.

3. Hockley, *Cinematic Projections*, 63–64.

4. Saxton, "Fragile Faces: Levinas and Lanzmann, 1–14.

5. Hillman, *Soul's Code*; Sardello, *Facing the World with Soul*.

of the blazing lamp of enlightenment."[6] The therapists who stay alive in this business are therapists who stay open to the arts. Arts re-vision, re-inspire, re-encourage. Through the balm of their restorative image and texture they soothe the soul and give it solace. Art and beauty are the essential portals into liminal realms.

Every human being is a living canvas. Psychotherapists get to view their richly hung galleries all day long. Not that such conscious, lovingly indifferent, clinical calm witnessing is without cost. Viewing any human art—the depth viewing or hearing or touching of any human art—requires the presence of soul and its assent to take image deep within the body-self. And such depth absorption is alchemical; it opens up self-chemistry to change and even to transformation. Entering an art gallery or the performance hall is always risky business. The soul is always at stake, whether acknowledged or not by self-consciousness.

And the highest art is raw, lived, opened-up human experience, no matter how initially desperate or tragic. Every day in my office is a moving stroll down the aisles of the Louvre or the Uffizi or the Prado. It's an event of fierce art-making, of divine aesthetic encounter. As Picasso said, "Painting isn't an aesthetic operation; it's a form of magic designed as mediator between this strange hostile world and us . . . God is really only another artist. He invented the giraffe, the elephant, the cat. He has no real style. He just goes on trying other things."[7]

The arts are the repository of beauty. And beauty is a vessel for catharsis, for the provocation of the cathartic soul that the ancient world felt was central and essential to full, abundant living. At sites like Thebes, Epidaurus, the Acropolis, Delphi, or Rome, visual arts and powerful community theater were used overtly to provoke the appearance and presence of the soul and the divinity the soul serves. Some people collect art in their homes to evoke such transformative grief. I collect film in convenient DVD form, and there is almost nothing I enjoy more than privately screening favorite films—particularly scenes of soulful beauty. It warms and soothes my heart, and it often constellates creative insight and movement in my personal and professional life.

Beauty is the very face of the liminal Other. Beauty is not just the sweet. Beauty, real depth beauty, surges with palpable, haunting darknesses. There is even an iridescent evil in beauty. Milton's Lucifer is an awesomely

6. Moore, *Re-Enchantment of Everyday Life*, 197.

7. Picasso, *Picasso: Masterpieces from the Musée National Picasso.*

beautiful luminary intent on lustrous acts of revenge. Georgia O'Keefe's orchids have a dark soul that terrify on closer inspection. Beauty prisms not just light but dark; that is why she is the queen vessel of the liminal.

The soul has a special affection for beauty. Beauty *is* soul. Beauty is the core narrative of existence, the central carrier of truth. Beauty knows the secret workings and meaning of the universe. Beauty carries the master DNA sequence.

Beauty is the voice of authentic grief, joy, transformation, ecstasy. Beauty is the organizing One Reality (what Jung, borrowing from the ancient mystics, called the *Unus Mundus*—the One World) under all the projections, fears, distortions, cruelties, violences, and chaos of the outer world. Beauty is the ensouled clock face of Kairos-Eros time, not the fractured clock face of Chronos-Logos time. Repeatedly, I experience patients whose healing comes in the immediate wake of a beauty experience. Whether in the throes of profound grief, depression, anxiety, dread, the experience can come in the form of a vacation to an achingly beautiful earth-place, as a sunset, a sea view, animal encounter, or a sexual/love encounter. It tips the scales and beauty floods in to irrigate a parched soul. The Navajo have a Night Way healing ceremony where the beauty chant is the central tracking, pacing metaphor:

> In beauty I walk
> With beauty before me I walk
> With beauty behind me I walk
> With beauty above me I walk
> With beauty below and about me I walk
> It is finished in beauty
> It is finished in beauty.[8]

Beauty gives us strength. Beauty helps us endure. Beauty is the inner constellation by which we can navigate our way back home to the deep abode of the good and the true. Beauty gives us the resilience to face, confound, and transform the monstrous.

Art is the cultural and spiritual medium we have invented to house and preserve the healing medicaments of beauty. But beauty is not just what we find in galleries, performance halls, and film. Beauty is the living world itself; it is every living being within that world. Being-ness itself is the core of beauty—and it has demands of us, ordeals even, if its exquisite aromas are to be enjoyed.

8. Matthews, *The Night Chant*, 145.

A dispirited woman rides silently in the backseat of a car travel-
ing into late afternoon mountains. The elderly driver and his com-
panion silently observe the verdant glades all around as they ascend
a curvaceous side road to a stolid mountain cabin bathed in late-day
alpine light. The sorrowful woman in the back seat seems like a little
girl out on a Sunday afternoon drive with mom and dad. The elders
caringly accompany their passenger into the house and promise to
return soon from their walk back into the village from which they
just ascended. They will leave her the car keys.

The sad woman is now alone. She seems greatly unnerved
here. One would guess she is an urban sophisticate with no taste or
trust for these rural wilds. The elderly couple left their dog, a svelte,
wary creature who hovers close but snaps and snarls if the dysphoric
woman attempts connection.

What is one to do but put on the nighttime face-cream mask,
smoke a vesper cigarette, and go to bed.

Dawn.

She bolts awake as the morning sun bakes her face. She rises
and pads down the second-floor corridor and knocks at the master
suite. It has been undisturbed. The couple did not return; their room
is empty.

Well, a vigorous morning walk to the village is in order, as she
worries whether her elder friend has suffered a heart attack. The dog
marches with her. Birds sing. Fields shine brightly in early morning
dew. It will be fine, she assures herself. Then the dog yelps. He is
ahead just around the bend. He nurses a bruised paw. She guard-
edly looks all about. Nothing is out of order. She edges ahead. Still
nothing. Then she slams into thin nothingness—empty space has a
punishing volume. She recoils. She leans forward timorously. Her
hand touches the plexiglass like barrier. Like a mime, she walks it
out, left, right, up, down. It is solid. It is a clear void wall. Shocked,
she stumbles back to the cabin to try and shake it off, to understand
it, to normalize it.

Shortly, she returns to the barrier to confirm it is there. She then
retraces her steps past the cabin, higher up the defile road. She sees
an elderly couple. The wife is on the porch, the husband is pump-
ing water—a reassuring scene. She hails them, then runs into the
barrier. She can see them; they ignore her. They are frozen in place,
voided like the barrier, empty of awareness and conscious being. This
is becoming a nightmare in broad daylight.

She is a reluctant guest of the 2012 film, Die Wand ("The Wall").

Encounter with depth beauty is a "shimmering" moment, where dead conscious life meets renewing eternity.[9] We do not always cherish its visit, but every trip to the art house is an opportunity to rescue and restore lost being and let it fly us back to our true home. Just how do the arts mediate shimmering liminality so seamlessly, so perfectly? This chapter picks one of its most eloquent disciplines to help us explore that mystery—film.

Film is beauty's favorite narrator, always attempting to restore beauty to our distorted world experience. Film is the great vessel of lost and restored beauty. And beauty is the essential handmaiden of compassion and mercy. As a therapist, I simply witness people's often anguished narratives of abuse, darkness, and despair in the hope that they can recover the living thread of this Self-and-Other, compassion and mercy, which always seems to survive dormant and safe under the withering forest fires of this world. Film and its beauty escort these singed souls through the liminal portals into the betwixt and between worlds so that long deferred inner healings, heart healings, spirit healings can commence. In the mildly dissociative, boundary-crossing state induced by film, we can experience a mending of our torn and battered souls in ways that we may not even be aware of, but which can have lasting, practical impact on our lives. Film viewing and immersion catalyzes the deep-tissue, psychic-healing that this book is concerned with.

Film is about core beauty and Eros, as well as the destiny that is revealed within that awakened Eros and beauty. *The Bridges of Madison County* (1995) evinces this deep eternal essay on awakening/guiding Eros at the core of all good cinema and art. Eros both enflames us and it restrains us. Unconscious Eros enflames and conscious Eros restrains. In *Bridges*, an on-assignment photographic stringer for National Geographic gets lost in Iowa farm country. He wanders down a corn-lined drive to ask directions of a farm woman. Her family has just left her for the state fair, while she has elected to tend the home fires and enjoy a much-deserved break from the grinding daily tedium of small-family farming.

The first glance between them down the driveway is charged, filled with what depth psychologists (following such traditions as Jacques Lacan) would call the primal "Look." On initial impression, these two make a strange pairing. He is a world-traveling loner in Republican Iowa, a vagabond hippie in a pickup whose bed is full of beer and cameras. He is Dark Eros.

9. Kaylo, "Imagination and the Mundus Imaginalis," 120.

She, on the other hand, is Ivory-soap pure. A mother of two adolescents and the faithful wife of Piers the Plowman. A little strange in that she was born and raised in Italy, but redeemed from that small blemish by having married her homeland-liberating G.I. and moving with him to his Midwest Shangri-La. She is Light Eros.

He is a lost Dionysos. She is a found Mother-Earth. She agrees to go with him so he can find the old wooden national-landmark bridges he has come to photograph. There, in the late afternoon as he disappears under the bridge and she hides in its cool shadows, we sense that archetypal bridging—not old wooden bridging—is really what this story is about. She will guide him into the light-Eros richness of everyday depth-intimacy and communion with the Other. He will initiate her into the dark Eros of soulful curiosity and abandon. In the end, they each will live and bridge more easily between both worlds.

> When I think of why I make pictures the only reason I can
> come up with . . . it just seems that I've been making my
> way here . . . all I've ever done in my life is making my way
> here to you . . .

—Photographer Robert Kinkaid,
The Bridges of Madison County

Life is about destiny and destination. Like in great initiatory epics such as Dante's *Divine Comedy*, it is always about deeper initiation into that destiny, of always finding guides and mentors to take our weary, terrified inner and outer Pilgrim closer to its true home and soul. One way to gauge how accurate and true one's life path has been is to assess how frequently one experiences synchronistic events and the fortuitous appearance of just the right teaching/guiding mentor. If one goes through long dry spells without such manifestations, one might get quite suspicious about how much one is trying to live a life of anxiety management and comfortable accommodation rather than a life of True, Bold, Adventuresome Being.

Film is an initiatory medium. The films we often stumble into on a weary Friday evening might be filled with synchronistically vivid images and scripts. They might burn into the very heart of our being, raising questions and specters that arouse us to a fuller state of being. Such clarion moments of soul-call frequently manifest around art—for art is always an initiatory medium that calls us from the ancestral beyond into a more whole soulfulness and embodied-ness in our lives. Life and its essential destiny is about the suffering-earned joy of arriving at that full moment and place of vocation that deep art always celebrates, mirrors, and lures us toward.

A singularly rich example of a true response to soul's vocational call is in Michael Mann's *The Last of the Mohicans* (1992). Though the overt narrator is Hawkeye, the implicit, depth narrator is Cora Munro, daughter of the British Commandant of Fort William. This narrative layering is not unusual in our era, when one way to view the consistent archetypal patterns occurring and re-occurring in almost all cinema of our late patriarchal era is a return of the Deep Feminine and a recovery of lost childhood innocence. Cora Munro voices and enacts much of this patterning in *Mohicans*.

Set in the eighteenth-century French and Indian Wars, two daughters of a British wilderness fort commander are traveling to join him via Albany, New York. Unaware that the frontier is aflame with ravaging raids instigated on behalf of the native tribes' French and English allies, the women stumble into a nearly disastrous ambush staged by their erstwhile guide Magua. They are saved by Hawkeye and his adoptive family—his father, Chingachgook, and brother, Uncas. In the immediate wake of this vivid encounter and the remnants' retreat into the deep forest, Cora's whole Anglo-patriarchal worldview begins to dissolve. She enters a primal world where life and death, masculine and feminine, heaven and earth, soul and spirit mean much more than the upper and lower classes of monarchial capitalism.

Cora is shocked when they leave the bodies of settler women and children unburied—the Cameron family, slain and mutilated in their own front yard. Later, in the dark night, laying silent as hostile bands glide past them in the deciduous gloom, she is surprised to discover that the Camerons were very close friends of Hawkeye. He left them unburied so that tracking enemies would not know they had been there and thus begin to stalk them. Upon this realization, however, she speaks a simple, heartfelt apology to Hawkeye.

He replies, "My father's people say that at the birth of the sun and of his brother the moon, their mother died. So the sun gave to the earth her body, from which was to spring all life. And he drew forth from her breast the stars, and the stars he threw into the night sky to remind him of her soul. So, there's the Camerons' monument. My folks' too, I guess." "You are right, Mr. Poe," says Cora. "We do not understand what is happening here. And it's not as I imagined it would be, thinking of it in Boston and in London . . ."

"Sorry to disappoint you."

"No, on the contrary. It is more deeply stirring to my blood than any imagining could possibly have been."

In Jung-speak, Cora Munro is moved from the ego-patriarchal world of Crown and London to the Self-matriarchal world of wilderness and myth. She is dropped into the unconscious and its soul-world treasures and dangers.

> But consciousness, continually in danger of being led
> astray by its own light and becoming a rootless will o' the
> wisp, longs for the healing power of nature, for the deep
> wells of being and for unconscious communion with life in
> all its countless forms.
>
> —C. G. Jung[10]

In another example of film's initiatory power—not only individual initiation but initiation within our surrounding family and social systems, is *Rachel's Wedding* (2008), which explores a family's struggles to awaken and to move on. The *mise en scene* is a transition ritual: Rachel's wedding. But the subtext is the greedy, sticky demands of past and unclaimed grief. We can never fully claim all our sorrow, never make full amends, never let memory fully let go of its clutch on tragedy and loss. Rachel's family knows this and has tried to distribute the burden, as families do, across all its members. There is the sainted daughter, whose burden is too much light, too much vision, too much goodness. There is the Lilith daughter, an addict, whose burden is too much darkness, too much gloom, too much violent unfinished-ness. Families always unfairly deal out the deck of coping agendas. There is always too much of something in everyone's basket of being. That's the way of our broken, jarred existence, ever since Elijah sat in that ancient valley of broken shards.

And the cleft of these primordial, gaping ancestral wounds is sutured in a frenzy of noisy event. Empty exploding calories of effort propel families and their constituent cultures past the menacing abyss—anything to move beyond the aching void of negative sorrow that waits to grab and consume us all into full annihilation.

The wedding-enacting family has a home full of gifted young and old, two generations doing anything to escape the maw of that untouched grief: music playing, soulful toasting, shriek laughing, floral arranging, wedding

10. Jung, *Collected Works Vol. 5: Symbols of Transformation*, 299.

tent erecting, reception dinner planning. For weddings—like funerals, baptisms, and bar/bat mitzvahs—threaten to rip open the thin scab that staunches this ancient flow of savage loss more than ordinary daily passages. And for Rachel's family it works, but not fully. The awkward, devastating truth seeps into nearly everything of the event. It stains deep into the edges of the pretty white silk of innocence, the material with which we attempt to clothe these rituals, forgetting that—like all real ritual—they are a reminders of our wound, our impermanence, our frailty before violent gods and fate.

At Rachel's wedding, the devastating truth flares its dragon's breath in a spontaneous ritual of hilarity: a generational challenge between father and new son-in-law. It is a mock joust for the incestuous privilege of claiming the fair virgin daughter prize. And the old man is beating the inexperienced young man's dishwasher loading time, even adding the flourish of extra dishes and rinses. In an effort to drive home his electric victory, the father roars for "more dishes, more dishes!" The dark daughter responds by discovering more plates for him to add from the cupboard. The plates fly off the fresh stack until, there, buried in the middle, is Ethan's plate—little baby Ethan, the child who drowned when a sixteen-year-old babysitter lost control of her car on a bridge. The room is filled instantly with the pall of funeral silence. Yes, weddings are a generational and existential death if they are anything, and the father, ashen faced, flees the room. Dark Lilith is left alone, as always, with the burden of ancient guilts and shames that never can be fully expiated. The residue of lost childhood destinies really do haunt us forever—probably in this life and beyond.

Innocence is the most precious commodity and gift of achieved consciousness. *Moonrise Kingdom* (2012) is an homage to the preciousness of such achieved consciousness. It is a moving cinematic recognition that we are all orphans in a trauma-hardened world, an often cruel, materialist world that seeks nothing more than to make us regimented servants of its infernal regularities and consumerist addictions. The film's bitter hardness can be found in the most altruistic of youth scouting movements, in the best of normal-appearing families, and in the rhythms of the most pristine of police departments. The lie is exposed—and renewing consciousness achieved—when one of the film's orphans escapes the asylum of deadening reality, runs away to the reanimated wildness of Primal Earth, elopes away with a stolen lover, and builds life anew in the savage wilderness miles away from their crushing, nihilist reality. And, once there, making naïve love in an idyllic waif child's tent under a fulminate moon on a fairytale beach, the protagonists discover and fully inhabit their Moonrise Kingdom—and come for the first time to the fullness of their being.

The trouble is, most people never make that heroic run. They never steal their life back from the clutches of threatening normality. They never defy conformist families. They never cut their way out of a confining scout's tent. They never risk forbidden love. They never make outlandish, lavish promises of spontaneous heart and soul with whomever has the matching courage to meet them, soulful outlandish for soulful outlandish.

But the denizens of Moonrise Kingdom, almost and maybe to the very last soul, have fled from their own prisons of personal despair and self-betrayal by the end of the original orphan's journey. A whole community has awakened and begins to be fully alive.

This is Wes Anderson's gift to us: a cinematic fairytale of redemption, not just for the occasional, courageous orphan, but for us all.

Into the Furnace (2013) is a poignant film exploring in a very different way the difficulties of successful soul initiation and survival in this post-modern soft hell we live in. Its hero is a good man, a steel worker in a dying Appalachian mill town. He's living with a good woman, a nurturing and animated teacher of young children. His father is dying of an industrial plant-induced emphysema, spending his last days on a small, reclining bed in a cheap wood-paneled den, sucking oxygen through a tube while his brother and sons tenderly minister to him through the hours of his passing.

Our solemn, good Everyman also has a beloved brother who is home temporarily between his third and fourth full-year military deployments in the current cycle of the endless War on Terror. He is badly PTSDed and seeks to soothe himself in a compulsive, impoverishing gambling addiction. His heroic older brother secretly underwrites this compulsion to keep him from being gripped by the cruel and sadistic reach of the loan-shark underworld.

But, in one of his missions to the saloon-owning local agent of this violent syndicate, our Everyman hits the rear end of a car backing out of a blind driveway and kills a mother and her child. After serving his prison sentence, he returns to a world where his father has died, his lover has moved on to the town police chief, and his kid brother is fighting in bare-knuckle matches in abandoned mill hells.

The film has a signature dual-track switchback scene structure. In one track, the older brother and loving uncle are hunting deer in the woods. In the other, the younger brother and his reluctant syndicate mentor head into the deep backcountry for him to throw a fight-match hosted by the rapacious, evil clan running that neck of the woods. Two brothers, both hunting for a better, more abundant life in the same mythic Mid-Life Wood; both backtracking in search of lost pre-war and pre-prison innocence; both seeking the pubertal lost Mother. When the older brother has a lovely sixteen-point buck in his sights, he passes on the kill, unable to deprive the world of such innocent majesty. On the other side of the holler, the younger brother is mercilessly beaten and later savagely shot by a monstrous backwoods beast named deGroot.

In the wake of his enormous tsunami of non-stop loss, our heroic elder brother lures deGroot to an abandoned mill lair, where he beats him, wounds him, and then goads him into a hopeless run for it—really a crawl and stumble for it. Finally, he places DeGroot in the sites of his deer rifle and drops him while the police chief, helplessly watching at a distance, cries out in disbelief and protest.

It is all over. The Mother is dead. The Father is dead. The Beloved Brother is dead. The Lover is dead to him. The mill is dead. DeGroot is dead. Good is dead. Evil is dead. America is dead. Hope is dead. There, in an empty mill slag field under an anemic winter steel-grey sky, all the gods have fled or have just simply vanished. Even his prey—whom he kept alive long enough to squat next to and ensure he knew who had killed him and why—even this sadistic, addicted, evil gnarled man grunts in begrudging tribute to this man's clever accomplishment of tribal honor. The Great Hunt is no more. Maybe the soul of everything is dead, the light fully gone out of it all at this dusk.

Such gifted filmmaking reminds us that life is an ongoing initiatory ordeal and challenge. We live to discover, realize, and achieve our destiny. Film awakens the fragile ping of the locator beacon that fate has installed in the core DNA of our being, the locator being that awakens and draws us forward into the effort and agony of accomplishing our destiny. And as time races by, as it dashes to its rendezvous of passionate engagements and surges onto the rocks of its destiny, we often grow numb and indifferent to that crucial life impulse impelling us. Film, effective film, disperses that fog of forgetting. It reminds us to look for its clues, the scent of its hidden path in the simple rituals of life and time passing, most of all in the structure and mystery of our family and ancestry structures.

Since the first cave people painted images on the pitted and grooved surfaces of their cave sanctuaries and shelters, we have been a movie-going people. It is now a wide consensus that these ancient cave shrines, when not used for housing, were evidently initiatory chambers where the young were nudged into adulthood by inciting and apparently transformative rituals. There exists an increasingly clear parallel between the emergence of human consciousness and its intuitions about the meaning of its life and spirit and the appearance of and manipulation of image. Image, then, especially moving image, is essential to our well-being—physical, emotional, spiritual.

The Cave of Forgotten Dreams (2012) assumes a contemplative, mature audience, the kind of audience that can engage with its almost imagistic chanting. In exploring the images of an ancient Paleolithic cave, it documents the birth of a dramatic, sudden new "fluidity and permeability" of soul that burst upon the blank screen of human consciousness 35,000 ago. Its director, Werner Herzog, intones during the film's voiceover narrative that only Homo sapiens—not Neanderthal or any of our other closely allied higher primates—constellated imagistic consciousness. Other evolutionary cognate cousins had a developed forebrain, an opposable thumb, made tools, and had language, but only our species created image. It is the profound novelty of this suddenly manifesting image lighting up and mirroring the numinal landscape of both inner and outer mystery that moves us in these ancient cavern precincts.

These were initiatory Paleolithic cinemas. The animal intermingled consciously with the human, masculine with feminine, stalactite with stalagmite, heaven with earth. These caves smelled of must, scat, and soul in an ancient, urgent perfumery. And on these green algae-coated walls of mystery, our forebears felt impelled to leave their literal tinted handprint and their images of majestic herds roaming pristine, primal landscapes. They invented film then. Over thirty thousand years ago, they opened the first movie houses with their undulated herds moving across these majestic walls animated by their flickering torches. There, film invention meets us at that primal wall and dares us to cross over into the alluring, dark, mysterious, and probably dangerous, worlds beyond.

There really is only one story. A Master Story if you will. There is only one authentic story about us, about the Other, about the cosmos. It is about getting calm enough, non-anxious enough, awake enough to let the story touch our hearts and souls. This story is the only true thing there is. What we imagine to be true—the solid world of time and space and sense is really just a part of this story. Even science and its astro-and-relativity-physics is but a story within this story. The Master Story embraces all these sub-and-counter plots and diversions. Jung, after the mystics he so loved, called this story the *Unus Mundus*—the One World Story. And it is always about the Lost Child. Getting Home. Love, really. Just plain, brown paper love.

In these caverns, we feel that fascinating and tremendous awe that nearly a century ago Rudolf Otto associated with the certain appearance of numinous divinity.[11] We are transfixed. We feel childlike and innocent and afraid and eager and anguished all at once. Image, instruction, initiation become reconnected as they should be, and the whole makes a quiet, complete, cosmic sense. We feel at home again.

And film is always after telling that story as simply and honestly and gently and soulfully as it can. Even darker forms of cinema—pornography, violent action, horror flicks—get tripped up on themselves and end up wanting to just tell this simple, pure story of love, meaning, wholeness. "Destiny" is maybe the best one-word wrap-up for film's vocation: narrating the Story of True Destiny—the authentic, passionate tale of finding the Lost Child and returning her to her true home.

There exist indigenous, aboriginal tribal groups in Australia who create exquisite clan-art forms. These dot groupings and paintings flow from communal creation. Everyone literally has a hand in their birthing. The clan sits on the ground in the painting space and merges into a communal reverie of blended improvisation around traditional sign and symbol forms. They murmur and laugh among themselves in a mild clan trance while these breath-taking forms emerge as though bodily from Earth herself. I have witnessed Tibetan monks merged in a very similar process around the creation of their tonka paintings, and I have similarly seen indigenous plains Amerindians communally create a Sun Dance or Yuwipi Ceremony. Film is just such a tribal reverie. No one person can encompass or control the whole technological-imaginal chorus of processes necessary to produce a profound communal art form. Film, like the soul, contains us. It welcomes us in from the cold, rainy night and bids us to warm ourselves by the dancing embers of its image-fires.

Film heals. We all know that it entertains, that it facilitates us escaping hard times and moments in our lives with a renewing two hours of adventure and laughter in the dark. Film as documentary or fact-tinged fiction may even inform and enhance our lives. But, more crucially, film

11. Otto, *Idea of the Holy.*

heals. It is a moment, an event of genuine depth therapy, what the ancient Greeks would have called *therapeia*—deep, true healing. It mediates many forms of healing.

Often, the essential healing is a grieving of what we lose by living amid the broken vessels of this world—the lost dreams, visions, ancestors, children, friends, health, and eventually our very lives. We weep in the cinema-cave-dark with strangers over our universally tragic state. The ancient Druids staring into the cinemas of the ceremonial fire and the ancient cave shamans burning their film dreams into the fire-danced stone intuited this tragic loss millennia ago, and their keening, lamenting voices underscore the soundtrack of all contemporary film.

The logos of the soul . . . implies the act of traveling the soul's labyrinth in which we can never go deep enough.

—JAMES HILLMAN [12]

Film, like myth, lives in the in-between world. In fact, cinema is always mythic, and myth is always cinematic. Robert Zemeckis's 2007 film, *Beowulf*, is a masterful case in point. At first, the dialogue in the mouths of his capable cast seems wooden and almost buffoonish. It rolls across the screen in awkward broad strokes, almost like old-fashioned community theater melodrama. Life in King Hroogar's mead-feasting hall, Heorot, almost seems done by Disney animators on amphetamines. Colors are too bright. Horror too dark. Lines delivered too loudly. And it accompanies seemingly overdone cinematic pyrotechnics that appear to deepen the very deep hole Zemeckis is digging for his film.

But then, subtly, it starts taking effect. The mind is eased back into those primal moments between temperate and Arctic zone, between pagan and Christian gods, between fall and winter, between dusk and night, dawn and day. We are now ready for the epic struggles of Beowulf with the fearful Grendel and his even more monstrous mother. We are in the mead hall and we tremble together at the loud unearthly knocks on its massive entry doors.

We all live in between: the abyss and the summit, the nadir and the zenith. There are peaks and abysmal canyons we can never willingly visit alone but only contemplate from afar—and we fear this strangeness that we yet so deeply yearn for. Driven mountaineers try to conquer tall peaks as obsessive deep-sea divers reach for the depths, but the highest and deepest

12. Hillman, *Dream and the Underworld*, 25.

often escape their uninitiated, anxious grasp. Film at its best is a vessel of reconnaissance where we can explore the very personal, challenging route of our destiny—the ordeal—and its unique ascent and descent into such realms. It works so well because film lives in these in-between lands. Film moves from a place of incompleteness toward the complete. It never fully leaves the former or achieves the latter. But its trajectory is always toward the whole, the self, the fully animated Soul of Things.

Patriarchy lives frozen in this dark in-between place. It is Beowulf's mead hall, where he broods on his big lie, *the* big lie. Its bleak landscape is filled with the bleached bones of the dispirited seekers who gave up in this foreboding land and soul-died.

> *I like to see all the stories we human beings (and our*
> *culture in general) have collected as a transitional space,*
> *the reservoir of the collected creativity of all human beings*
> *in the past and in the present.*

—VERENA KAST[13]

All religions know how to plot a course into liminal territory. The renowned Persianist scholar Henri Corbin spent his lifetime tracking and mapping such realms. A Protestant by core creed, he encountered the magnificent landscapes of Islamic mysticism early on through the medieval guidance of Schwardi. Through this poet-scholar's work, Corbin discovered Ta'wil, the essential organizing, imaginal, archetypal core of our being. James Hillman's whole post-Jung school of archetypal psychology received significant theoretical trajectory from Corbin's work here, as well as from its companion notion of the *mundus imaginalis*, the imaginal capacity of our consciousness that allows us access to and interaction with ta'wil. As Tom Cheetham points out, "[Corbin's] attempt to find unity in the astonishing diversity of the religions of the Book—Mazdaism, Judaism, Christianity, and Islam—by focusing on the freedom of the Holy Spirit as the 'Angel of Individuation' must be characterized by a fundamental fragmentation and flight from any socially or politically unified center."[14]

It is by imaginally finding and relating to this "Angel of Individuation" that one achieves one's full destiny—one's meaningful dignity and destiny of being. And in achieving this dignity and destiny of being, we serve not just ourselves but the world, the world spirit or *Anima Mundi*. By staying

13. As quoted in Hockley, *Cinematic Projections*, 5.
14. Cheetham, *All the World an Icon*, 34.

awake to the struggle between our inner forces of darkness and light and being equally vigilant about these oppositional forces in the outer world, we achieve a full and life-giving relationship to the true angle of beauty and soul at the core of our being. "Every creature of Light has an Angel," writes Cheetham, "—a being who is its 'double' and eternal Twin and to whom it is battling to return. We live in a time of 'mixture,' struggling to separate the Light and the Dark, and we are involved in a battle for the Angel, for our own individual Heavenly Twin as well as for the salvation of the world."[15]

Again, film lives between worlds, two different but related angels-of being. The world of conscious and unconscious, seen and unseen. It's a magical, almost mystical medium that no one can fully explain. There are important perspectives from perceptual psychology, physics, philosophy— that is the seen and conscious part. But the full explanation of how an alert human being can be taken into a dark room and shown dancing images across a wall to which they accede full conscious attention within thirty seconds is still just plain, awesomely mysterious—that is the unconscious, unseen part.

Bernardo Bertollucci's *The Dreamers* (2003) poises itself on the borderlands of justice and ethics, between inner life and outer world. Three young people meet at school: a bright, though naïve American man and a brother-sister set of French twins. The twins invite the young man into the home of their famous author father and scholar mother. The American is touchingly received and invited to stay with them while the parents leave on a multi-week holiday.

During the interim, the American loses his innocence and virginity to the sensuous twins. He discovers their incestuous and fetishistic relationship. He falls in love with the sister. He confronts and attempts to implode the twins' deepening enmeshment even as he joins their growing isolation from the 1968 Paris Student rebellion which is unfolding in the streets outside their trysting apartment. The parents come home unexpectedly early and find the naked sybarites sleeping innocently entwined in a silk tent they fashioned in the living room. The youthful hedonists awaken to discover signs of this parental visit and the inevitable horror of shame and guilt enter their Edenic dream. The strife of the street bellows outside their paradise's windows, and they pour into the streets with all the other youthful protesters. The twins impulsively move forward with a violent anarchist faction. The American tries to restrain them, holds back, and then sadly

15. Cheetham, *All the World an Icon*, 45.

disappears into the crowd in the opposite direction. Somehow, we know he will thrive with his new worldly knowledge while the twins may tragically wander on into ever deeper incestuous emptiness.

Paradoxical borderlands. Age and memory, twin and Other, male and female, protest and tradition, sensuousness and restraint, impulse and wisdom, despair and achieved destiny. Film always insinuates itself closely to such paradoxical interfaces and borders. It rarely solves its constellated conundrums, but it always faithfully tells their story. It is story, individual and collective, that fuels politics; it is story that is the origin and aim of the political process, the community narration.

Many if not most of the world's most sophisticated spiritual and psychological systems honor—even privilege—this liminal meeting place. In fact, it is the place itself and its numinous qualities that are valued more than any personality changes or gains that are achieved. It is really both a place and a moment simultaneously, a place and a moment where the essential ingredient is an eros of connection between self, Other and the numinal divine. It embodies an eros of relation that awakens an awareness that this relational eros is the eros infusing and enlivening all reality, all the cosmos. In tantric practice, the goal is not clichéd hot sexual experience; in fact, the system is an instruction on how to awaken physical eros in service of this deeper relational eros. The experienced practitioner seeks not the releasing orgasm, but the moment and place just before the orgasm—one of its poignant descriptions is a hovering "before the gates of cloud and rain." In that hovering ecstatic moment, one rests in the embrace of this pan-relational eros of connection and being. Film achieves this relaxing of outer world attention and tension and induces us into just such an eros-saturated reverie of being.

Film revels in its plasticities. It bends time, space, gender, mortality. In film, the dead return to life (in innumerable zombie productions), aliens invade our blood stream (*The Invasion*, 1993), ordinary people can become presidents (*Dave*, 2007), the young can instantly become powerful thirty-year-old Madison Avenue executives (30 *Going on* 13, 2004). Film warps ordinary time in the service of extraordinary Being—it is always serving soul and its initiatory presence and development in our midst. It breaches all mundane barriers and phenomena. It sees right through them. It lives beyond them.

Cinema has a special affection for those vulnerable moments of punctuated forward leaping in the individual and collective life cycle. Film never tires of its chief role as a mentor, a teacher of all things soul necessary for full growth at such moments. One of its favorite visitation sites is young adulthood, when we make our first major stab at adult beinghood. In *Mr. Woodcock* (2007), a mid-twentyish self-help guru revisits his hometown. He discovers his mother marrying his junior high gym coach, who had abused him as a child, only to discover the man has something soulful to offer—both then and now. Or in *Superbad* (2007), three geeky young men find depth voice, sexuality, and soul all in the same mad, drunken, adventuresome, poetic night out on the town. Or a young woman finds herself in the surprise of winning with her Nascar entry, a conscious VW "Beattle" named *Herbie* (2005).

There is a central scene almost dead center of Fellini's masterful film essay, *La Dolce Vita* (1960). It is what the French would call a salon, a gathering of stimulating elites from the music, painting, literature, journalism, science, and philosophy worlds. The camera has us enter the room with the film's key narrator, and the explosion of warmth and animation from that room greets the full frame of the cinema house and leaps across the viewing gap into our viewer's body. It is not a perfect gathering and it is not a perfect time or world. The dialogue and images remind us of this frequently. These people all suffer the secularist anomie and quiet despair of untethered meaning we all feel in these uncertain cultural times—so vivid and current even in a film now a half-century old.

There is an undercurrent of soulful music and moving dialogue amid the comedic banter of all such occasions. There is even profound spiritual commentary. The gentle, wise, softly world-weary host is even inveighed upon to play his audio tapes of natural sounds—wind, water, storm, birds— in the Italian wilds. The room is absorbed into a deep, contemplative reverie. The host takes our journalist narrator, a younger good man filled with a similarly soulful angst, into a nursery. Here, the host's very young son and daughter (a healthy child duo we had seen earlier when they were delightfully drawn to the adult's salon-room by the recorded sounds of primal nature) lie asleep behind protective white gauze screens. The mood is full of a fully awake and functional father's unconditional, fierce guardian love.

The salon becomes literal liminal space, constellating a communal soul, a *communitas*. Our soul-sad narrator, so filled with this liminal resonance, centrally convenes the peace and vibrating spirit of this place and this gathering. We all know that any reproduction of this mood is impossible to predict, but there is a higher chance of its ritual arrival in the hands of such a centered, awake host. It is a liturgy. This community is a worshipping congregation—worshipping the constellated presence of the soul and the hovering gods on the balcony of this high-rise Roman apartment. The unbearable awfulness of our lives finds momentary, releasing, even transcendent beauty here in the cracks of being opened by this liminal liturgy of deep presence.

Film burrows deep into liminal crevices; it's most alive there. It believes the best, healing, most essential narratives upon culture, art, and spirit come from these often abysmal cracks in our individual and collective being.

Film instructs us about the soul. What comes next may sound shocking and esoteric; it is both, but nonetheless true. It is a living medium, an animate membrane between this world and the world of spirit. Image is the professor of soul. Film is one of the most urgent contemporary and ancient voices this professor of image uses to instruct and influence us about the healing qualities of the soul. Film is a living museum of image. Film is a living diorama.

I recently took a photography seminar in Yosemite National Park. One of the reprieve mantras was, "paint the light; not the thing, the light." Depth psychotherapy teaches something very similar: see the soul, not symptom.

On that same weekend, we saw an original photograph by Ansel Adams. In viewing *Winter Sunrise* (1944) at a distance, you see three broad bands of light. At bottom is a meadow with a spotlight of cool winter solstice light bathing a grazing mare. In the middle of the photo is a black bar—a menacing, ragged, high Sierra ridge. At the top is a brilliant, high series of peaks zebra-spotted by black ink depressions.

Perhaps this photo is a spontaneously brilliant apperception of the ego's journey through unconscious purgation to gain a peak-experience soul. The liminal abyss has to be traversed and known if the soul is to be achieved. The animal-raw innocence and purity in us can only be kept in the light and its destiny fulfilled if its innocence is honored by the suffering ascent.

Film seeks to scramble real-time life. It unhinges our space-time chronologies and sets them creatively adrift in non-linear sequences that force us to exercise unused aspects of our physical and psycho-spiritual sensorium. This is exactly what medial-liminal phenomena accomplish in their scrambled unhinging of ego-dominated encasements.

Film generates synchronistic experiences and recognitions. A colleague reported arriving at a cineplex in high dudgeon to see a particular film. It was sold out. The energy drained from his expectancy bubble and he set to staring vacantly at the remaining possible bill of fare. He and his wife chose and stumbled mutedly and synchronistically into *Gone Baby Gone* (2007). Its tale of a dark-motivated detective seeking a lost child, executing a pederast along the way, and becoming a replacement father-babysitter for the recovered child while her crack mother went out into the night to indulge her addictions, awakened startling recognitions in my colleague of his own inner executioner of bad mothers and fathers. Discovering such dark urgency at the core of his own experience allowed him to discover a yet deeper, purer desire to execute soulful parenting of his lost inner and outer selves, as well as to deploy more consciously compassionate parenting with his own outer, real-world children. The film would not leave his consciousness and empathic sorrow for days. Fate became a synchronistic awakener, integrator, and healer through the primal transformative magic of cinema.

All life is a balletic *pas de deux*. It is a dance with the Other, often awkward, occasionally turbulent, always gripping, and full of a strange grace and wonder. Film is a mirroring *pas de deux*, an echo of our dance in the dark liminal space of the cinema hall.

Aristotle once promoted a dramatic model of cathartic healing. It was the conceptual basis of why the mandatorily enacted plays at the sacred shrines—at, say, Delphi or Epidaurus—worked; why comedy and drama was essential for deep, transformative healing to occur. Jung borrowed this model once in explaining the cathartic impact of dreams and dreaming. The essential elements were the cast of characters, an exact setting in time and space, a plotline that culminates in a climactic/resolving moment or event, and a calming denouement. The denouement was essential so that the truths revealed, the sorrowful depth resolutions seen and felt in the dream, could be absorbed by the opened-up psyche. The ancients understood that theater was psychic surgery, in the heated enactments of the stage the psyche was torn open, the vulnerable soul exposed. Film is the best and most widely experienced of our contemporary forms of sacred theater.

Depth therapy is a theatrical event. Each session is a one-act play; a successful, therapeutic sequence, a full repertory season. The art of therapy is assuring, as much as possible, that the denouement process is contemplatively performed so the patient is not cruelly thrown, unprotected, back into the savage routines of the ruthless world.

Film is theater that restores and cleanses the soul. It does not debase it. This culture has flattened image traumatically. In the service of power, greed, and consumption, it has slung sloppy, noisy image on every available, conceivable space all around us. We are submerged in shallow, gaunt image everywhere—on subways, buses, televisions, cell phones, magazines, license plates, breakfast cereals, Nascars—everywhere. Shallow image enslaves us. It is pornographic, mocking, and compulsion arousing. It rubs our noses in our debasement, making us lust emptily after more image even with fresh, undigested image hanging tattered and unchewed out of our mouths and eyes and ears.

Cinema's image soothes and tries to lead us back home. Even in multiplex places that are sadly being filled with pre-film infomercials, expensive and expansive in-film product placements, and post-film handouts and lobby billboards, film opens up our grieving, saturated hearts and souls to transpersonal clarions often only dimly noticed in the darkened theater. But every trip to the cinema is a trip back to the soul well, and our parched core is moistened just a bit.

The humble philosopher-father of modern existentialism, Immanuel Levinas, reverently warned us against the kind of image idolatry that violates the landscape of our era. Although he recalls the Torah admonishments of his faith—the "prohibitions against representation"—he seems to suggest that a soul-connected generation and projection of image such as we find in depth art and cinema is an honoring of the Other—the mysterious, deep human and transpersonal divine he calls the Third. This use of image is not flat, dead representation. It is embodied honoring. This use of cinema creates no "effacing" or "defacing" of the Other, "but rather cherishes and expands the Other." It opens a resonant inter-space of subtle connection and cross loving. This is symbolic image at its best, an imaging that does not live on the surface and eat up all the meaning, resonance, and mystery of the other but compounds and amplifies it. This is soulful image at its best.[16]

The image is condensed expression of the psychic situation
of the unconscious as a whole, and not merely, nor even
predominantly, of unconscious contents pure and simple.

16. Saxton, "Fragile Faces," 5.

—C. G. JUNG[17]

There exists a contemporary conversation about chaos in the natural world. There are studies from correlational mathematics that suggest there are embedded geometrical objects in all apparently random events in the phenomenal world—natural organizing structures in everything from clouds to jagged coastlines to emotional patterns. These conversations further describe a universal scaling of events through time that will reveal these structures in time through cascading or avalanching occurrences. There is an almost magical moment, or what this correlational narrative calls "phase transitions," where the heretofore unseen geometric object appears in the phenomenal world in both its temporal and spatial aspects. Film is just such a phase transition, where aspects of collective imaginal experience pop clearly into conscious awareness and access.

In the closing sequence of *Cashback* (2006), an artist-as a-young-man narrator named Ben Willis takes his earnestly sought and won beloved out into a night snowstorm to show her a secret he has mastered—the stopping of time. He had discovered this technique while in an insomnia-laden phase of his life. While helplessly wallowing in the traumatic wake of a lost love affair, he remembered the awesome beauty he observed in the naked body-form of his family's Swedish nanny as she walked from her daily shower. Fueled by this intense memory of numinal beauty, he suddenly manifests the capacity to stop time in his droll graveyard shift job at an all-night convenience mart. While time is stopped, he undresses women's bodies and incessantly sketches them—especially one particularly present and soulfully sad young woman named Sharon Pintey. Eventually, they begin dating in regular flowing time. This results in her discovery, at his gala art show, that she is the outer object (her facial image movingly and repetitively blown up all over the gallery walls) of this intense inner journey between time and space.

Then and there, he decides to initiate her into this liminal world. Fairytale style, he draws her across the threshold by a kiss. He takes her outside the art gallery into the snowstorm. They walk between the frozen-in-time-and-space snowflakes. They are the alchemical king and queen of primal love and beauty dissolved and melded into One in an ancient alchemical flask of cold, snowy fusion. There they become living quantum physics. We, the viewer, become living quanta in the same flask. We all become the unitary world beyond the artifice of time and space constructs. We are Jung's

17. Jung, *Collected Works Vol. 6: Psychological Types*, 745.

Unus Mundus. It takes us back to Heidegger's fourfold (*Geviert*) of earth, sky, divinities, and mortals.[18] From this timeless place (which Heidegger most reliably discovered at a mountain writing cabin he owned for years), we can re-access a memory of the beauty and meaning of existence often lost and mangled under the cruel treat of Chronos-time grinding on and on. We can't heal or even change things from happening, but we can get some reflective distance from them so that when we return the world will be more bearable. The underlying meaning-core will be remembered, referenced, and cherished in the often horrific din of the everyday.

"I've always wanted to be a painter," says Ben. "Maybe have my work hung in a gallery one day."

Sharon: "I've always wanted to meet a painter."

"Why?"

"I think," Sharon responds, "it might have something to do with their ability to see beauty in everything."

A similar initiatory, snowy landscape is seen in Quentin Tarantino's *Kill Bill: Vol. I* (2003). The Bride and O-Ren Ishii (a.k.a. Cottonmouth) are two women assassins who duel to the death with samurai swords in a snow-covered winter Zen garden. The Bride had attempted to break away from their ruthlessly bloodless master: Bill. In a jealous rage (she was his favorite assassin mentee), Bill tracked her down with his posse of dark samurai warriors and slaughtered the whole wedding party—including the pregnant Bride and her fetus (or so she thought throughout the first film).

But by oversight, the murderous posse missed that The Bride was still barely alive under all that body-stacked carnage. She awoke from a deep, year-long coma and clawed her way to recovery and revenge. In the film's climactic scenes, she dispatches Cottonmouth as soft snow falls on a seamlessly white Zen garden, the blood of pure revenge splashing on Cottonmouth's white ceremonial robes and snow. Like in *Cashback*, the innocence of the scene almost stops the snowflakes and, as in *Cashback*, the culminating action here constellates a mature, conscious self-mastery and calm that resides at the timeless and spaceless core of things we call the soul.

Hattori Hanzo, the master sword-maker of the blade that dispatched Cottonmouth, says: "I'm done doing what I swore an oath to God twenty-eight years ago to never do again. I've created, 'something that kills people.' And in that purpose I was a success. I've done this, because philosophically,

---

18. Gauthier, *Martin Heidegger*, 128.

I'm sympathetic to your aim. I can tell you with no ego, this is my finest sword. If on your journey you should encounter God, God will be cut."

The liminal world remembers everything. Everything—material and spiritual. And it seems fond of encoding all that memory in holographic, affect-rich image. *The Tree of Life* (2011) explores that coding in a haunting exposition of a mid-life male thrown into liminal in-between-ness by the deep memory of his connection to a gifted younger brother who died at nineteen. We are never quite sure what triggered the cascade flooding of decoded image. But as he navigates the normal round of real-time high-rise, high-end professional services he peddles to the world, his inner journey is unfolding across exploding universes and volcanic molten terrains. His (apparent) mother's sensual, caring voiceovers wash over us, filled with urgent, pithy commentaries on the core essences of living and the cosmos. Early on, she intones that there are two choices, two ways of this reality of being we are ensnared in: nature and grace, and that grace is the best.

Again, in brief reprise and restatement, film is ancient. It is one of the most ancient artifacts of civilization and its sacred images. It even precedes consciousness. The eminent twentieth-century philosopher Immanuel Levinas, a cultural critic always suspicious of surface-held, shallow-felt images, talks of a "*meaningfulness* prior to representation." Film holds this meaningfulness in the palm of its empty camera hand. In that brief empty moment, in the space of silence and darkness when the house lights go down and we anticipate the originating flicker of the projector, there all meaning exists. Deep, true film image then responds in devotional service to these ancient discourses of soul.[19]

Painting is just another way of keeping a diary.

—PABLO PICASSO[20]

LIMINALITY, BEAUTY, AND GENRE

Each genre of film is a description of a particular aspect of the soul and its activity in the world. Take the Western and its brooding essay on the redemptive solitary warrior, for instance. Take a modern version like *Roadhouse* (1989) or classic selection like *High Noon* (1952). They both work soul with equal and similar genre effect.

19. Saxton, "Fragile Faces."
20. Picasso, *Picasso: Masterpieces from the Musée National Picasso.*

Or consider the romance genre. *Last Love* (2013), for example, celebrates the way liminal worlds are always there before us, but reflects that it takes a jarring experience of grief and suffering to open up our perceptions to their Weaving Goddess presence—Weaving Goddess because our destiny is a woven thing, it is a tapestry composed of the various threads and colors of our fated being.

The film shadows the desperate, grey grate, dead-ember life of a widower three years after the painful cancer death of his beloved wife of many decades. A philosopher and father, he has no interest in either vocation anymore. He cannot locate himself in this world. He is a shade, a specter who ghosts through the streets of his expat home city, Paris. He cloaks himself in sack cloth and ashes. He has become invisible in the way age and loss cloak us all eventually, because the world cannot bear to look on this ultimate fate of things, this grey, empty, colorless world of pre-death. So, the world gaily and noisily or even violently (anything but grey deadness) dashes on by as Mathew slogs invisibly by on busy streets and buses to return to his silent, empty art deco apartment to stare blankly out at dark, empty night streets below.

Until, on a bus, he and a young woman catch each other's eye. A quiet spark, subtle and intense. Mathew walks on by down the central bus aisle. But the glance lingers. He looks back and gazes at the back of her head. He then proceeds, but as the bus lurches to a stop, he stumbles, falls into the seated body mass of frustrated passengers. They yell at him until the sparked one rushes back, helps him off the bus, steadies his stance to dignity, and walks him home. Suddenly and quite unexpectedly, Mathew is not alone. The world is peopled again. It has eros, connection, a little recovered meaning.

Then the flirting begins. He discovers she is a dance teacher. He tracks down her studio. It is Latin dance day. He is awkwardly pulled onto the floor and, despite protests and disclaimers, he stomps and trips and laughs—yes, laughs—his way through the first hour of dance instruction in his life. And all the while he focuses on Pauline, her joy of being, her simple lightness in an often heavy world.

They meet for dinners, for drives into the country. They are in platonic love. Literal, physical, cross-generational enactment would befoul this. It is different, more real than mere coitus. She later admits she is attracted to his aloneness in this world, his orphanage, an aloneness recognized by her orphanage in the world. He tells her she is the one thing in his life that he cannot cipher. He returns to the studio, this time swinging through another hour of Pauline; fixated light and joy.

All this until his adult children (a son and a daughter) come from America after he "botches" a suicide attempt. He had seen Pauline with another and remembered his aloneness. He felt that leaving this world was the only final, responsible thing to do in that there was no more role or place for him here. He left his boxed library for Pauline, this orphan whose abandoned circumstances did not permit her the education that Mathew, a Princeton professor emeritus, knew her brilliance deserved.

Pauline discovers he is not alone, that he has a family who cares for him. She sees the rage in his adult son Miles, especially, an adult son longing for the father who abandoned him for Paris; the adult son who is five weeks into an unexpected divorce from a wife who abandoned him for another. Paris now full of abandoned others.

Pauline challenges them both to recover their relationship, to see and cherish what they have, what she will never have in the same way—living, connected family. It is difficult, fraught work, but she stays at it and the two men gradually wake up to it. They rediscover the nobility and good intentions hidden in both, for both, by both. There is reconciliation, especially after a battle royal over a coastal home beloved by the wife and husband, a beloved home of beauty that Mathew seeks to deed to homeless Pauline even over her protests that it belongs to his children.

And along the way, Pauline and Miles fall in love, which flashes jealousy in Mathew and ultimately deep delight, for he sees that Pauline has the same touching, transparent, good-to the-bone soul that his beloved wife had. In his final words to his son, after the son admits to seeing that same soul light in Pauline, Mathew urges him to never let go.

Then, Mathew can suicide successfully. It is not a morbid suicide. It is a suicide of a man finished and accomplished in this world, ready for the next. A father who loved his son openly and can now leave his blessings and finances and love for the son to realize. Pauline is flesh and blood, but fate also infused the Gnostic salvic Sophia through her into both their lost hearts. And Pauline is opened to their fatherly-brotherly-loverly salvation, as well. She is no longer orphan. After a post funeral trip to care for his own son, Miles will return for her. He promises. She assents, she will wait. There is redemption. The light of Mother Joan lives on into the soul, Anima Mundi work of the next generation; liminal space found and honored and cherished so that dead life can be reborn and redeemed.

Films are complexes, both personal and collective. The complex was a central research recognition by Jung. He based the construct on early career, empirical research into anxiety-fueled interruptions in the brain's neural response to associated stimuli. Taking this early data, he was able to generalize key clinical observations and healing interventions across the rest of his practice lifetime. He came to understand that human beings associate and cluster certain feeling-toned responses to anxiety-promoting events in their lives. The original template for these clusterings were early life traumas (both physical and psychological). These are the complexes, and Jung became famous for certain popularized cartoons of these complexes, such as mother, father, power, and inferiority complexes.

Film lights up these complexes. It resides within them. This is why horror genre films get so creepily under the skin and why action flicks get the heart pounding and the blood racing.

Westerns awaken the Alone One. Westerns—good, solitary ones—are full of howling, empty, wind landscapes. They are giant, empty canvases full of the unfinished, unfulfilled, undreamed, unknown. If we feel alone, landscape—the Earth—now, she *really* knows alone.

The Stalking Moon (1971) haunts me with this aloneness. It is a Western version of a Biblical hermit Joseph finding a family and hearth of love in his later years. Only he is an Indian Scout, not a carpenter, and his child is an Apache. But a narrative of a dangerous desert exile and a transformative journey is all there. Good, mythic stories bear retelling in new clothes all over the world all of the time. It is the core way our species remembers its best soul self and survives.

The Western, the classic raw Western, is a stark narrator. At the high point of Western storytelling in the 1950s, color was available, but gifted directors often chose to shoot their Westerns in highly distilled, high-clarity black and white. This starkness revealed the vacant emptiness of the desert that our taciturn Everyman rode through at film's beginning and returned to at film's end. It revealed the anguished emptiness under the façade of our noisy, frenzied culture.

Westerns often originate in this landscape from a lack. The Western is a narrative of lack. In late patriarchy, it is often a tale of the patriarchal cut off from its matriarchal mate. It is the incomplete gunman seeking the whole justice man, the violent man becoming a peace-man sheriff, the bad–good, the partial–whole. In sentimental, incomplete Westerns, our dark hero meets the "girl" Other and rides off into the sunset with her. But in the best Westerns, there is a moody interlude where he wanders off for a while to brood on what events this unexpected heart opening have taught him. He has always known violence, but violence connected to love, to justice, to his inner and outer lack, now *this* is something unexpectedly and puzzlingly different. Shockingly different. Gary Cooper, having survived a precipitous shoot-out in *High Noon* (1952), does wed and give up his guns, but there is an aftertaste of bittersweet wisdom—the world of this new love is deeper, with a more complex fleshiness. He drives off in a nuptial buggy into that empty space, but it is an empty space filled with more portent and possibility than ever he imagined before.

In the iconic closing scenes of a two-hour account of a decade-long revenge rampage, John Wayne's Ethan in *The Searchers* (1956) returns the torturously achieved Deep Feminine back to the dark cavern of the ancestral home, but he rides off as alone as when he arrived: a middle-aged, wiser male who is more alert to his brokenness, more complete in his sorrow. He will probably die alone, still woefully incomplete, but closer to the shores of the complete after his liminal wanderings in the desert land of lack.

Jason Stratham experiences a profound transformation in the modern Western *Transporter* series (2002, 2005, 2008), in which the sleek thoroughbred horse has been exchanged for the shiny BMW. But it is still a post-modern desert terrain full of emptiness and lack. In his liminal journeys through this parched earth, our estranged world-weary warrior-monk finds his Deep Feminine Other, learns how to cherish her, and then receives her teaching about the Wise Sage within. In all these better Westerns, our hero is often a beat-down middle-aged man worn ragged and frazzled by emptiness and patriarchal demands. But he is able to be influenced at a deeper level by more soulful instincts and urgings.

So, it is not by accident that so much of film is fascinated by disaster, by catastrophe, by the unexpected, for such moments give the ongoing ontological challenge to meaningful experience. For an annihilating disaster strikes a strong nihilist register. It empties the proximate moment of significance. It renders all as a yawning vat of painful, bottomless emptiness.

Often, film deals with the soul-disastrous in dark comedic fashion. Take an elegantly simple dramatic film, *Dan in Real Life* (2007). It traces a holiday trip home by a middle-aged widower and his three young daughters. By an innocent set of circumstances, he discovers that a woman he has just met in an intense eros-charged moment is his brother's beloved, brought to the same family event. Our narrator, Dan, must now cloak his just-opened heart (the first such bold opening in four years of bereavement) behind a persona of accommodated family-of-origin behaviors. We all know how demanding a persona task it is to go home for the holidays and keep the persona intact on "normal" occasions. Every family is an affective minefield, and within minutes of arrival before the ancestral hearth we can be reduced to the inner confusion of a four-year-old by a subtle, barbed comment from parent or sibling—regardless of how many years of analysis we may have had or that we have walked into the room encased in a middle-aged body. In this case, the sad widower must weather this normal incitement while masking his secret knowledge of newly discovered love.

The director tightens this complex screw wondrously, and for two hours we live in its slowly ratcheting tension. The complex starts out up there on the screen and ends up in the seat beside us. By film's end, we are the complex full of all the inner shame, embarrassment, rage, love, sorrow, and hope that any standard family-of-origin visit entails.

Freud felt that one of the most powerful evocations of the unconscious is uncanniness, its strangeness (*unheimlich*). When gripped by its unheralded presence, one can be taken into sometimes terrible and awesome places. These psychic places can often be filled with subtle terrors and voiceless indictments that can haunt long after the strange moment has evaporated into the psychic mists from which it precipitated.

Film can insinuate itself into these same terrible essences. Everyone has seen an unsettling film that lingered in an anxious foreground of awareness for days, months, even years with its strange uncanny. It has reached up from the graveyard of unconscious, introjected burials and filled awareness with the silent screens of a wordless, ancient terror. For me, Nicolas Roeg's adaptation of Daphne du Maurier's *Don't Look Now* (1974) and *White Noise* (2006) had such an effect. Films like these seep into the cracks of our anxiously enforced and settled worldview. They awaken ancient Beowulfs of being who rage and howl at the edges of our precarious modern pretentions. They insidiously suck us down into the liminal living realms of the dark gods and demons.

It is interesting that in film violence and horror film genres often predominate in times of chronic collective stress, splashing projected collective anxieties across the Friday night cinema screen in ghoulish images of blood and dismembered body parts. They provide a contained space for a cathartic acting out of nighttime terrors in hopes of a more sanguine individual and collective re-memberment and integration. They are offered up in service of a more productive psycho-spiritual accommodation of conscious and unconscious energies. Only such a terror-purged psyche can attain the contemplation of the core beauty and harmony of the All.

Incestuous violence haunts us all our lives. Do we guiltily live in service to the violent, brooding father, incest-conquered and diminished, or to the compassionate, concert pianist mother? Who will win? Who will be conquered? Who will be transformed? In *The Beat that My Heart Skipped* (2009), a young man twists on this petard for two agonizing, suspenseful hours. He is a Parisian enforcer for his dissipate father's gray-zone real estate holdings—intimidating, beating, harassing competitors for these holdings as well as illegal squatters. He is young, handsome, and edgy—bursting into spontaneous displays of rage and verbal/physical savageries. He hates his dad's character failure—his dependence on young, vulnerable women, his deteriorated physical self, his lack of vision and value in his life.

The young man has a recessed secret that surfaces on one of his dark forays into real estate mayhem—he had been a promising pianist as a young man under the gifted tutelage of his concert-performing mother. Her untimely death forced him to bury this vulnerable art and heart until, on this dark night, he crosses paths with her former high-end agent and is invited to audition for him.

Between bloody head knockings and chain-smoking illicit affairs with business partners' wives and Russian mobsters' prostitutes, he revisits the dusty keys of a baby grand in his apartment. He resurrects old Hayden symphonies and finds a Chinese prodigy instructor who speaks no French but teaches him in a ballet of gesture and silent, intense, shared passion for the keyboard and its hidden ecstasies. The best of the lost mother and the worst of the invasive father are erratically but certainly converted into new soul alchemies of reclaimed beauty, purpose, and love. And the violence plays a key role in this chemistry—a key and necessary role, as it does in all our lives. There is no liminal peace without accommodation to her violent, terrifying portals. She is always as much Kali as Hestia, and only a fool is unaware of this dual-faced numinal reality.

FILM AND COMMUNITY

There are no hard rules in psychology and spirituality. It is impossible to claim the centrality of either nature or nurture, heredity or environment in the making of our personality and fate. They are both inextricably linked and require cooperative interdependence for maximal healthy result.

So it is with science and spirituality. There will never be a conquest of the one over the other—they interpenetrate each other's being and are both functionally necessary to the processes of cosmic evolution. So it is, too, with art and science, art and spirit; individual and community, the political and the spiritual.

Film, much more than an individual "auteur" art form, is both a collective production and a collective experience. A key integrating theme in Jungian psychology is the centrality of the opposites. Oppositional tension is necessary for the ongoing generativity of the life force itself. The engine of evolution is the tension between poles, opposites. In many ways, film is simply a faithful narration of this tension and a witnessing of its trajectory through both time and space. Film achieves this witness from the perspective of an almost "super reality" where it seems, at its best, to nonanxiously cast its observing eye on the full horizon of human and numinal experience.[21]

Please don't let me fall asleep.

—FROM *INVASION* (2007)

Film is inherently a political medium. Politics is the art of managing and distributing power. Film reflects on this management and distribution. It is a politics of image, and its images not only reflect, they direct and correct. Film shuttles back and forth in its liminal fluid between the collective and the personal. It addresses both aspects of the psyche and, paradoxically, lives in between this paradoxical twinship of psychic reality. It always serves wholeness and justice in both these dimensions.

The film *Invasion* (2007) is a case in point. The third attempt on the same theme (*Invasion of the Body Snatchers*, 1956 and 1978), this most recent iteration is a science-fiction noire series that begins in ordinary time and slowly twists the image coils into a horrific extraordinary time. The key narrator is a divorced psychiatrist and the mother of an early latency-age boy. They live in Washington, D.C., where they wake up to the shocking news that there has been another shuttle crash spewing debris across thousands of square miles through the central section of the country—almost up to the steps of the capital itself. This opening image is the Rosetta stone clue of the film: it is about something tragically crashing through the

---

21. Hockley, *Cinematic Projections*, 40.

heartland of our shared public commons. It is a film about the American polis—the Greek word for the unique political-cultural interface psycho-spiritually shared by people.

Early on, a key political operative of the state (the director of the disease control wing of government) is met by a child outside a military tent where some of the debris is quarantined. With the Washington Monument in the background, this young girl hands him a piece of what looks like insulation tile and he painfully pricks his hand on the artifact. As the film quickly unfolds, the object that pricked his hand is a deadly alien virus released throughout the atmosphere on its fiery descent. The country has been infected by extraterrestrial plague. The government operator, it turns out, is the former husband of our psychiatrist narrator-protagonist and her child's father.

And it is not by accident that she is a psychiatrist or that the most prominent book displayed in her study is by Carl Gustav Jung. The film wants us to know that this virus is as much an internal virus—what psychological therapy would call an introject—as it is an external entity. And introjects are toxic elements of a parental-guardian's undigested wound in her/their unprocessed rage, terror, and grief, which they inject into their child's innocent psychic body as a place to dump and hide its horrific influences.

The ancient Greeks talked about the *polis*, both the political will of the people and the place of that political enactment. They called this *topos*, or place. Within, it was holistically inclusive of all things physical, spiritual, and aesthetic. Martin Heidegger, the famed modern German philosopher, speaks movingly of the polis/topos:

> *Polis* means, rather, the place, the there, wherein and as which historical being-there. The *polis* is the historical place, the there *in* which, *out of* which, and *for* which history happens. To this place and scene of history belong the gods, the temples, the priests, the festivals, the games, the poets, the thinker, the ruler, the council of elders, the assembly of the people, the army and the fleet.[22]

In other words, the polis, the political place, act, and being of a people, is a complete historical moment that gathers in the full cultural and spiritual essence of a people. It is inherently an imaginal topos/place, for only imagination can embrace the full human and transpersonal dimensions of

22. Heidegger, *Introduction to Metaphysics* (1953), as quoted in Gauthier, *Martin Heidegger*, 99.

such a political soul. Film in our time is such an all-encompassing political imagining.

But it needs to be a political space reconnected and re-contained within the ultimate polis: Mother Earth. The most visceral of containments are the seasons themselves. This knowledge is as old as the shaman-druids. They organized their inner and outer lives by the seasons' compass. Film, too, walks the margin of the seasons and lovingly lays down their protective borders all around us viewers—often beyond our conscious awareness. A vivid cameo of this phenomenon can be seen in *Notting Hill* (1999). Our erstwhile narrator, grief stricken by love's traumatic abandon, is followed in one long dolly-tracking shot through the four seasons as he strolls down Highgate Street in Notting Hill. He sadly trudges through the street's maze of venders, babies, fruits, art, and pregnancy unseen in his anguish. The street is ablaze with Eros even as his deadness wraiths through its midst. No one sees but the seasons, which are breathtakingly rendered in almost high-Renaissance still life. The seasons see and know him and grieve with him. So, the ancient Druids knew, seasons rightly acknowledged heal a wounded, broken soul. Time, season time, literally does heal all wounds.

In the same film, in one of the oscillating moments when love is kindling, our protagonist and his new beloved pass one of those London pocket gardens artfully slipped between the protective walls of residential mews. She goads him into joining her in scaling the fenced-off preserve. They land in a moon-bathed enclosure of fairy silence and still beauty. There, in that time-stopped garden, the lost innocence of the young, the lost innocence of the old, and the lost innocence of the middle-aged become a secret garden where children play, young couples make love, old couples cherish, dead ancestors are remembered, and new generations are anticipated.

Film is, most of all, such a garden of receptivity and containment. Film never tires of wrapping us into her renewing embrasure. In such succor resides the eternal hope that the lost child of soul innocence can be found and restored to a weary life, body, and world. That is why we never tire of returning to film's sacred, containing precincts.

It is to this Great Mother, political space of rich, liminal re-imaginings that we now turn.

POLITICS

*So if we want to understand the psyche, we have to include
the whole world.*

—C. G. JUNG[1]

ONE OF THE OLDEST cross-cultural archetypal stories involves a hunter on
the savanna setting down her spear after a long day's hunt. She roasts the
day's hare as vesper light bathes the plains, then drifts away into a light
slumber as fatigue and strain seep into her weary bones. But suddenly she
snaps into full consciousness, alert to her surroundings. The savanna mood
is different. There is a deeper silence to the silence; a new brooding presence in the stillness. Then she finds it—two glowing eyes in the deep brush
on the other side of the fire. Her spear is over there, too. Nothing to do now
but to blend back into the high grass behind the screen of the fire. Once
deep into the dew-dampened grass, she turns and begins to run.

The hunter runs alone and free at first, but soon is pursued by the
sound of stealthy, heavy paws parting the grass close behind. Hers is a desperate sprint for life. She runs and runs, her hunter's muscles firing beyond
the point of belief, her lungs as raw and fiery as a mating Frigate Bird's chest
plumage. She is near collapse and facing certain death, the great cat predator just two steps behind. But just as she is surrendering to her inevitable
fate, the ground explodes below her feet and she is falling, careening into
the deep abyss of a great rift. Spinning all akimbo, she plummets until a
large cliffside vine snags her hand. She grabs its roots with a death grip.

1. Jung, "Archetypes and the Collective Unconscious," 9i:56.

She dangles and twists, rotating like the spitted hare she was preparing for dinner moments before. The stillness a suspended, timeless silence. Lion spittle splashes her brow as the great cat claws the air above her. Deadly spiked rocks await in the darkness thousands of feet below. The scene becomes eerily hushed—a blank screen of pure sensory awake-ness. No fear. No desire. No hope. Just empty awake-ness. Then the hunter sees a ripe, full-season strawberry on the end of her life-saving vine. With her free hand, she plucks the fleshy fruit and puts it into her mouth, reflecting on its exquisite, infinite sweetness.

Such receptive emptiness is what we and our weary, ragged world require just now.

A middle-aged patient dreams of walking down a streambed in an arid region with a younger woman companion. It is late in the day, and she and her young friend become aware that they are being followed, stalked actually, by a large cat—a cougar or panther. It crisscrosses the shallow stream water just behind them. As it closes in, she elects to turn and face the creature. She pleads for the life of her friend who at this moment transfigures into a female cat. The large male cat agrees. She pleads for her life. The large cat again accedes. All three—a human and a potential large cat breeding couple—then turn and proceed together. They travel through a financial district urban canyon, bonded as a new community in the twilight silence. The threat of death has been transformed by an act of conscious courage into a moment of cross-species renewal for this weary, craven capitalist world. The wounded old patriarchal Fisher King may yet receive the healing balm of the Cat-Grail unguent in his jaded 120th-floor Wall Street suite.

This chapter explores the possibility of developing a liminal politics that is loyal to seeking and respectfully enacting a conscious, receptive emptiness. Without it, I fear we will be devoured by the instinctual darkness all around us or crushed by the deadly abyss below. Like Dante, we are precariously cast into a collective hell. We must calmly wake up and begin a patient return to the true, full Home that awaits us (or that constellates amongst us) so that we can fashion a resilient, respectful, and compassionate numinal politics.

Cultures benefit from liminal immersion as much as individuals do. Cultures can be starved from liminal drought, just as individuals can be. In fact, cultures evolve very similarly to the way that individuals individuate. If conscious interaction with and retention of the liminal moment is encouraged by a mature culture, each individual's descent into liminal reality can broaden, deepen, and intensify cultural resilience and impact.

I once witnessed an indigenous coming-of-age ceremony. The opening chanter came out and, in native language, proposed three simple questions and a declaration:

- Is everybody here?
- Is everybody safe?
- Is everybody awake?
- Everybody will get home.

These questions and declaration are essentially cosmological. They are, in fact, cosmological necessities.

Is everybody here? What a core liminal question—maybe *the* core liminal question. We are not really here, safe, and awake until *everybody* is assured that they will be able to get home. The ancient Greeks in their city-states knew that this was the fundamental political requirement of the polis: to get every citizen safely Home. And this safety can only be certain when we are sure the gods are with us, that they accompany us on every step of the journey back home. Politics, authentic politics, walks in liminal worlds.

All life is political. We all live in a cosmic polis, a universe designed for fundamental community and correspondence. And the political is the subtle interweaving of conflict, the teasing out of distaff harmonies. Jung centers his psychology here, averring that its central fueling essence is this multi-positional dance.

Tradition asserts that Socrates, in his 70th year, was offered a plea deal at his famous trial. He was offered the chance to live and be pardoned if he promised to stop being a philosopher, to cease practicing the care of souls. His elegant, no-holds-barred response is a timeless mirror of the courageous response we must make to the plea deal being offered both professionally and culturally in our own era:

> In his often-quoted answer to the possibility that the jury might acquit him if he would promise no longer to practice philosophy, Socrates tells the jury that he would say: Gentlemen of the jury, I am grateful and I am your friend, but I will obey the god rather than you, and as long as I draw breath and am able, I shall not cease to practice philosophy, to exhort you and in my usual way to point out to any of you whom I happen to meet: Good Sir, you are an

Athenian, a citizen of the greatest city with the greatest reputation for both wisdom and power; are you not ashamed of your eagerness to possess as much wealth, reputation and honors as possible while you do not care for nor give thought to wisdom or truth, or the best possible state of your soul? [And then he goes on to say:] I shall treat in this way anyone I happen to meet, young and old, citizen and stranger, and more so the citizens for you are more kindred to me. Be sure that this is what the god orders me to do, and I think there is no greater blessing for the city than my service to the gods.[2]

It takes courage to live a liminal life. In a culture addicted to noise, distraction, and other such psycho-spiritual mayhems, to grow silent and offer voluntary self-entrance into liminal absorption is to commit a revolutionary act. The collective always tends toward the dissociated. To be liminally in touch is to be animated, fully awake. The body and the subtle body both glow like the sky in a summer sunset. You stand out. Everyone on the street knows you are reposing in that dangerous liminal realm where there are no safeguards. There are no safety railings where unexpected deep-well affects of unexplored sorrow can gobsmack a liminally wide-open ego.

The collective prefers the carefully prescribed stage of set things. It likes the chronologically precise order of things. A steady job. A permanent address. A predictable income. A routine rotation of family holidays and their engrained ritual observances, right down to the pumpkins, rice, and cranberries. The collective uses such steadiness to anaesthetize the ever-threatening liminal demonic antagonists.

Of course, it's artificial. It's a storefront diorama, a Sears and Roebuck catalogue kind of ingenuous certainty. But it keeps the power grid up and the light on at dark so that the more real and trickster forces of Deep Psyche cannot pry our comfortable ego loose from our threat-dulling deceptions.

The professions participate in this culture-soothing charade as much as any other sector, maybe more. For when the scientism of our times really takes hold, its evidence-based nostrums are chanted to keep the unpredictable, model-shaking genies of the unscientific nether world from fully shattering all such surface certainties.

In the mid-19th century, Jung was very interested in fantasist novelist and philosopher Edward De Novalis. Here is how De Novalis disrobed the over-clothed Empirical Emperor of his times:

---

2. Belah, *Religion in Human Evolution*, 385–86.

When the soul hovers uncertainly between life and the dream, between mental disarray and the appearance of cold reflection, it is in religious belief that one seeks solace. I have never been able to find relief in the school of philosophy which merely supplies us with maxims of self-interest or, at the most, of reciprocity, leaving us nothing but empty experience and bitter doubt. Such a philosophy combats our moral suffering by deadening our sensibility, like the surgeon, it knows only how to cut the organ which is causing the pain. But for us, born in an age of revolutions and upheavals which shattered all beliefs, raised at best to practice vague religion based on a few outward observances and whose lukewarm devotion is perhaps more sinful than impiety or heresy, for us things become quite difficult whenever we feel the need to reconstruct the mystic temple whose edifice the pure and simple of spirit fully accept traced in their hearts. The Tree of Knowledge is not the tree of Life. And yet can we rid our mind of all good or evil implanted in it by many intelligent generations? Ignorance cannot be learned.

I have higher hopes in the goodness of God: we may well be approaching that era when science, as predicted, having accomplished its entire cycle of synthesis and analysis, of belief and negation, will now be able to purify itself and usher forth the miraculous city from chaos and ruin.[3]

De Novalis saw profession and our full citizenry to be vocations after truth—seeking the true oath of Destiny, both personal and collective, that his soul, Jung's psyche, called us toward. *Vocatio.* The call of the true inner and outer *Daimon.* We have no ultimate choice, if we seek the full life, other than to follow the lead of this embodied beacon of ensouled destiny.

Democracy is an esoteric practice. Its primary artform, its essential tool-craft, is politics. Numinal-based politics. Its deepest garment of presence, mystery. Politics is projective alchemy writ large. And depth political alchemy requires us to consciously suffer our internal splits into a deeper integration. Authentic transformational alchemy brokes no partial solutions. This esoteric process has broken even the finest practitioners who failed to finish the last painful miles of the life-long marathon after wholeness. Take Thomas Jefferson, the founding American esotericist, as an example. Jefferson's political work projected onto the public screen his complex private demons. He raged against public debt even as his private debts raced toward an almost perpetual insolvency. He wrote elegantly about the inalienable rights of all even as he prodded and abused his personal slaves on to

3. Jung, *On Psychological and Visionary Art,* 35–36.

greater labors.[4] Ultimately, Jefferson could not honorably acquit his debts and free his slaves. This chapter is about politics, small p and capital P. It is about our personal political hygiene and our integrity in dealing with both our complex intrapsychic dialogues and our equally complex interpersonal relationships. It is about the politics of corruption within the professional healing culture. It is about corrupted national politics and, most urgently, it is about corrupt global and species politics.

In this chapter, I talk about the political economy I know—that of the industrialized West. But I am convinced that most of this chapter's arguments and reflections apply globally, for, as they say, patriarchy is a global disease. It operates, unconsciously, very similarly across global religions and political cultures despite the vast surface differences between economies and theories of exchange and value. Patriarchy is not clueless about our bind. The conflict and its earnest desire for a soulful resolution saturate Western artforms.

Take a very garden-variety example from the cinema of nearly 70 years ago: a 1951 film entitled, *The Man Who Shot Liberty Valance*. A Western genre film, it had an odd twist for its time in that it featured two screen icons modeling very different "ideal" masculine personas. The first, Ransome Stoddard (played by Jimmy Stewart), is a dweeb—an Easterner fresh off a stagecoach with only a bag of law books in tow. Having come West full of a Horatio Alger-like passion to seek his true destiny, he arrives in a one-horse town almost comedically named Shinbone, and he arrives unconscious. His coach had been robbed just south of town, and he'd received a vicious beating from the outlaw leader for having taken a lawyer's umbrage at the violence directed toward a woman passenger. He is discovered in his beaten state and brought into the town by the other male character—a steely-jawed, self-made, fast-on-the-draw wilderness cowboy named Tom Doniphon (played by John Wayne).

Neither man is a cartoon. Stoddard is the best of the civilized man, humbly earnest in his democratic ideals, courageous in his embodied advocacy when necessity demands. Doniphon is the real-deal Western hero, taciturn in his clear-eyed, cynical appraisal of a dangerous world that must be met with armed, no-nonsense strength. One man fights with law books, the other with a six gun.

And both love the same woman: a bright, salt-of-the-earth farm woman working in the town restaurant. Hallie Stoddard (played by Vera

---

4. Ellis, *American Sphinx*, 284–85.

Miles) is fierce, passionate, and soulful, and both men love her for it. In an unusual turn, both men honor each other's love for the same woman. In fact, we sense that it is through her that they meet each other in common, begrudging admiration. Through her, they wordlessly know they complete each other. The good desert cowboy needs the good urban scholar to be a complete man, soul-softened and made whole by encounter and transformation within the Deep Feminine.

In the end, after Doniphon surreptitiously kills a threatening thug who would have murdered Stoddard, Stoddard "gets the woman." But it's really both men she loves, both men who get her in the end, even as she leaves a blooming desert cactus on Doniphon's pine box coffin in the empty back room of the Shinbone undertakers. Stoddard becomes a world-famous statesman, Doniphon dies a penniless rancher. But in the end, both men end their lives in Her full embrace.

Our postmodern, dystopian world often lives the way a John LeCarre espionage novel reads—drenched in impenetrable moment-to-moment dreads. Such a postmodern world posits no real choice between compassion and violence, but only between a less-immoral violence and an absolute, evil violence. It is an angst-saturated world of real politic. It is a cynical world where one survives only by being quick, alert to every potential threat in the shadows. It is a world that knows we never left the jungle, never really got out of the caves. It is a world that celebrates only the apex predator. It is a world that is all Tom Doniphon and no Ransom Stoddard.

We need to bring Ransom back into the story and then get both men to dance again in Dame Soul's embrace. I want to believe that our world—our violent, patriarchal, predator world—will find a way to die and be reborn in Her arms.

Entering liminal realms is not for the faint of heart. They are charged realms and dangerous. This is especially true in our own era, though maybe every era fancies for itself the same ultimate crisis. And it is hard to awaken our fellow citizens to the danger because it is so cleverly camouflaged. America is a cruel place. But, she insidiously hides her cruelty in her piety, which is the most insidious and deceptive form of cruelty. It is violent annihilation behind a velvet glove of disguise. Entering the political arena for action, protest, or relief is like entering a giant minefield that could explode all around you at a moment's notice.

As a result, most people's relational connection to politics is fraught. People's political sensitivities are fretful ones. We mostly live in fear—of our families, of our neighbors, of our communities, of the state. We are afraid because the "other" has inevitably failed and violated us. The initial trauma, as we have seen, is very early and very primitive. It is a trauma generated when our early guardians reach the limits of self-soothing for their own trauma and turn our infantile vulnerabilities into objects of scorn and derision. At that moment, we are forced to interrupt our gradual evolution into the world's ambivalence by unexpected, often violent, behavioral renunciations. We seal off our terrified, needy selves and act un-needy. Often, we become as silent and invisible as possible to avoid further repetitive scapegoating.

Ultimately, our fear of everything outside of ourselves is fear of this unexplored and sealed off trauma within. So, in a capitalist society, porous with the unspoken but omnivorous presence of the military-industrial establishment and its obsessive desire to control all markets, cultures, and behaviors so as to amass unchallenged wealth and power, we learn to be afraid quite early. This outer political fear is reminiscent of the inner failure and violence of failed parental attunement. We consume and conform as a way to accommodate the implied threat of social stigma and exile—even imprisonment and death if our social norm dysfunction is provocative enough, as Abraham Lincoln, Martin Luther King, Jr., Malcolm X, John and Robert Kennedy, Anne Frank, and others so painfully discovered.

We fail to see that most of this consumption and accommodation is violent itself, depriving the world of precious resources out of an incessant attempt to assure ourselves of social status and desirability. Such consumption is really cowardice.[5] It is a backing away from authentic affirmation and from voicing a grounded, other- and earth-connected Soul-genuineness. It is an anxious fear that a more liminal, real way of living will draw the annihilating attention of state and police.[6] If we are honest, it is part of the primitive anxiety that grips all of us when we go through a Transportation Security Administration (TSA) screening at the airport or pass under a ghostly surveillance camera in the street. There is an alarming growth of economic empowerment by the mega wealthy over everyone else in our society, a society in which the criminal, control-enabling, wealthy elite remain unindicted and un-convicted while those in the streets are incarcerated at record levels for often the most farfetched of perceived infractions.[7] We

5. Soelle, *Silent Cry.*

6. Soelle, *Silent Cry.*

7. Klein, *Shock Doctrine.*

come by our political terror honestly, but we can't continue to live that way healthily.

> No amount of fiddling with capitalism to regulate and humanize it . . . can for long disguise its failure to conserve the wealth and health of nature. Eroded, wasted, or degraded soils; damaged or destroyed ecosystems; extinction of biodiversity, species; whole landscapes defaced, gouged, flooded, or blown up . . . thoughtless squandering of fossil fuels and fossil waters, of mineable minerals and ores, natural health and beauty replaced by a heartless and sickening ugliness. Perhaps its greatest success is an astounding increase in the destructiveness and therefore the profitability of war.[8]

As with individual trauma-protection reflexes, collective trauma politics use two recurrent patterns—projection and displacement. Germans projected their shadow onto—and murdered—six million innocent Jewish victims. Euro-America displaced its anti-Semitic shadow and guilt onto a relatively innocent Palestinian Middle East. Instead of creating what was essentially another concentration camp on Cyprus after the war, the Axis could have taken a page from Theodore Herzl and guaranteed a safe and abundant Jewish Homeland in the Rhineland based on Herzl's basic Homeland principles. Always, the collective finds an innocent projective scapegoat into whom to pour our inexhaustible rage and helplessness.

All of us dance with sociopathy. Similarly, all politics—our collective persona—dances with sociopathy. There is a narcissistic core to all political enactment. Somewhere, somehow, the primal mother is trying to be located and appeased. There is always a desperate attempt to heal her attunement wounds, to make her feel less lonely and abandoned by the world. If the political individual can get glib enough, tall enough, high enough, and violent enough, they might just save her or, failing that, punish the sadistic world that harmed her fragile flesh in the first place. Even in the shriveled soul of a most heinous Hitler, where the personal mother is not sought, but rather annihilated in sadistic reprisal, it is the primal, Pure, Mythic mother of the All whose loving embrasure is desired.

> *A client dreams of being lost in a vast forest. She burrows down into a deep, self-dug trench of hiding, there to discover an adult companion who constantly needs her diaper changed. She cowers there*

8. Berry, *Wendell Berry, Poet and Prophet.*

until a Superman comes, a man who learned to be Superman by
"burrowing through water and air with real transpersonal power."

A democratic polis is closer to the burrowing psyche than a soaring-sky representative one, which is a local, close, smell-able government—a government of spring wilderness and baby poop fragrances.

A patient dreams, in a lovely quadrilateral dream, that it was their wedding day. It was the at the U.S. Capitol building. The opening morning-gathering event was at a coffee shop in the Northeast corner of the Capitol building, then the service was held at noon under the auspicious Capital Dome. There were to be both Jewish and Catholic officiants present. They never showed, but the Bride and Groom found another informal but even more sanctifying way to tie the nuptial's sacred knot. The day's celebration was to be ended at a coffee shop in the Northwest corner of the building. The beautiful ageless Bride was a Fusion Bride of the patient-Groom's real soulful and earthy Hestia woman and a woman in a handsome power suit. Hope and joy suffused the dream, a cozy sense of the best of the personal and the public Polis being joined in sacred matrimony.

There has been a shattering of the depths of the spiritual commons all around the globe. In this dream, the U. S. Capital building stands as an American symbol for this global yearning for a gathering of all peoples in all our varying ethnicities, genders, religions under a common Dome, a sacred/secular Cathedral Dome of justice, peace, and compassion, an especially vulnerable symbol given the insurrection riots of January 6, 2021. The dream also alludes to the Native Indigenous notion of the sacred importance of the four directions. In many of these traditional cosmologies, each direction contributes something essence-unique from Mother Earth and Father Sky toward the healing and integration of our individual and collective lives. From the East comes the sun's morning rebirthing-blessings/visions after the often recurring darknesses of Soul Loss and destruction of the long night of despair. The South brings the fertile winds of the harvest and the nurture of its crops. The West brings the wisdom and reality of death and the ancestors; a grounding soliloquy of healing Memory and Presence. The North direction represents the cold bracing winds from the North; their sweeping away of the detritus and dead visions of the past to make way for the new visions coming on the dawn. And in the middle of this sacred compass there is a wedding, an alchemical conjunction/joining; a sacred liturgy of the days where the service begins in the Matins dawn and ends in the Vesper evening. This ritual transforms secular, mundane coffee shops [in themselves a favorite commons place to study, converse, and enjoy life] into a sacred space, bonding with the Soulmate/Bride/Groom that always lays alchemically hidden in the most ordinary activities and gatherings of our temporal lives.

Politics is liminal because it is a ritual activity. Politics is a sacramental enactment. As we observed in the first chapter, the word "liminal" itself became academically popular several decades ago because, in great part, of the anthropologist Victor Turner and his field work with African tribal groups. He noted that something measurable occurred, measurable both subjectively and objectively, when individuals and their local communities underwent rites of passage. The ordinary "time" and everyday "space" of things became extraordinary and numinous (charged by the mysterious and mystical Otherness of things—the numen) when the individual and the tribal community entered a carefully prepared ritual. The Eros of things became a visible register—bodies became naked or ethereally arraigned, everyday language was discarded for chant and dialect, pedestrian body movement became sacred dance and orgy, "dependable" daytime perception became nighttime dream, trance, and vision. And the changes effected struck a collective register as much as an individual one.

Liminal political events hover because they are dynamic, not static, chains of happening and encounter. These liminal occurrences and the gods they mediate are always exploding, gyrating, luring, and inciting around us. But our strict codes of reasonable, rational framing exclude them from awareness. They are the enlivened fire always just below the crust of our moribund, patriarchal world.

> Since the individual is not only a single entity, but also by his very existence, presupposes a collective relationship, the process of individuation does not lead to isolation, but to an intense and more universal collective solidarity.[9]

Psyche convenes political space. And psyche is soul, so soul convenes political space.

> As described by Heidegger, the polis is constituted by everything from supernatural entities (the gods) to buildings (the temples) to various classes of individuals (the priests, the poets, the thinkers, the ruler) to rituals (the festivals, the games) to political institutions (the council of elders, the assembly of the people) to military institutions (the army and the fleet). As the "foundation and scene of man's

9. Jung, "Two Essays on Analytical Psychology," 7:155.

being-there," the polis is the "point" at which supernatural deities, classes of individuals, rituals, military and political institutions "meet" at the site of history.[10]

Cities, at least some cities, are magical portals. Cities are where the best and the worst of our species come to roost. Cities perform our best symphonies, sing our most elegant arias, and chant our most soulful poems. Cities also enact our most heinous acts of violence on each other, for cities breed our racist gangs, house our chattel brothels, distribute our lethal drugs, rationalize and even lionize our capitalist hoardings. Cities construct our most gravity-defying buildings, house our truly precious art, and dispense our latest medical mercies. Cities are showcases for the best and worst of human vision. Cities are, indeed, magical portals, for cities are where the deepest clues to our individual and collective destinies are to be found. Cities are almost pure liminal space, for, at their core, they defy the limits of time and space in the unquenchable urge to discover and live at the very edge of human experience in a quest for the outskirts of living divinity.

Perhaps no city is more magical for our current global civilization than New York. No city lives as such an arousing metaphor for the mine where the richest destiny-seeking ore is to be found. Yet destiny always resides in close proximity to the abyss. And the abyss, where the destiny quest is lost, must be visited to discover our true individual and collective destiny. New York and all similar great metropolises are full of such Abyss:

> Consciousness itself lives over the abyss, and the attainment of a fullness of life means, at some point, a return to that abyss . . . Though the experience is intensely personal it is just as intensely, and always, political.[11]

Our cities, our sanctuaries, are magical because they are birthed invariably in magical, liminal, abyss-discovered connection to the living earth. These connections sustain and house us. And our modern, dystopian, secular culture has for the most part forgotten or scorns such sacred places of origin.

As an everyday example, I remember once being a member of a mainline Protestant parish in the Pacific Northwest. They wished to build a new church in their rapidly growing suburban corridor. They did what any good

10. Gauthier, *Martin Heidegger*, 99.
11. Dourley, *On Behalf of the Mystic Fool*, 231.

marketing plan in our era would encourage. They hired trendy market experts who tutored them in where the new super highways, shopping malls, and high-tech factory campuses would be and advised them to buy and build to maximize access to these population chokepoints.

Almost as an afterthought in this frenzy to grow (so typical of "can-do" America), they interviewed selected members of the congregation to survey their ideas about the best building sites. When they called me in, there was a stunned, almost disbelieving, silence when they heard what I seriously proposed. I suggested consulting with the medicine people in the local Native American community, both to ask their wisdom about the best sacred places and to solicit their permission and blessing to build there. I indicated that we were lucky in that the First Peoples in our area still lived in their primordial precincts. The Northwest tribes were the only indigenous communities generally not "conquered" and "genocided" by United States government policy. I asked the parish committee to remember that the vast majority of the great cathedrals in Europe were built consecutively on the sacred places, wells, and openings in the earth where people had experienced healing dreams, visions, and events. These are places where the walls between human and divine thinned and the transformative could manifest in ensouling ways.

Well, you could have heard the proverbial pin drop. Very anxious, the committee almost stumbled over themselves to facilitate my early departure after expressing their rushed, overly-effusive thanks for my time and thoughts. What a fly on the wall would have heard as they talked and laughed nervously in my absence, I can only imagine. But I was sincere. I tried calmly to tell them the truth, that I sincerely wanted their success. They subsequently elected to build on a data-chosen site recommended by the consultant.

The church stumbled through some hesitant dozen years and now is descending into permanent dispersion. They had the site, but a shovel never touched the ground. If they had chosen and built on holy ground, I believe they would have had a chance to genuinely and deeply thrive as sacred community.

THE FATAL CONFUSION OF THE POLIS WITH THE ECONOMIC, THE PSYCHE WITH PRODUCTION, COMPASSION WITH CONSUMPTION

To be hopeful in bad times is not just foolishly romantic. It is based on the fact that human history is a history not only of cruelty, but also of compassion, sacrifice, courage, kindness... And if we do act, in however small a way, we don't have to wait for some grand utopian future. The future is an infinite succession of presents, and to live now as we think human beings should live, in defiance of all that is bad around us, is itself a marvelous victory.[12]

Capitalism has lost its esoteric, alchemical ardor. It was birthed in an era when the whole West had been in the quagmire of the "Dark Ages," where human life was mean, local, and brutal, and when little was left of the psycho-spiritual grandeur that had been the height of Egypt, Greece, and Rome. Capitalism was birthed in the spirit of exchange. It was the exchange mostly of the hard goods of survival—the swapping of life-assuring, complementary staples between one village and another, one region and another, one continent and another. It developed quite clever exchange metrics to assure the volume transfer of bulk commodities across vast distances. Traded commodities accommodated a more dimensional existence for everyone—more and more persons could have home larders comfortably laden with spices, fish oils, salts, fabrics, and the novel cultural and religious ideas that came with them.

Capitalism, not surprisingly, was birthed at a liminal transition zone where land met sea, where interior solidity and fecundity met saltwater-born wildness and danger. In Chapter Two, I discussed an incident in my visit to capitalism's birth city—Bruges. The Hansa, the trading league, spread across the vast reach of the Baltic Coast and incubated the exchange notion of capitalism in that marsh-wreathed realm at the delta of some of Europe's great freshwater river systems. The Hanseatic League invented modern accounting systems, cargo manifesting, even modern insurance where crews' families were guaranteed a share of the cooperative capitalist company's profits if their craft were to go down in the turbulent northern seas.

Original capitalism was relatively free of contempt. It was competitive. It was earnest. But it did not lean toward the indecorous, engorging

---

12. Zinn, "Optimism of Uncertainty."

economic beast that shadows the planet today. Remember, the liminal seems to be allergic to contempt.

> *But now, three-quarters of a century later, we are no longer talking about theoretical alternatives to corporate rule. We are talking with practical urgency about an obvious need. Now the two great aims of industrialism—replacement of people by technology and concentration of wealth into the hands of a small plutocracy—seem close to fulfillment. At the same time the failures of industrialism have become too great and too dangerous to deny. Corporate industrialism itself has exposed the falsehood that it ever was inevitable or that it ever has given precedence to the common good. It has failed to sustain the health and stability of human society. Among its characteristic signs are destroyed communities, neighborhoods, families, small businesses, and small farms. It has failed just as conspicuously and more dangerously to conserve the wealth and health of nature. No amount of fiddling with capitalism to regulate and humanize it, no pointless rhetoric on the virtues of capitalism or socialism, no billions or trillions spent on "defense" of the "American dream," can for long disguise this failure. The evidences of it are everywhere: eroded, wasted, or degraded soils; damaged or destroyed ecosystems; extinction of species; whole landscapes defaced, gouged, flooded, or blown up; pollution of the whole atmosphere and of the water cycle; "dead zones" in the coastal waters; thoughtless squandering of fossil fuels and fossil waters, of mineable minerals and ores; natural health and beauty replaced by a heartless and sickening ugliness. Perhaps its greatest success is an astounding increase in the destructiveness, and therefore the profitability, of war.*[13]

Capitalism and its evil spawn, the military-industrial complex, flood the commons of our culture more and more. Take policing, for example. No longer is the familiar tagline "to protect and to serve" the essential reality of community law enforcement. Increasingly, it is to control and to restrain, to surveil and to intimidate. Its source-pool for applicants is less and less the policing and criminology programs of community-based universities. Increasingly, it draws from military and combat-trained veterans. Its tactics are less and less relational; they are more and more tactical. Less and less beat cop; more and more swat team. Even the uniforms are more and more "black ops" and less khaki; more SS and less Bobbie. When police engage the streets, it is more to conquer and control them than to relate to and interact with them. Again, if our evolutionary arc has to be from conquest

---

13. Berry, *Wendell Berry, Poet and Prophet.*

and competition models to cooperation and compassion models, contemporary policing is in a deepening, dangerously regressive cycle.

With a military that rapes subordinates with impunity and teaches ethnic and racial hate as military-police policy, with a Supreme Court that ideologically decides before it hears, and with a higher education system that does not teach, this collective Western culture can ingrain a deep, contemptuous shame in its citizens.[14] It is shameful not to support the military. It is shameful not to support capitalism.

> But in the liminal realm it gains a dimensionality, a centrality, a texture that ordinary time washes out. As I write this, a single Norwegian right-wing bomber and gunman methodically has killed 86 victims, most of them adolescents on a wilderness island shot like so many rabbits in a caged warren. The world awakens from its numb denials as evil probes the good yet again and the best of us and in us attempt to comprehend this dark visitor that shows up with such merciless abandon on a summer Norse afternoon. Initially, we join the panicked call for renewed vigilance, legal reprisal, fierce damnation for the mindless killer, Gradually, later in the dusk-drenched reveries of our midsummer eve days, the specters of our complicit inner darkness and urges rise for recognition and confrontation.[15]

The deadened politics of the last two decades of the American Polis, especially, seem to be free-falling into this regressive abyss. Most often male, Anglo politicians enunciate fiery language and image with strangely little effect. It falls right to the ground from their often empty, lathered mouths. They earnestly want liminal fire (even if they cannot articulate or describe this desire), but they have no idea how to access it. They have forgotten the sacred path to the holy core of authentic political enactment.

Real leadership after 9/11 demands we transpose military solutions into relational-policing ones, transform brute force into justice. Our survival as a species will require no less. South Africa's dramatic Truth and Reconciliation process was a significant part of this beckoning evolution, an evolutionary process attempting to lure us to a more compassionate and wide-angle mode of communal existence. In this mode, humanity co-abides not just with itself but with all specie vessels of life and light. The contemptuous, flagrant, and cynical militarism and electoral abuse of the

---

14. Berman, *Twilight of American Culture.*
15. Gibson, *Private Personal Journal.*

last decades belie any consciousness of the urgent necessity to engage with such transformational beckoning.

The vast majority of the $2.3tn the US government has spent or obligated for the war [2001–21 Afghan War] has gone not to Afghans—corrupt or otherwise—but to US military contractors (and those who bought US debt): a reported 80–90% of US outlays ended up back in the US as a "massive wealth transfer" from taxpayers to firms in the military industrial complex, which have seen their profits and stock prices skyrocket.[16]

Trauma generally shuts the psychic system down. Much like the body's blood-clotting mechanism, psychic numbing and denial agents rush quickly to the point of impact and psychic inflation. They begin shutting down and sealing off the wound site to protect from further core cell damage. The effect of deploying these protective cloaking agents is reflected in the endurance of these measures across long periods of time. Most adults I see in Jungian psychotherapy attest to the resilience of these defensive structures. Decades after the original traumatic assault, depth areas of their core emotional selves slumber on in anesthetic reverie. It is often a herculean effort to awaken and arouse these developmentally delayed areas of psyche to seed a more fertile and widely-prismed emotional life and existential vibrancy.[17]

The Culture Psyche similarly numbs whole populations into comparable states of emergency hibernation in response to brutal, traumatic incursions from war, famine, genocide, economic panic, or despotism.[18] Such dystopic collective slumber can last centuries, even millennia, just to violently burst into life when fragile tribal, ethnic, or religious protective scabs are ripped off by unexpected outer events. Unimaginable violence and savagery burst out. The Armenian, Jewish, and Cambodian genocides of recent memory are distinct cases in point. As with individuals, when the protective barrier is violently ripped open, it is met by its savage intrapsychic twin. This twin responds reflexively, *lex talionis* style: eye for eye, dogma for dogma, exploded device for exploded device. Once unleashed, the beast can keep on killing and destroying for years until, vampire like, it runs out of blood to feed its addictive rage and slumps into a dormant stupor to await the next frenzied feeding.

16. Vine, "Defeat Was Inevitable."
17. Kalsched, *Trauma and the Soul.*
18. Singer and Kimbles, *Cultural Complex.*

But occasionally, a paradoxical event occurs. Once the eruptive, reflexive violence runs its course, instead of a re-numbing dormancy, an awakened compassion fills the bloodied void. With 75 million corpses stacked up all around, post-World War II Europe entered one of human history's most evolving and sustained exercises in building a compassion culture. Universal health care, human rights establishments, the European Economic Union: all became manifest symbols. In North America, the spreading fabric of gay rights and inclusion might not have been possible without the psyche-wakening tsunami of the AIDS epidemic and its tragic mass loss of life. In paradoxical response to these spirit-numbing events, depth psyche awakened rather than re-slumbered.

Why? I postulate it is because the trauma wedge of these nihilist Armageddons drove so deeply that it penetrated into the molten liminal zone of individual and collective psyches. Its animating image and energy rushed through the breach. These artesian openings into renewing soul—the soul for which the original emergency blockades had been protectively created—could not be re–sealed against the enormous hydraulic force. Soul is always hungry for soul, inner world for outer world. Once the long-lost beloved was relocated, once the Berlin Walls of trauma had been breached, nothing could turn back the sorrowful joy and release of reunion with the core "Soul of the All."

This phenomenon happens, just not on large epic canvases. It occurs in micro moments of every great collective upheaval. The stopping of time after John. F. Kennedy's death, the slow, mourning dirge-walk of stunned New Yorkers across the George Washington Bridge on September 11, 2011, the grieving in the streets following Martin Luther King, Jr.'s assassination—all liminal balm compassionately pouring out onto parched Chronos streets. "What should we do," asks philosopher Catherine Malabou, "so that consciousness of the brain does not pure and simply coincide with the spirit of capitalism?"[19]

Sometimes the political can become intensely personal, all at once. Visitations to the liminal realms assure us we are not alone in the universe. Such visits vouchsafe that our suffering is not in vain and provide us an embodied experience of being compassionately witnessed.

Some years ago, I heard on the radio news while driving to work that my favorite film director, Wim Wenders, was in town being honored by the University of Washington for his gifted film craft. I spontaneously decided

19. Malabou, *What Should We Do With Our Brain?*, 12.

to drive up to Seattle and join in this honoring. It took place in the University's largest lecture hall, where there are over a thousand seats. It was packed and unusually hushed, and I suspected many others there shared the sense of grateful devotion toward the richness of what this man has created and shared with our world. Wenders gave a moving talk on film as perhaps the most universally accessible and understandable art form, perhaps being our best hope for saving ourselves and our planet. It was eloquent and moving, and English is his second language. No small feat.

He politely asked for questions as we all stared at the four mics positioned on riser platforms ascending up the rows of the amphitheater-style chamber. It is no small hubris to break the ice of conversation in front of a thousand informed strangers, even if your dialogue partner is a man as receptive as Wenders.

Then, almost unnoticed, a diminished, haggard-looking young man cleared his throat before the most distant mic. He brokenly apologized for being first, but he had what he felt was an urgent question. He explained that since his fiancé's traffic death nearly a month before, he had been vacantly wandering the streets of the university and its urban surroundings. Lost in his unbelieving anguish, this had continued until the evening before, when the local cinema house was playing one of Mr. Wender's most beloved films—*Wings of Desire* (1987)—in recognition of tonight's award. It was a film, according to Wenders, that began with a sketchy storyboard; something about two angels in Berlin, one of whom falls desperately in love with a circus tightrope performer and wishes to incarnate into this world to be with her. The only other aspect of the initial sketch was that Wenders wished his good friend, Peter Falk, to play a former angel who had constellated himself into this living world of blood, joy, and suffering. The rest, as is characteristic of all Wender's projects, was fleshed out in improvisational choreography with the full, film-making community on-site.

The young man explained that he knew nothing at all about film, but after wandering and viewing the piece he had one question. With his voice choked by a suppressed sob, he asked, "Do you believe in angels, Mr. Wenders?"

The room grew very silent. You could almost hear the young man's silent weeping. After a long interregnum, Wenders huskily began by explaining his basically agnostic worldview. He briefly said that the film was initially just an idea that came to him and possessed him like all his projects: a possession that would not cease until honored and the film made.

Extraordinarily, this film, about a deeply caring, wise angel incarnating and falling into this world right in front of the Berlin Wall, appeared a scant two years before that Wall fell festively without a shot fired. Wenders insisted that the film was a relational fantasy and that he was more interested in the compassion narrative than the angelic one. Nonetheless, and here he paused and started to cry himself, he said the cast had experienced such unusual events together in the making of that film that he knew without a doubt that we are not alone in the universe. He grew silent. The young man by now was openly sobbing, as were we all, and the night almost ended with this one question and these tears.

There was a reborn Child of Innocence in our midst. Liminal angels had visited the city. A thousand of its citizens experienced an acceleration of their compassion intelligence. That starry night we all drove home a little more whole, our spirits a little less fractured, hope a little closer at hand. A university lecture had become a moment of the best kind of transformational, liminal politics.

> And this sacred dimension often comes to presence during the suffering of the individuation process in the image of the child . . . a part-divine innocent child whose life is the preoccupation of mythology the world over. The human/divine child, in other words, does not belong entirely to "this world." And neither do we.[20]

The liminal bridges the dual. The West, especially, has been perplexed by this "double-tracking" of life. There is life and there is death. There is sorrow and there is joy. There is a conscious life and there is an unconscious life. There is a wash cycle and there is a rinse cycle. It is an Ecclesiast's kind of world. The mystical traditions of the West saw this oppositional dynamic as the *via positiva* and the *via negativa*, the positive and the negative way. A wise, liminal politics threads this narrow passage and weaves these dual engines of creation together into a unified and soul-based vision and praxis. And by "soul," I do not mean a narrow, dogma-inscribed phenomenon, but the core liminal essence of a people acting with full collective justice and compassion in their time.

Politics should be about the creation of a wise public commons. It should primarily be about the task of creating wise citizens. It should be

---

20. Kalsched, *Trauma and the Soul*, 15.

both a modeling and an intervention toward protecting (always), repairing (when need be), and cherishing the collective soul as Gandhi once observed:

> It is beyond dispute that a child, even before it begins to write the alphabet and gathers worldly knowledge, should know what the soul is, what truth is, what love is and what forces are hidden in the soul. It should be the essence of true education that every child learns this and in the struggle of life be able more readily to overcome hatred by love, falsehood by truth and violence by taking suffering on itself.[21]

Political space warps. Just like personal space, political space expands and contracts across the moods, the fears, and the courage of the population it serves. Yet, really individuated people, like a Gandhi, a Dorothy Day, or a Martin Luther King, Jr., may be able to contain and transform whole sections of a corrupt public space and hand it back to us cleansed and renewed. As Jung mused once:

> . . . infinite greatness and infinite smallness are infinitely true, and it is quite possible that we contain whole peoples in our souls, worlds where we can be as infinitely great as we are infinitely small externally—so great that the history of the redemption of a whole nation or of a whole universe might take place within us.[22]

We must come to celebrate cultural-theological diversity if we, as a diverse species, are to survive. Diverse, adaptive organisms survive and thrive; isolated, non-engaged organisms become extinct.

> Sketched in its broadest sense Jung's cosmogony and theogony coalesce in affirming that the Goddess creates consciousness in order to become conscious in her child. She births the various religions to provide a diversity of access to herself. The stories of their Gods, the substance of their beliefs and their ritual initiations and constant reenactment serve primarily and forcefully to identify and access her deeper movements in the human psyche. She is the presiding divinity, the one true Goddess and source of all the others.[23]

21. Faegheh Shirazi, ed. *Muslim Women in War and Crisis.* Austin: University of Texas Press, 2010.

22. Jung, *Visions Seminars,* 1:59.

23. Dourley, *Jung and His Mystics.*

Politics, at its core, is never secular. It is always theological theater. For politics is about fulfilling individual and collective destinies, individual and collective souls. And theologies, particularly fundamentalist theologies, endanger and degrade our global politics on all sides. Theologically rigid traditions and faiths tend to project their unaddressed individual and collective shadows onto other traditions and beliefs. Such a reflexive, siloed response to the world becomes a recipe for eventual inter-Nicene violence and savagery. The only solution seems to be a bottom-up formulation, one where growing numbers of a society's individual members risk personal, experience-revealed transformations. Where they integrate their own shadowed "otherness" and the threat to it sufficiently enough to prevent its toxic projection onto relatively innocent others:

> Jung's sociology names the archetypes that inform and bond modern forms of communal political faith such as the collective utopianism of the "benign" father of fascism and the power of individual reason and interest unbridled in a democracy leading to state totalitarianism. The strong suggestion in his theory of society is that its members become fully aware of the archetypal power at the heart of their communal cohesion as the sole protection against losing their identity and freedom to it. A society based on this kind of consciousness or self-consciousness has yet to exist and may be itself a utopian goal but its approximation is the only protection against the tyranny of whatever the bonding archetype offers. It is both humorous and tragic to see religious bodies bonded by the self in religious form make a distinction between the religious and the secular. The implication is that religious forces are not equally archetypally bonded by whatever form of faith unites them. As this is realized the ability of a specifically religious body to uphold religion in the face of a secularity allegedly divested of religious commitment is a vapid claim. Rather the split between religion and the secular from a Jungian perspective is a split between competing faiths, values, and their communities. Neither has the right to call the other irreligious from a position wholly free from the unconsciousness endemic to collective and personal faiths.[24]

Only such a resurgent, bottom-up individuation process could liminally re-enchant a liminally dispirited, post-Enlightenment, techno-drenched,

---

24. Dourley, *Jung and His Mystics*, 8.

capitalist-entrenched era. And this only once it had reached a healingly infectious tipping point:

> In his extended analysis of secularity, Charles Taylor identifies a societal malaise described as a widespread "mind-centered disenchantment," a term initially coined by Weber in the nineteenth century. Taylor frames his discussion in terms of the question "Why was it virtually impossible not to believe in God in, say, 1500 in our Western society, while in 2000 many of us find this not only easy, but even inescapable?" The question leads him to distinguish a shift from a medieval "porous" consciousness to today's "buffered" mind.[25]

Psychotherapy is inherently a political event, a religious event, a healing event all at once; a surfacing and interweaving of these fierce crosscurrents of sorrowed being into a more satisfying narrative of meaning and connection for both the individual and the community. Analysand and analyst co-abide in the depth polis. What they uncover and enact between them travels out into the wider polis that surrounds us all.

In years past, I regularly visited Lakota Sioux friends on the Pine Ridge reservation in South Dakota. When there, I was invited to participate in tribal sacrament, most often the sweat lodge. This was a medicine family with generations of tribal religious leadership. My friend, the sweat lodge leader, would introduce the profound and sacred ritual. He would outline the simple structure of the rite:

East was the first door. After the rocks—generally twenty-one—arrived steaming from the fire pit, the buffalo hide door would be closed, water poured over the glowing stones. Intensely penetrating, the almost scouring steam would pervade the eerily dark chamber. The East door was a doorway into the new, the unfinished, the creative in our life; it lay dormant and awaiting our conscious attention and nurture. Then the buffalo skin flap would be opened. Cool night air would rush into the hot interior. We would then prepare for the South door—the portal into the seeded inner soul—and awake attention with careful, conscious husbandry. Then the West door, the death door, door of the ancestors. The humbling door that reminds us of the sweet, short interval we all have within which to deliver the compassionate, moist gifts of personal and collective soul that are our assigned destiny. And, finally, the North door of the bracing polar wind

25. Dourley, *Jung and His Mystics*, 9.

and its penetrating, urgent visions of what is required of us to wake up and serve the Life Spirit in a holy, respectful fashion.

After this brief introduction in the late-sun embers of dusk, he would point to the buffalo skin-covered lodge to the east and the fire pit twenty paces to the west and he would say the path in between was the Great Red Road, the path of soulful living between birth and death. This lodge was designed to help us remember, honor, and return to the honorable path after our anxious detours and dalliances. Indigenous communities, at their best, behave like a postmodern philosopher's dream—all local and all global all at once.

Conscious politics is sweat-lodge politics. It's Great Red Road politics. A bindi marks the spot in the mid forehead that represents the Third Eye in India, the eye that sees the depth dimension of life and spirit. The 2009 film, *Outsourced,* stars an expat narrator who spends the film training Indian workers how to sell cheap, useless tchotchkes to Americans. Over the course of the film, however, he discovers that India is training him in cross-cultural compassion. Upon his return to his bland Seattle condo, he places a bindi sequin on the forehead of a kitsch George Washington plate—right in the middle of the esteemed Founding Father's mid brow. It's the last still from the film, representing how much that spiritual depth is missing in American political culture. It's the national treasure that has slipped between our fingers. George Washington, the Mason, had that deep-spirit aesthetic and discipline that kept him humble and destiny-tracked [though, like Jefferson, he knew the vile evil of slavery, he never manumitted his slaves].

But such humbleness is growing rare in our fast-paced, hubristic, can-do culture. *Homo habilis.* Handy[wo]man. Toolmaker. Culture builder. Technology savant. Much interest and concern has been shown in recent years about the power, the almost numinal power, of the creations of human invention and imaginative prowess. Its medicine has radically increased the scope and quality of the life cycle. Its genetically-modified seeds promise an agrarian revolution where famine no longer enters the lexicon of human experience. Its digital grasp now reaches for the farthest corners of the known universe.

But is there a dark side to this "artificial intelligence," this machine-based "other" which has so rapidly evolved to almost co-share this world and life with the organically-embodied us? Politically, this artificial other has begun demanding increasingly political empowerment and voice.

Corporations, its capitalist iteration, in many places now insist that they have civil rights, that they have standing before our courts, that they can suffer injury and thus require the redresses of the justice system for inflicted pain.[26]

For me, that standing is easily tested. For something to have rights, to have a true voice, to be granted a real say in things, it must have a soul. And a soul is simply an authentic capacity to discover, regularly transit, and exhibit an evolving depth and maturity. As a visible artifact of that transit, it must be able to negotiate the liminal portals between this world and the numinal worlds beyond. It would, in other words, have enhanced capacities for and demonstrations of compassion, justice, goodness, tolerance of complexity, non-reactivity, and [inter]personal grace, as well as a deeper relation to all life, personal and impersonal, human and divine:

> This would make of Jung's myth a revelation without making him a messiah. His personal revelation implied a relation to the divine common to all and the figures in it ones that peopled the universal psyche from which they came into his conscious life in a form appropriate to the historical situation of that life.[27]

Given this simply definitional test, if R2D2 came to me for psychotherapy, I'd have not a moment's hesitation granting enthused service in honor of R2D2's obviously evolving capacity for such behaviors. If Goldman Sachs entered my office, I'd have enormous hesitation. For one thing, I don't know what Goldman Sachs looks like. Is Goldman Sachs its CEO, its Board of Directors, its legal department, its lobbyists? Who is the true face of Goldman Sachs? Its true voice? Its true effect beyond the ultimately decimating, earth and culture destroying greed it leaves everywhere in its wake? There is no place on more intimate terms with dark capitalism than a psychotherapist's office, and there in no place more likely to discover the grassroots healing medicine necessary to transform the devastation of rampant capitalism. In a pandemic era of toxic political and biological contagions, what we need is a liminal, initiated sense of global compassion and justice.

The professions need to renounce their increasingly deep-bondedness to capitalist modelings. Do not let capitalism near anything that requires empathy. All the professions require empathy. Justice, healing, deep

---

26. Taibbi, *Divide*.

27. Dourley. *Jung and His Mystics*, 3.

education or depth therapeutic encounters demand empathy; all research and humanities wisdom indicate that empathy is a core interpersonal element toward effective healing outcomes. Capitalism has bleached out empathy, fearing, rightfully, that it is often antithetical to the bottom line.

Capitalism confuses the essentials. Capitalism gets inflated and believes that *it* is the essential. Capitalism is an economic idea. It is not a moral one.

CAPITALISM AND THE MILITARY AS WARRIOR-CLASS TWINS; WAR AND PSYCHE AS POLIS PRESSURE POINTS

My Baby Boomer, war-protestor generation initially did a noble job of de-valorizing the military. We defanged it. Now it has roared back more aggressively, more dazzlingly jarring than ever. How in the world did this happen and on the watch of the same aging Baby Boomers?

> It seems to be easier for us today to imagine the thoroughgoing deterioration of the earth and of nature than the breakdown of late capitalism; perhaps that is due to some weakness in our imaginations.[28]

Violence boils deep in the human psyche. Some of the oldest psychological systems on the planet locate their origins in the root chakra, at the base of the spine. Shit and rage apparently are close cousins. All of us have primal rage simmering away down there in the central crock pot of our being.

> *I just want to kick some bad-guy butt.* ~ A young trainee describing in a Public Radio interview why she wished to become a Marine, November 24, 2014

It is hard to talk about veterans, an emotional topic saturated in patriotism, pride, and much nation-state prejudice. And the veteran is at the vortex of this complex conversation, for veterans are most often enlisted into this frequently life-long status in late adolescence. Furthermore, the enlistment vehicle relies heavily on the preconscious and often pernicious mechanisms of cynical corporatist propaganda and the psychic manipulation that engulfs public media. The rest of us feel this coercive group-think pressure to both send off and then welcome back these warriors, these

---

28. Frederich, *Seeds of Time.*

heroes of the bloody corporatist wars to which they were consigned. All of us then, veteran and general citizen alike, are expected to avoid any mention of the often dark, distorted, deceitful economic self-interests that sent them off in the first place. And we most certainly must avoid any discussion of the heinous acts and atrocities committed in service to these soul-tainted agendas.

The level of collective entrancement to this warped, wealth-and-power-driven agenda of blood varies across time, culture, and circumstance. In my youth, the charade of becoming conscripted into the warrior-veteran miasma was perhaps at its most transparent moment in American history. Nightly, we saw images of innocent Vietnamese and Cambodian blood being spilled, we saw the innocent forests engulfed in the nefarious Agent Orange, we were made privy by an awake, generally dutiful, media to the compromised military-industrial agendas that induced and maintained these toxic atrocities of "super-power" entitlement. And we were all implicated—in the Spring of 1968 every eligible male was vulnerable to the draft. Finally, unable to bear the dissonance of potentially losing our lives for such a violent collective lie, the streets flooded, the war eventually stopped, and a sitting American President was dethroned. None of these three things had ever before happened in such productive concert in American history.

Those veterans had great sympathy for non-combatants because of their own conscription—many did not volunteer. They were impressed. Some non-combatants, however, behaved with savage emotional violence toward veterans—many of whom were victims of the military-industrial agenda. The veteran became the proxy scapegoat. In the projective fear and frenzy of the protest-activated streets, the lines between the cynical corporatist designers of this war and the conscripted enactors of the war became tragically blurred.

Veteran sympathy is harder to discover in the current environment where all enlistees are "volunteers." The military-industrial complex cynically wised up and removed the draft. It cuckolded the media—embedded it in its propaganda cycle and vision. It removed all images of dead Americans, even their flagged-draped coffins upon their return to Dover Air Base. Only the bodies of the "bad guy" are displayed. Only the graft and violence and savagery of the bad guys are reported. There are no My Lai's in this war, no Wounded Knee battlefields here. It is a sanitized, propaganda-enhanced, pure war. Which makes these veterans more isolated than perhaps any veteran cadre before. The promised mission of undiluted glory

148

upon enlistment has to be permanently sutured, split away from the dark incidents of violence and savagery that inevitably follow.

Political tension is always ancestral tension spilling out into the public square. I can remember walking down demonstration streets as an angry young man with other angry young men and women protesting the Viet Nam War. On one especially memorable twilight, fresh on my arrival to graduate school in Boston, we were marching down Beacon Street to the Boston Commons. We were shouting an obscene, mesmerizing chant: "One, two, three four, we don't want your fucking war." We shook our fists at the Boston Brahmin leaning out from their cocktail hours, safe in the cover of their elegant townhouse balconies glaring at us in the amber dusk light. They were surrogates for our parents. This collective outrage was an individual family-of-origin moment of catharsis for our terror at having been thrown under the military-industrial draft-and-death bus. How could our culture do such an evil thing? It had happened to black slaves, to geno-cided indigenous, to Red Scare Eastern Europeans, to interred Japanese Americans, to Hispanic migrants, and now, in 1968, it was happening to all of us as a protest-enraged General Hershey drafted every single university graduate of 1968. How could they do this to us, their innocent young? The streets were as fully awake as perhaps ever in American history to patriar-chal savagery, a savagery like that of the Greek god Chronos who will even eat his own young if power-threatened enough. Liminal political leadership seemed absent inside the trope-hyped American "cathedral" of democracy.

Politics is sacred theater. The politician's task is to perform this sa-cred theater authentically—speak and be the truth. They should not play to please or avoid audience displeasure, but to perform true, authentic, healing civic action. That is a real politician, a real statesperson. It is a rare thing, indeed. In ancient Rome, Vitruvius was the father of the master ar-chitectural plan for Rome. He fixed upon three fundamental principles for the structure:

- Firmitas-solid foundation/structure
- Utilitas-utilitarian purpose
- Venustas-beauty/aesthetics

The liminal experience introduces and favors these factors in stabiliz-ing and growing the core psychic structure of the individual and the culture of which the individual is a part. Our current national and global structures are undermining all three of these fundaments in the ongoing onslaught of hard capitalism. Both aspects of a healthy, full existence—a vibrant spiritual life and a vibrant civic life—are threatened by its ever-widening intrusions:

> Everyone has a double duty in life, to maintain a cultural life and a religious life, and the laws of these two realms are often diametrically opposed to each other. The duty of the church (whatever the creed) should be to assist people with their religious life, which involves seeing past duality and advancing consciousness. The cultural life consists of choosing between good and evil and keeping the human side of life in order and proportion.[29]

It is hard to keep one's bearings in an increasingly dystopic culture. It's hard to avoid self-soothing addictions to ease the deepening ache of our growing internal and relational isolation. It often takes profound courage to keep at the task of developing healthy, creative engagement with this dysthymic, armored capitalist edge. It takes will and gift to penetrate the silence and aloneness left in the often devastating wake of hard capitalism. And yet, this crisis must be turned around by returning to shared, sound, social, depth re-structuring, communally-shared utilitarianism, and commensally-experienced sacral beauty.

Capitalism is surrounded by malice and hostility. Health insurance carriers don't care about me, my health, my doctor, our relationship. Economies should serve the polis, not undermine it. Capitalism was a great idea a thousand years ago. It will destroy us now if we do not evolve beyond it. Cooperation and compassion, the psycho-spiritual method in relationship, is what will bring the human and divine Home. Capitalism is an old, neo-feudal idea born of the primal commercial awakenings out of the Dark Ages doldrums. Democracy is the new idea birthed in the transformative, often contradictory fires of 17th-, 18th, and 19th-century intellectual and physical revolutions. Capitalism rewards even as it extinguishes—hopes, dreams, forests, coral reefs, the poor, the vulnerable, the planet. Like the discovery of fire, capitalism was initially a good thing, even a great thing. It is fast becoming a catastrophic thing, a species killer. It must be absorbed and transformed by the broader egalitarian cooperation fundamental to the democratic ethos if our species consciousness and destiny are to move forward.

Democracy and capitalism are incompatible, often contradictory, ideas. Capitalism and democracy—their collision rather than their collusion is inevitable if the democratic ideal trumps the militarist-industrialist-capitalist

29. Johnson, *Balancing Heaven and Earth*, 173.

stacked deck. Best case, democracy absorbs capitalism and transforms it, not the other way around. Disconnected, far-right thinking would wrongly argue that the Dark Age capitalist idea absorbs and reduces the New Age enlightenment notion of democracy.

This is not just economic reflection. This is profound psycho-spiritual reflection. Psychology—depth psychology—is the most essential nursery for transformative economic ideas. Psychological activity is the generative voicing of primal need; it is the traction for individuated citizens to gain consciousness and make culture—the twin engines of cultural renewal. It is, indeed, always a bottom-up process of transformation and transmutation.

Money is power in capitalism. It is access. It is better health care, better jobs, better income. Money buys justice because representation is financially based. The poor don't make or successfully break the laws. The monied do. This is as it always has been. Such brute aggression may have been necessary to get us out of the caves and swamps. But it is a trajectory for evolutionary extinction now.

There is a pyramid of participation in American attempts at economic justice. While spearheading the burst of progressive populism that marked his era one hundred years ago, Theodore Roosevelt observed that judicial attempts at repairing economic injustice were too slow, remedial, and limited. He advocated regulatory repair, which he felt was quicker and more preventative.[30] What this chapter suggests is an even broader platform of participation, correction, and achievement of economic justice—and justice of all kinds, actually. It suggests the conscious individual pursuit of one's personal and collective individuation.

Liminality-mediated compassion uproots. Dislocation is in its very DNA. It upends cosmologies and dinner plans alike. It wreaks creative havoc in the name of eventual peace and moments of compassionate solace. Politics is a sorrow factory. It distills compassion. It produces soul when it is fully functioning.

We must all become compassion's whistle blower. The whistle blower has always been the essential engine of American democratic reform. The courage and individuated consciousness of whistle blowers has fueled collective awakenings time and again.[31] It has always been thus in justice-restored human community, from Socrates's brave defiance and death until now. The shadow of greed and power always seeks to extinguish justice, to

30. Goodwin, *The Bully Pulpit.*
31. McCullough, *Truman,* 273.

annihilate liminal space. In our era, it is hard capitalism that annihilates liminal space.

There is a city in northern India called Vrindavan. It is a city of refugees. It is an exiles' city. And the exiles are widows who, under traditional caste law, have no societal rights and protection once their husband and father sponsors are dead. It is a tragically sexist and violent tradition that flourishes despite a modern democratic legislative overlay. In 2011, a gifted contemporary artist named Fazal Sheikh made their plight his photographic crusade.

Yet for the women who live there, Vrindavan often becomes a liminal place of transitional soothing and comfort. There are numerous anecdotal reports of many of these women experiencing spontaneous succoring visits from the God Krishna. Either in dream, trance, or vision, or simply with a vivid sense of his presence, these women often report being assured of their belovedness and essentialness. This succor stabilizes and enriches their lives with a pervasive and productive contemplative action. Resentment over their violent casting out, terrors over their resulting poverty, and even their fears of death diminish and calm into a stream of meaningful existence in the moment.

Nothing can get more liminal than that. In their dream-mediated visitations, I wonder if these women meet real emissaries of the "numinal others"—beings who instruct them in the techniques of relinquishing anxiety while abiding in the true "Kairos" [soul] time. Beyond the madness of our chronological time and beyond blunt capitalism's daily brutalities.

Economies exist to serve people. They exist to serve the deep psyche. Economies do not exist to serve hoarding and disparity. They ultimately exist to serve the consummation of the cosmos in its ultimate consummative task of compassion and creation.

> The more we freed greed from laws and regulations, the more we would prosper; and the more we prospered, the more we would become enlightened, happy, and decent. This is, of course, the fundamental moral argument we associate with the rise of capitalism and the market economy, the dominant economic philosophy and institution of the modern world. Capitalism, in order to become so dominant, had to convince people, against all the weight of tradition, that greed really was a virtue. That transvaluation may have owed much of its theoretical argument to an Edinburghian

philosopher named Adam Smith, but it found the greatest receptivity, its most zealous believers, among Americans.[32]

THE ETERNAL PROGRESSIVE-CONSERVATIVE CONTINUUM

Let justice be done though the heavens may fall.
Fiat justitia ruat caelum.

We need a politics with a moral, liminal core. We need a politics that can shame in a motivating, transforming way rather than in an annihilating, destructive way. Our politics are a pietistic politics. They are embedded in a post-rational consciousness that split off the embodied feminine, the dark earth, and the irrational Eros dimensions of a full psycho-spiritual Being. Puritanical consciousness is a conditional consciousness, a conditional morality. There is no unconditional love or exception in a puritanical worldview except for the power-holders and the rule-makers.

Recently, an energized family holiday dialogue reflected our culture's deeply entrenched Pietistic Psyche. It was a family circle with a nicely-balanced chorus of progressive and conservative voices. The topic was health care. The concern was escalating costs.

The conservative family voice proposed that people be penalized for their "destructive," body-threatening behaviors. The progressive voice advocated for a non-coercive response to such persons: a universal-access, single-payer vision in which all would be unconditionally welcomed to the table of non-judgmental, freely available health care. This voice promoted the idea of "unconditional" for its capacity to induce healing, suggesting that no one should be shamed for "being fat" or for "being a drunk." The progressive family voice saw "incentivizing" individuals through pricing to be implicitly about shaming and asserted that it was as much about public exposure as it was about cost. Power-holders and rule-makers engage in accumulation strategies to make vast exceptions for their unbridled greed, this progressive voice argued. And until that dark, greedy drive is tamed, it would be abhorrent in the context of a social contract to support a policy of means-based behavioral access to the health care system.

I am not a patriot. I am not a Christian, or a Jew, or a Muslim, or a Buddhist. These containers are too narrow and self-enclosed. They are

32. Worsten, *Wealth of Nature*, 14.

clan-loyal, not species/cosmos-loyal. Containers either get bigger, more inclusive, more matriarchal, more compassionate, or we as a species—and maybe the whole cosmos of meaning—will not survive. If democracy implies an on-going, simultaneous dialogue between the paradox of individual need and right and the collective need and right, then the liminal fluid between them is the place of resolution and deepening. If democracy in America maintains enough central sovereignty to govern while preserving maximal individual liberty within reasonable, functional, limits, it will survive and flourish as a society. An authentic, liminal democracy preserves justice for the collective by limiting the abusive excesses of individual liberty and vice versa.[33]

The liminal realms are the places for such delicate, minute acts of individual and collective transformation, where aggression is de-formed and destructive violence ended. The liminal is where democracy is preserved, where maximal liberty is achieved for the individual and the collective. By contrast, the individual and cultural "child" is mutilated or destroyed without the nurture of a democratic, liminal compassion or the success of an authentic healing power:

> As is true for personality disorders, codependence is an expression of the problem of power. The world, the adult, and the caregiver have power while the child does not. Power itself is neutral. It is merely the expression of energy between two entities. When caught in a complex, it can be demonic. When the world misuses power, the child is obliged to adapt in profound ways in order to survive. In effect, codependence is an anxiety disorder because the power of the other is implicit in all relationships, having been transferred reflexively from the historic to the contemporary. As one's security lies with the other, so one becomes, reflexively, defined by the other and one is obliged to adapt one's truth to serve the demands of that other. One learns to cover one's actual feelings lest they prove costly in evoking the displeasure of the other. How many individuals do you know who say something painful, and then laugh, as if to mask their pain lest they, fearfully, be taken seriously for having uttered their truth?[34]

Deep healing must always address the core dilemma of chronic anxiety over the abuse of inauthentic power and its concomitant fear. The goal is to authentically locate dysfunctional individual and collective anxiety

33. Ellis, *American Sphinx*, 333.
34. Hollis, *Archetypal*, 114.

clusters, to bring the soothing balm of reflective, embodied consciousness to the aroused individual and to the collective psyche. In any given era, dysfunctional concentrations of individual and collective anxiety tend to affix to one polarity or the other. The trace footprint of such a toxic concentration of anxiety is the virulent expression and enactment of both covert and overt contempt—both interpersonally and interculturally. As is well known in depth therapies, virulent self-contempt and shame are often anxiously projected outward onto convenient scapegoats. Such scapegoating is abundant in disruptive collective moments.

The worst frenzy is that produced when a nation goes to war, which is always a dysfunctional, negatively-cathartic moment of mass projection. Roxanne Dunbar-Ortiz suggests that such war-psychoses became an intentional strategy of conquest in the West beginning with the Crusades and culminating in the brutality of the American military-state. America and its settler colonizations and genocides created a unique and grotesque apex example of how a whole culture can become liminally blind to its own bloody hands and hearts.[35]

> Our nation was born in genocide when it embraced the doctrine that the original American, the Indian, was an inferior race. Even before there were large numbers of Negroes on our own shores, the scar of racial hatred had already disfigured colonial society. From the sixteenth century forward, blood flowed in battles of racial supremacy. We are perhaps the only nation which tried as a matter of national policy to wipe out its indigenous population. Moreover, we elevated that tragic experience into a noble crusade. Indeed, even today we have not permitted ourselves to reject or feel remorse for this shameful episode. Our literature, our films, our drama, our folklore all exalt it.—Martin Luther King.[36]

In my lifetime, I have witnessed three such collective psychoses—Korea, Viet Nam, and the two, almost-merged Gulf War events. These wars, like most wars, inevitably went bad. The power of entrenched, self-interested capitalism injected itself into the cultural bloodstream and insidiously inflamed the body politic in defense of an ostensibly threatened democratic ideal. In reality, it was roused in hidden service to corporate profit and capitalism's insatiable need for natural-resource fuel.

---

35. Dunbar-Ortiz, *An Indigenous Peoples' History.*
36. King, *Why We Can't Wait,* 110.

Politics channels the collective soul. Its engine is the confusing maze (what the alchemists and, later, Jung called the *massa confusa)* of viral tensions active in any collective body. It is a messy business. But it is an inherently *soul* business, intent on individuating the collective just as analysis is intent on individuating the individual. Hard capitalism has become insidiously ingenious at wedding religious sentiment and imagery to its very spiritually-debased appetites and greedy agendas. Its circus tent, where the alchemy of dark transformation occurs, is a fusion of patriarchal evangelism, patriotism, and fundamentalism. The toxicity of the resulting devil's brew threatens to destroy Western—perhaps even global—culture. Meanwhile, our culture is almost blind to these toxicities—as are, indeed, all cultures, for the East has its own parallel brand of patriarchal brutalism. Toxic patriarchy is truly a global disease.

The new, liminal "politics of Psyche" will no longer value faux evangelism, patriotism, and fundamentalism, but instead will value inclusiveness, global-ness, and progressiveness.The liminal emerging in the fluid, post-institutional world in which we live will be an individuated and evolved liminal energy. This liminal politics won't come in the collective arousals of the unconscious, anxious dogma of the past. Rather, it will come from authentically lived individual experience compassionately shared with others in soulful reception of the common, animated Depth Collective Soul. The liminal exists between ideal and real, beyond them and under them. It blends the real and the ideal in its constellating ignitions. It consumes their exoteric essence as the fuel of its esoteric processes. It resolves their tensions and harnesses their joint dynamisms:

> But what is that resolution? It is always something ancient and precisely because of this something new, for when something long since passed away comes back again in a changed world, it is new. To give birth to the ancient in a time is creation. This is the creation of the new, and that redeems me. Salvation is the resolution of the task. The task is to give birth to the old in a new time. The soul of humanity is like the great wheel of the zodiac that rolls along the way: everything that comes up in a constant movement from below to the heights was already there. There is no part of the wheel that does not come around again. Hence everything that has been streams upward there, and what has been will be again. For these are all things which are the inborn properties of human nature. It belongs to the essence of forward movement that what was returns. Only the ignorant can marvel at this. Yet the meaning

does not lie in the eternal recurrence of the same, but in the manner of its recurring creation at any given time.[37]

We are swimming in a sea of toxic testosterone. The Great Patriarchal Beast is urinating to mark his hyper-anxious boundaries in wider and wider arcs of false security, twenty-four hours a day. Capitalism is to the War on Terror what slavery was to the Civil War—the hidden core issue obscuring morality. The lurking beast? Unaddressed issues of soul congruence, a deafness to the deep, healing, compassion-bearing melody of the singing spheres of the Cosmos.

POLITICS AND SILENCE

He who loves the people remains silent.

—C.G. JUNG[38]

We need to rediscover a politics of contemplative silence. What if, after 9/11, America had been convened into an awake, sorrowful silence by a liminal leader? Instead, we cowboyed up, and over one million Iraqi citizens are dead as a direct result of our impetuous leap to a violent solution. Patriarchy and its implicit and explicit violence always tend to corrupt our personal and collective redemption-seeking narratives.

In the 2010 film *The Next Three Days*, a loving and socially earnest family is devastated by the almost viciously rushed arrest and conviction on murder charges of the innocent mother. Multiple years and judicial appeals later, she is still incarcerated, and the increasing desperation of her obsessed husband drives him to cross the violence line. A quietly brilliant community college professor of literature, he teaches Don Quixote by day (quoting Don Quixote's notion that "belief in virtue is more important than virtue itself") and plots his wife's jail break by night. His efforts to fund his operation through the legitimate sale of his home are interrupted by inevitable red tape, so he robs, arsons, and shoots drug dealers for their ready cash. He then drives his reluctant, jail-sprung wife and his beloved young son through a nail-biting, shoot-on-sight race against rapidly deployed police roadblocks. Violence for violence, no matter how extenuating the sympathetic script narrative, is still eye for eye, desperate unconsciousness.

---

37. Jung, *Red Book*, 311.
38. Jung, *Red Book*, 317.

Death and the maiming of more innocence is the ever-likely possibility of desperate unconsciousness.

A contemplative awake-ness and a conscious compassion can never make these "pragmatic" accommodations with violence, regardless of how amplified the goad of circumstance. Even when one is the possible victim of violent injustice, one is called to remain calmly awake in the midst of great sorrow and suffering. Our evolution to a more substantial platform of being requires this paradigmatic shift beyond primal "fight or flight." Something of much broader horizon is required if we are to survive as a species and if the Omega of creation's evolutionary design is to be fulfilled. We must seek always, no matter how intense the suffering, to find that lucid, silent beacon at the liminal core of our being.

Don't talk unless you can improve the silence.

—*JORGE LUIS BORGES*

POLITICS AS SACRED ENACTMENT

I have now seen quite a number of people die in the great transition, reaching as it were the end of their pilgrimage in sight of the Gates, where the way bifurcates to the land of Hereafter and to the future of [wo]mankind and its spiritual adventure. You had a glimpse of the Mysterium Magnum. ~ C. G. Jung[39]

Jung confronts contemporary humanity with the question of whether it is up to suffering divinely based conflict in the immediate precinct of human interiority, the matrix of all the Gods, without breaking containment and destroying itself as it destroys the projectively scapegoated, evil other. Failure to meet Jung's challenge would only continue the sad current situation of externalizing the conflict and blowing up, in the name of the demonic, whatever contradicts one's own truncated personal or collective compact or testament with the divine. Thus, the recall of the Gods and the internal resolution of their mutual enmity as the precedent of external peace is currently at the heart of hope for the species. Can humanity survive its God and religion-creating proclivity? It is the fire of this wider hope that the analytic process fans through addressing whatever conflict it faces in the individual circumstances of the analysand. Each individual gain in consciousness contributes to the contemporary emergence of

39. Jung and White, *Jung-White Letters*, 306.

*a myth informed by a more universal sensitivity and wider inclu-
sion now sponsored by the unconscious in its role as the maker of
history.*[40]

Psyche rarely becomes so concerned about our botched efforts to find our
true way that She sends us a beacon soul, a guiding spirit to help us locate
the liminal portals between human and divine so that we do not lose our
authentic path entirely. Perhaps She sends us a brooding figure such as
Jeanne D'Arc or Abraham Lincoln. Perhaps she sends buoyant figures such
as St. Francis, Gandhi, Martin Luther King, Jr., or Maya Angelou. She sends
such figures to pull us back from the annihilating brink. And the ultimate
price for such figures is too often that they die, that we may more fully live.
But Psyche is not cruel. She sends gracious, tender warnings, as though to
help the chosen epochal one prepare, to get their final things in order. This
is what happened to Lincoln:

> *About 10 days ago, I retired very late. I had been up waiting for im-
> portant dispatches from the front. I could not have been long in bed
> when I fell into a slumber, for I was weary. I soon began to dream.
> There seemed to be a death-like stillness about me. Then I heard sub-
> dued sobs, as if a number of people were weeping. I thought I left my
> bed and wandered downstairs. There the silence was broken by the
> same pitiful sobbing, but the mourners were invisible. I went from
> room to room; no living person was in sight, but the same mournful
> sounds of distress met me as I passed along. I saw light in all the
> rooms; every object was familiar to me; but where were all the people
> who were grieving as if their hearts would break? I was puzzled and
> alarmed. What could be the meaning of all this? Determined to find
> the cause of a state of things so mysterious and so shocking, I kept on
> until I arrived at the East Room, which I entered. There I met with
> a sickening surprise. Before me was a catafalque, on which rested
> a corpse wrapped in funeral vestments. Around it were stationed
> soldiers who were acting as guards; and there was a throng of people,
> gazing mournfully upon the corpse, whose face was covered, others
> weeping pitifully. 'Who is dead in the White House?' I demanded of
> one of the soldiers, 'The President,' was his answer; 'he was killed by
> an assassin.' Then came a loud burst of grief from the crowd, which
> woke me from my dream. I slept no more that night; and although it
> was only a dream, I have been strangely annoyed by it ever since.*[41]

40. Dourley, "Jung and the Recall of the Gods," 48.

41. Lamon, *Recollections of Abraham Lincoln 1847–1865*, 116–17.

These figures tend to spend their last vibrant days, months, and years almost fully enveloped in liminal realms. They simultaneously address both the fallen world of moment to moment and the eternal world of compassionate oneness, and they translate one world to another, human to divine. Healing, deep healing, is a liminal accomplishment. Individuals, their families, their societies, and their cultures cannot heal alone. We need the presence and cooperation of the gods.

POLITICS AS EVOLUTIONARY AROUSAL: EMERGING COMPASSION-CONVERGENCE ZONES

Grace comes from elsewhere; at all accounts from outside.

—C. G. JUNG[42]

Climb the mountains and get their good tidings. Nature's peace will flow into you as sunshine flows into trees. The winds will blow their own freshness into you, and the storms their energy, while cares drop away from you like the leaves in autumn.

—JOHN MUIR[43]

We live in dangerous, alarming times. Maybe all times seem this way, but now it seems that the extinction of our species is in the air.[44] Our only hope is a recovery of Earth connectedness, a connection to Gaia, the ancient Earth Goddess.[45] She is the keeper of the alchemical secret of balance that has evolved the life force on this planet—the balance between life and death, between creation and destruction. She is the Wisdom of Ecclesiastes, the sister of White Buffalo Woman. In our unbalanced, logos-driven, patriarchal frenzy of corporatist consumerism, we have more than muffled Gaia's voce, we have throttled it:

A client dreams of being with a community of progressive folks in Eastern Montana. They are worried that the growing cultural darkness will get even worse and they have established a community of resonance and aesthetic reliance that is intended to outlast and

42. Jung, "Psychological Commentary," 11:482.
43. Muir, *Mountains of California*, 482.
44. Kolbert, *Sixth Extinction: An Unnatural History*.
45. Lovelock. *Vanishing Face of Gaia*.

influence the coming storm—to help the "world not have to fully
bottom out before attempting to recover its sanity."

Late afternoon in August they see an ominous squadron of pro-
peller bombers descending on their area. One plane drops a sinister
large hay bale payload that floats to earth and lands surprisingly
without exploding. The woman and her community retreat to their
well-appointed cave of community hollowed out of an adjacent
mountain.

It is a moment of reckoning. Not just individual reckoning but species reckoning. Sinister black hay-bale payloads land all around us. The level of liminal awakening and consciousness that we must achieve seems beyond the possible. Without a liminal miracle, it seems as though we are surely doomed. In an age of the greatest income inequality ever recorded, the streets are anaesthetized, asleep in front of the hypnotizing blue gleam of our smart phone and computer screens.

We must hope that just under the badly fractured surface of our common culture, more consciousness has been evolving than we had dared notice. That now we can deeply relax from our orgy of rapaciousness and surrender our arms to an ever-offered celestial grace. We must first wake up, and then, after we apprehend the alarmingly dire gravity of our predicament, we must calm down, dig in, and start working together on our common redemption.

A patient arrives with one daydream and a three-part night dream.
The daydream arrived as she drove across Utah deserts in spring. It
is of her two adult children as bright night-sky meteors bursting over
the horizon. They burst through the birthing vessel of her body and
on into separate trajectories over the far horizon. The night dream
first has her in the mudroom of her brother-in-law's lake cabin, only
it is now a lovely wood-paneled intimate room with a fireplace—
warm and cozy. Then she is on the deck of the same lake home the
night of the first human landing on the moon—watching up into
the mysterious magnitude of the heavens. The third nighttime image
is of a new condo development rising up over and down along the
lovely meadows of a lakefront peninsula, dirtying the natural seren-
ity with greed-driven development.

In the reverie of our analytic conversation, the concept of cardinal directions pops up. I experience her vision and dreams as four directions of a shamanic compass. The meteor image is the birthing East; the mudroom house is the fertile, incubating South; the brooding condo virus is the ever-threatening personal and collective death of the West; and the deck visions are the cold, reorienting north winds that bring renewal to staid lives. The patient weeps quietly. I weep quietly. We sit in the middle of the liminally constellated compass hologram. For a moment, both of us are fully located and at peace.

Finding that moment, a moment that is both fully and consciously located and peaceful, connected to grounding earth and soul, is easier said than done. It requires the best that the accumulated archetypal wisdom of our race has offered about depth ritual and contemplative practice. It requires that there be an exponential increase in the number of persons capable of both locating liminal precincts and opening up to them. We are such an anxious species. We have found and lost these sacred precincts and their liminally renewing practices in countless cycles of foolish squander. In recent travels, I stumbled across one such site of soul both found and lost:

> There is a deep rift that runs roughly north and south through Iceland. In one place along that dark, almost sinister cataract a crystal waterfall plummets to be thrashed upon sharp volcanic stone at the bottom. An aqua-blue current braids itself around the middle of the white-foamed cataclysm.
>
> Nearby is a promontory atop which sits the Lögberg. This is the Law Rock, where once a year since the 10th-century arrival of Norse settlement the Law Speaker would recite all the canon of covenant that held the assembly of wild clans together in a tapestry of order. He would chant the law here, on the groaning fault line where the North American and European continental plates duel for terrestrial dominance.
>
> Geography is the gods—divinity made immediate and accessible. Geography is sacred, and those places where geography most visibly moves and animates are all the more divine. These places are liminal, where tell-lines tell tales of the gods.
>
> So, it is not by accident that our warlike species came to such awesome planetary sites to calm violence-fretted brows. It is in such places of numinal magisterium that compassion's voice of restorative justice surfaces in our best individual and collective dreams. Dreams are where the gods come to whisper hints of how to slake our bloodthirst and use its essence to water the cosmos and calm the fiery embers of our instinctual greed and grandiosity. Indeed, legend has it that deep dreaming from soul-activated and accelerated psyches more easily occurs at these high-frequency earth shrines.

Yet sometimes even such sacred places and their calming beauties are not enough. Even in the soulful shadow of the Law Rock, righteousness-inflamed new Christians tried to extinguish their ancient pagan Druid truths by drowning innocent and spirit-gifted women within earshot of the sacred Law Bringer's voice. In this "sacred pool," panicked converts tried to obliterate the sacred healing witch for claiming her rightful place of wholeness by the side of her patriarchal consort. What was remembered after was the rule and the punishment without the beauty and the healing. Only half this lovely sacred glade is honored. And we will extinguish ourselves if the missing Fault Sister is not rejoined to her Fault Brother.

My visit here was not born of an idle pilgrim's whim. I came to Iceland because her dying glaciers are the canary in the global-warming mine. We are seemingly perched above an abyss—extinction-event—where a rapid biodiversity kill-off is frighteningly underway.[46] *And the weapon of mass destruction this time is not an asteroid or climate change generated by wobbling in orbit. It is a virus; a human apex-predator virus. We are apparently cutting our own throats as our glorious Earth burns to the ground all around us, pathologically torched by our imperious species' conceit.*[47]

We desperately require the co-evolution of a more substantive financial and political cosmology. Evolution itself is an achieved liminality. Collective individuation is the wide outer envelope of a process of personal individuation. To the degree we evolve and tolerate more and more liminal consciousness, the Collective and the gods evolve as well.

Increasingly in our age, depth-sensitive therapy will be responding to collective images of urgency and crisis about the rapidly spreading environmental chaos flooding our weary planet. All of these dreams will be full of deep psyche suggestions about how to best respond—individually and collectively—to this seemingly unavoidable catastrophe. A new Dark Ages seems looming. And in earlier feudal ages of our species, the individual and collective dream always possessed the best alchemies of soulful response and remediation, even though remediation usually required centuries and generations of consciousness-seeking effort:

A patient dreams of being in the flooded basement of a Seattle office campus surrounded by much water and debris—limbs, rocks, cans, silt. He walks to another part of the campus and ends up in a little bistro. People are drinking in silence; shocked, stunned. He sits next

46. Kolbert, *Sixth Extinction.*
47. Gibson, *Journal.*

to an awake, caring woman. They hold each others' hands as they
commiserate in the crisis. He is holding a little takeaway container
of corn relish. The dreams ends as he and a friend talk with some
concern about focusing on the increasingly demanding addiction of
another friend.

For us to survive the individual and collective demands of an increasingly high-risk era, we must compassionately share as much of the Corn Goddess's Earth larder as we can.

Jung observed that as the world grew up out of the unconscious, things appeared more separate, real, and substantial. But as he tracked the unconscious energies in himself, his patients, and the world, he noted they receded into more inchoate and amorphous mystery and depths. These depths seemed, on deeper penetration and pursuit, to have a silent connection and interrelated cohesion; their primary energies seemed to recognize a common source.

Jung noted that modern physicists had observed the same phenomenon: that the substantial realness of the everyday world receded into a materialistically indecipherable subatomic world. There, substance was less a meaningful description than it was a relationship; separateness was less probable than interconnectedness. This was a place where space and time, cause and effect, became more fluid and plastic; where yesterday and tomorrow, here and there, became less like meaningful descriptors and more like a profound, non-local fraternity linking all things to all other things, all life to all other life.

This holographic omni-locality is the liminal world. It is the place where everything that "is" comes into focus, where the subatomic matrix and the amazing cohesion of the cosmos abide in primal, organic, dynamic Presence. It is where our chopped up, fragmented chronological time disperses into a fluid comprehensive Kairos, or "being" time. It is where our tightly boundaried, possessed, highly abstracted, almost claustrophobically constricted sense of space becomes a spacious Commons that compassionately houses all who arrive.

Lucy, Luc Besson's 2014 film is an essay on liminal reality. It seems to completely accept Jung, modern physics, and their revised revelation regarding our subatomic destiny as individuals and as a species. Lucy is an intellectually and culturally naive young woman traveling on a whim with her boyfriend to Taiwan. She suddenly finds herself an enslaved drug mule whose body cavity is filled with a pouch of synthesized neural-growth hormone destined to become the latest addictive, highly profitable drug craze. Only her pouch leaks, and its aggressive impact on her neural networks stimulates a runaway synaptic evolution of brain function that moves her useable brain capacity from the typical 7% of our species to, eventually, 100%. Along the way, she learns to collapse time and space, and she discerns that time itself is the key primordial yeast at the core of the batter of life. Time is infinitely plastic: at one moment a single point of presence and, at the next, the expanse of all cosmic activity occurring from the beginning of time dissolved into the present, only time—Now.

As Lucy morphs through these dynamic changes of awareness and perception, she moves from species-typical patterns of territoriality and violence to a cosmic, non-violent compassion and presence. The film begins with a scene of her paleolithic ancestor alive and foraging in a primal swampland. It is the ancient "Lucy," one of our oldest extant full Homo sapien skeletons. Near the end of the film, our morphed, contemporary Lucy is able to meet this ancestor. Through her developed ability to collapse time and space, she greets her progenitor with a profound, respectful, compassionate presence as they reach forefingers to one another, Sistine Chapel-style.

Some economic systems are closer to liminal time than others. Evolution is, itself, liminality achieved. Our depth-psyche-landscape looks collectively dismal. But it seems that is a typical condition for this temporal plane of existence. This world always hovers between the awful and the beautiful. The trick is how to bear it, how to be conscious of it, and how to experience depth transformations of soul within its hammerlock. The final chapter attends to this dilemma. For Jung, the healing supernatural is located within and down, not without and above. This is a stance opposed to most Western institutional forms of religion. It is an imminent divine, not a transcendent one; it is an elemental, animate "other" *here*, not beyond. It is found in this moment between us, now, if we can learn Lucy's deep, contemplative calm. The psyche may be regarded as a fixed mathematical point and at the same time as a universe of expanding stars.[48] Lucy teaches us how to find that dynamic, centering Point of Being.

Liminal space is "superior "; it is not bound by ordinary clock-time or time-space.[49] Conscious immersion in liminal space " . . . allows us to see, behind the discrete processes, a universal interrelationship of events. A

48. Deloria, *C. G. Jung and the Sioux Traditions*, 70.

49. Deloria, *C. G. Jung and the Sioux Traditions*, 81.

pre-existent unity of being takes shape, and the seemingly incommensu-
rable worlds of physics and psyche can be understood as aspects of this
unity."[50] It facilitates the embodied discovery that we live not alone, narcissistically self-sufficient and self-sealed, but fundamentally conjoined and
related to all other life and life forms:

> It is as if you were a whole small universe inside, while externally
> you are simply a unit . . . as if each individual were a little universe,
> a little microcosm in the macrocosm. But as if inside [s]he were
> a macrocosm too, and contained many microcosms . . . You see,
> infinite greatness and infinite smallness are infinitely true, and it is
> quite possible that we contain whole peoples in our souls, worlds
> where we can be as infinitely great as we are infinitely small ex-
> ternally—so great that the history of the redemption of a whole
> nation or of a whole universe might take place within us.[51]

We really are doing planetary work. Evolution itself is essential liminal
process. What is sought here is not just an ecological green but an alchemical green. It is the greening *veriditas* of that first feminist mystic, Hildegaard
of Bingen.[52] It is the green fire of recognition between species discovered
by ecological land reformer Aldo Leopold in his grief over slaying the wild
"other."

> *My own conviction on this score dates from the day I saw a wolf
> die. We were eating lunch on a high rim rock, at the foot of which
> a turbulent river elbowed its way. We saw what we thought was
> a doe fording the torrent, her breast awash in white water. When
> she climbed the bank toward us and shook out her tail, we realized
> our error: it was a wolf. A half-dozen others, evidently grown pups,
> sprang from the willows and all joined in a welcoming melee of wag-
> ging tails and playful maulings. What was literally a pile of wolves
> writhed and tumbled in the center of an open flat at the foot of our
> rim rock.*
>
> *In those days we had never heard of passing up a chance to kill
> a wolf. In a second we were pumping lead into the pack, but with
> more excitement than accuracy: how to aim a steep downhill shot
> is always confusing. When our rifles were empty, the old wolf was
> down, and a pup was dragging a leg into impassable slide-rocks.*

50. Deloria, *C. G. Jung and the Sioux Traditions*, 72.

51. Deloria, *C. G. Jung and the Sioux Traditions*, 70.

52. Fox, *Illuminations of Hildegard of Bingen*.

We reached the old wolf in time to watch a fierce green fire dying in her eyes. I realized then, and have known ever since, that there was something new to me in those eyes - something known only to her and to the mountain. I was young then, and full of trigger-itch; I thought that because fewer wolves meant more deer, that no wolves would mean hunters' paradise. But after seeing the green fire die, I sensed that neither the wolf nor the mountain agreed with such a view.[53]

With liminal space, we are talking about the cosmic animate Green Dragon,[54] the green-fire-eyed wolf-Other that is the living cosmos.

CONCLUSIS: BECOME HAVEN-MAKERS

Ultimately, the liminal melds both false worlds—the worlds of gods and the world of humans—and melds them into the true One World, the *Unus Mundus.* As Lionel Corbett reminds us from the work of Kabir, "The lane of love is narrow. It cannot accommodate two."[55] We then discover that we live in a common continuum of being, that all time and space merge into one grand project of completing compassion and love:

> Trees cannot exist without animals, or animals without plants, or perhaps animals cannot be without [wo]man, or [wo]man without animals and plants and so on. And the whole thing being one tissue, it is no wonder that all of its parts function together, just as the cells in our bodies function together because they are a part of the same living continuum.[56]

The liminal zone is a safe-haven zone. It houses our fretted souls. It calms and repositions our anxious being. It gets us vision-adjusted. It reminds us of our skill to return to the everyday work of being confident haven-makers for others. For that is what psychotherapy does best, it helps people find Home. It is what true religion, true education, true law, true medicine, true politics, any true profession, does. It helps people and their communities find their ways Home, to the true Home, to the Home of the present, whole Soul.

---

53. Leopold, *Sand County Almanac,* 130.
54. Swimme, *Universe Is a Green Dragon.*
55. Corbett,. *Sacred Cauldron,* 259.
56. Jung, *Visions Seminars,* 2:205.

The liminal zone is a merger zone, a nirvana zone. Within its precincts, personal identity becomes conjoined with the All. Our personal dreads and anxieties, our dissociations and ambitions, become blended into the Home-yearning, the Home-leaning intentions that seem to fuel the trajectory of cosmic process toward its ultimate compassionate endings. This plain of worldly existence seems to be the necessary place where the naive soul sheds its omnipotent and grandiose innocence. Through suffering, that original naïveté is fired into a compassionate heart, opening to both self and other. And, in the final, liminal stages, it is open to the living, sentient Cosmos.

Divinity seems to co-share this transforming evolution. Divinity—animate, creating Otherness—seems to demand such intimate involvement as a prerequisite for its own transformation of primal Divine naïveté into the ultimate merged, compassionate Homecoming of the All. As Meister Eckhart observed 800 years ago, and as Jung re-discovered half a century ago, "as soon as God existed [S]he created the world."[57]

I have a recurrent daydream. It is a simple dalliance, but its recurrence bespeaks its core importance for me. I imagine that tonight, when I go to bed, only 2 or 3 percent of the world is awake—fully, liminally awake to their shadow crisis, both personal and collective, and desire its compassionate, conscious transformation. Then, due to whatever you call it—from morphic resonance[58] to the hundred-and-one-monkeys phenomenon—when the world wakes up tomorrow, three quarters of our species will be fully, liminally awake. Now that's a productive daydream.

In a way I cannot rationally explain, the more I do depth work with others and myself, the more I am convinced that everyone and everything will get Home. No one and nothing will be left behind. Like Eckhart, Kant, Hegel and Jung similarly came to discover, all will find conscious absorption into the compassionate cosmic All.

> It has always seemed to me that I had to answer questions which fate has posed to my forefathers/[mothers], and which had not been answered, or as if I had to complete, or perhaps continue, things which previous ages had left unfinished.[59]

57. Dourley, *Jung and his Mystics*, loc. 2294–95.

58. Sheldrake, *Morphic Resonance*.

59. Jung, *Memories, Dreams and Reflections*, 233.

Everything is family, everyone is related to everyone else. The cosmos is family, it is relationship. All is interconnected to all. No individual grows alone, our roots always enfold those deeper, broader roots of the ancestral forest. We are a cosmic family. We are a matrix of family. Within that thin, resonant, living tissue of ancestry we carry genetic memory from the beginning of time, the Matrix Boom Bang.

We all must become politically dirty. We must then all become politically purified. We must see collective action as being as crucial as individual action, collective individuation as imperative as individual individuation. We must work to become compassionate citizens of the world, of our species, of the cosmos, instead of partisan, reactive citizens of national, corporatist states.

Returning to our indigenous tribal clarities and psychic ceremonies, we must diminish ego bounded-ness, our self-talk, and our self-interest, and we must learn to talk from integrity to the integrity of other beings, other life species.

> Consequently, the most mature and profound individuals would be those people who have not only been capable of individuation but who have benefited from a number of experiences—the clarity of interspecies communication, for example, or the acquisition of power through the medium of the vision.[60]

It is only through such matrix movement and dialogue that we can attune our urgent personal destinies toward urgent cosmic destiny; from self-teleology to the teleology of all life and compassion:

> These individuals would be capable of receiving information in their dreams about where the physical realization of cosmic process might move.[61]

As I heard Bucky Fuller once suggest, when we jump on the surface of the earth there is a ripple on the other side of the universe.[62] Every aspect of our life and being has communal witness and implication. Every enactment in our life produces cosmic implications. In such a cosmos-encompassing view, there is not a wasted moment, never an idle gesture. Everything is fraught with etiological implication.

---

60. Deloria, C. G. Jung and the Sioux Traditions, 180–81.

61. Deloria, C. G. Jung and the Sioux Traditions, 181.

62. Fuller, "Lecture at Tacoma First Congregational Church."

... a human life is nothing in itself; it is part of a family tree. We are continuously living the ancestral life, reaching back for centuries, we are satisfying the appetites of unknown ancestors, nursing instincts which we think are our own, but which are quite incompatible with our character; we are not living our own lives, we are paying the debts of our forefathers.[63]

As cosmos-tenders, then, our politics should be our most profound relational statement in honor and in service to this vast responsibility. Each of us as political actors (and hopefully this chapter has convinced you of this grave personal stewardship for the political commons we share together) must seek to be as contemplative and awake in our political behaviors as possible, for political activity is the highest form of individuated activity. Our official collective representatives must be similarly challenged to so interact and deliberate. The ancient Greeks dialed this up right: political activity is sacred theater. It is cosmos tending; a watering and nurturing of the primal Tree of Being. And it is toward this Primal Tree of Liminal Being that the last chapter turns its Inner Eye.

> It is possible that one sets out to live the ancestral life right in the beginning, as most people do who develop in a reasonable and positive way; they grow out of several ancestral lives into all-around individuals.[64]

63. Jung, *Dream Analysis I*, 320.
64. Jung, *Visions Seminars*, 2:453.

Postlude

The first time I saw Brother Lawrence was upon the 3rd of August, 1666. He told me that God had done him a singular favor in his conversion at the age of eighteen. During that winter, upon seeing a tree stripped of its leaves and considering that within a little time the leaves would be renewed and after that the flowers and fruit appear, Brother Lawrence received a high view of the Providence and Power of God which has never since been effaced from his soul. This view had perfectly set him loose from the world and kindled in him such a love for God, that he could not tell whether it had increased in the forty years that he had lived since.[1]

THERE IS A LONG TRADITION of the tree as mystic symbol. It is perhaps the most anthropomorphic of vegetative shapes with its trunk torso, root legs, branch arms, and leafy crown head. It shakes and wags like a young woman dancing or an old man playing cards. The tree can move as frantically as a toddler at play or be as still as death. It seems sentient and, in the silence of a spring glade, as empathic as the most profound of lovers. When its leaves begin to quiver, it makes crystalline soul music that seems to connect its organism to the very gods themselves.

The tree is a portal between worlds. Its roots burrow deeply into our everyday, Chronos-dominated world of clocks, compasses, calculators, and computers, anchoring the tree snugly within the earthy realism of hearty soil and rock. But its leafy spires reach into the Kairos, numinous-time heavens, touching the stars and filtering the quicksilver impulses of the gods down onto this heavy world of matter and means. It was this tree

---

1. Brother Lawrence, *Practice of the Presence of God the Best Rule of a Holy*, 7.

touch that animated the mysterious magnetic presence experienced by Brother Lawrence. Across the decades of his career as a monastery kitchen pot-cleaner, scholars, popes, and queens all came to hear his deeply affecting story of a winter's encounter with an ice-clad tree.

This essay is about trees and, more importantly, the Anima Mundi—the spirit of the world that animates them. It argues that trees grow on the liminal fault line between humankind and nature, between ecological disaster and natural disaster. It posits that care and reverence for the tree will lead to deepening care and reverence for human souls and earth soul.

In Carl Jung's famous commentary "The Philosophical Tree," he reflected on a series of tree drawings by patients in deep engagement with the depth psyche.[2] Within that rich canon of therapeutically-generated images, Jung found a whole healing cosmology, a cosmology that goes all the way back to Plato and, through Plato, to our shamanic cave origins. The tree is a living *imago* of Plato's ancient world soul, which Jung draws on to explicate this connection between tree, symbol, and soul. The ancients called this *über*-earth spirit the Anima Mundi, the spirit of the world, one of the oldest consistent psycho-spiritual ideas in the West. The earth is pure psycho-spiritual space. This notion about the primary vitalism that underlies all sentient experience on the planet is probably as old as the Paleolithic cave sanctuaries, but certainly as old as Plato. It is a notion that the planet is alive, that she is mother, breast, and home to us all. The tree stands as an essential demotic of soul.[3]

Jung felt that the contours of the psyche were carved very closely to the contours of nature; that nature, if you will, was the mold, psyche the molten content. So, this Anima Mundi always bears the core imprint of nature, the *magna mater* of creation. To lose daily, maybe even momentary, connection to this nature spirit is to risk losing connection to life essence itself and, hence, the personal destiny that always leads us to our full home of being within Her.

My own home rises just above the glacial-carved waters of Puget Sound in Washington State. Less than a league to the south is the only remaining natural estuary in the South Sound—a federally protected wildlife refuge. And on the serpentine creek that waters this marshland stands the stump of a Douglas fir tree. The local Amerindian Nisqually insist on its

2. Jung, "Philosophical Tree," 251–342.

3. For a lovely amplification of tree and soul, see "Urban Trees as Mirrors of the Soul," in Gambini, *Soul and Culture*, 58–82.

preservation, for the Medicine Creek Treaty of 1854 was signed under its once-abundant canopy. Knowing the sterile materialism of the capitalistic Anglo, the Nisqually believe that, if that concrete symbol—that Treaty Tree—disappears, so does the memory of our promises. Dead roots still hold 150-year-old soul pledges.

We share the same skin with the earth. We live in each other's bones. We co-inhabit each other's dreams. We dance a cosmic *pas de deux*. And, as was the case on my grandparents' Kansas farm, we share a party line with all the animate beings on this planet. All of us listen in on each other's planetary calls. If someone needs help, we know it, and, if we are good neighbors, we respond caringly with all the resources we have to offer. We pitch in to address the common threat. If someone's home—or the home of some species—burns to the ground, we bring a potluck and rebuild. This is what good neighbors do. This is what we used to do, but not so much anymore. Arrogant apex predator that we are, we have grown impervious to what feeds us, to the great food and life chain that supports our being. When that chain collapses from our material and spiritual neglect, we collapse. Connection is that interactively essential—if one being forgets respect and gratitude for any of the other beings, the chain breaks apart. Anima Mundi is the connective tissue through which this essential chain communicates. She is the *admirandum mundi maioris mysterium*, the wondrous mystery of the macrocosm.[4]

But this Anima Mundi is not a benign, Disneyland essence; it is a wild and unpredictable telluric force. It is part Athene, part Kali; part gentle soul kiss and part savage-to–the-bone bite. She has the fangs of a Japanese tsunami, the devouring bowels of a West China earthquake. Anima Mundi is not a giddy archetypal presence. She is a close companion of darkness. She broods. She has profound capacity for experiencing and constellating what the continentals call *Weltsmertz*: world sorrow. She grieves because, often, we can't or we won't. All that lost innocence and violence, that rampage, that destruction and disaster—she is often as impotent to prevent it as we sometimes are. But she can mourn. Like the ancient aborigine, she has days of sorrow where she wakes in the morning filled with the agony of this plane of existence. She just walks up to a cedar at the western end of the camp, stoops beneath its fragrant bower, and stares off at the horizon, rapt in lamentation and grief.

4. Jung, "Philosophical Tree," 259.

Some recent distaff Jungian voices to the contrary, there is teleology to nature. There is a telos to consciousness. And it is human inclusive, not human exclusive—even in human-and nature-generated disaster. Our survival as a species seems to depend on our understanding this. So, in this book's final chapter reflecting on liminality and contemporary consciousness, I explore the threatened planetary Anima Mundi telos through the lens of two films—one narrative, one documentary—and highlight its essence and import for our current world as the central carrier of the transformative liminal.

> *Do you think that somewhere we are not Nature, that we are different from Nature? No, we are in Nature and think exactly like Nature.*
>
> —C. G. JUNG[5]

A NARRATIVE FILM'S ANIMA MUNDI VIEW

Film loves to imagine. That is its job. It is our collective imaginarium. Film is the collective dream. It is a repository of collective memory and a prism of collective anticipation. It looks both backward and forward, it has both retrospective and prospective lenses. It attempts to precipitate the future. It digests and gives meaning to the unfolding Mobius strip of lived experience. It wants to give context to that experience, to give it embodied meaning.

So, it is not by accident that so much of film is fascinated with disaster, with catastrophe, with the unexpected; such moments give the ongoing ontological challenge meaningful experience. An annihilating disaster strikes a strong nihilist register. It depletes the proximate moment of significance. It renders all as a yawning vat of painful, bottomless emptiness.

Narrative film is still a central arena for such disaster commentary. Whether it is of the cheap thrill-and-soothe variety or the more profound genre that disturbs and provokes, narrative film remains a principal vehicle for apocalyptic wonderings and wanderings. And, because it reflects the loss of a vitalizing connection to the Anima Mundi, the visual narrative is often subtly saturated with tree imagery.

---

5. Sabini, *Earth Has a Soul*, 24.

Here we are at the threshold.
This is the most important moment of your lives.
You have to know that here your most cherished wish will
come true.
The most sincere one.
The one reached through suffering.

—Andrei Tarkovsky (from his film *Stalker*, 1979)

One of the most generative of modern apocalypse narratives is Andrei Tarkovsky's last film, *The Sacrifice* (1986). Much has been written about this film, but nothing that explicitly addresses its close kinship to the threatened Anima Mundi and the coming end of times. Set in Sweden, the film focuses on a renowned figure in the national theater, Alexander, as he is turning 70. It opens on the day of Alexander's birthday celebration, as he walks down his coastal home driveway with a winsome-but-mysterious pre-pubescent boy, Little Man. Little Man's neck is bandaged, signaling a never fully expli-cated medical malady that renders him temporarily mute. They are going out to plant and then to water a small, frail, lonely tree that appears dead. It is their "Japanese Ikebana tree," which they place along the barren, arctic-shore drive. Alexander tells this boy—his son, we learn—about an ortho-dox monk who, following the instructions of his departed mentor, watered a dead tree for years. He watered as other monks around him wondered and snickered, watered until the one day, seemingly no different from the rest, he ascended the tree's mountain home and found the once lifeless tree full of blossoms.

An old man on a bike, Otto, the local postal deliveryman and one of Alexander's closest local friends, arrives to celebrate the birthday. Alexan-der's daughter, Julia, and her doctor husband, Victor, arrive as well. Two maids buzz around in response to the insistent commands of Alexander's brittle wife, Adelaide. The main room of the elegantly rustic home glis-tens with the repartee of family members and friends gathering for good drink and conviviality. The glistening, however, is insufficient to mask strong hints of a somber and depressed mood beneath Alexander's genial, but fragile, exterior. The viewer senses that, at 70, this man believes he has failed his life and all those he loves (including his younger, engaging wife and child). In all the commotion of birthday dinner preparation, Otto gazes intensely, probably for the hundredth time, at a copy of Leonardo DaVinci's "Annunciation" in a dark passageway. "I never did like this painting," he states. "It is brooding." Dark things often do presage moments of authentic, depth transformation.

At one point, Maria, the Icelandic maid, is burdened and then dismissed by the brittle hostess. She stares directly into the camera and says, "The plates, the candles, the wine." This is no ordinary birthday bash. A sacramental meal is being readied, and the group inducted into synchronistic, extraordinary Kairos time. And we, the audience, are just as deeply inducted into this rapidly-developing, alternative universe created by Tarkovsky.

Suddenly, the camera is outside on the beach moors. Maria walks across scruff grasses to her home, her day's labors over. She passes by a distracted Alexander walking in the adjacent woods, where he had just stumbled upon a model of his home on the ground. Maria explains that it was to be Little Man's birthday gift to him. It is a preciously elegant model. It reminds us that the home is our most ancient metaphor for the containment of the soul; that this film, if there were any lingering doubt, is about the soul and its abode. And it sits so comfortably in the embracing arbor of coastal scrub oaks, the sacred grove of long-forgotten Druid servants of the Anima Mundi.

Then, back in the house, eight crystal glasses on a tray begin to vibrate ominously. A glass cupboard door swings open as a shelved pitcher of milk sloshes and then careens to the floor, its contents pouring across the polished planks. There quickly follows a deep, unsettling screech of fighter jets, flying low in multiple waves over the house and out to sea. The partiers quickly find television and radio channels that inform them of the cause: the East and West have declared all-out war, and the jets are the harbingers of nuclear annihilation. The women scream and are medicated by the patriarchal doctors in the assembly. Then, a silent melancholy descends on the household. The end is near.

No dead tree will miraculously bloom tomorrow in Alexander's destiny-barren life or in the wasteland of a global culture that has destroyed itself. The film's pace (in keeping with all Tarkovsky's films, which never gallop) slows to an anguishing standstill. The darkening screen images are as breathless as the party participants. We are all doomed, awaiting our end.

The women safely drugged, the men get drunk. But off to the side, Alexander whispers his prayer of bargaining with Divinity: "I'll give Thee all I have. I'll give up my family, whom I love. I'll destroy my home and give up Little Man." This is the desperately earnest sacrifice that titles the film. Profound sacrament always demands profound sacrifice.

Otto walks over to his friend and conspiratorially whispers that Maria is a witch, that if Alexander would go to her in the night and sleep with her, the world possibly could be saved. Otto—the alchemist, the hermeticist—returns later as Alexander anxiously rests on a second-floor couch. Otto reminds him of his mission, and that he must proceed by stealth, using a ladder off the second floor. This is the beginning of a trip into another world. One can enter only by sacred, laddered ascents and descents. One cannot look at things directly, but only indirectly through cupboard glass and wall mirrors. We realize clearly now that Otto is Pan, the messenger god between our human world and Olympus, the flitting anxious god of imminent action, imminent disaster, imminent healing. Pan is a god of cunning and stealth. Pan never uses doors, only ladders and mirrors.

The screen goes pitch black. Then we hear a faint brass clinking, a cow bell. A soft mewling. Alexander has set out on his son's bike into the black hole of the arctic night. He's on his eccentric, mystic errand. He falls in the farm-road ruts and bruises a body already ravaged by seven decades of living. Amid the limpid night sounds of lowing cattle and barking dogs, he limps through the absorbent sponge of this infinite night to the witch maid's threshold and knocks. Another dog barks. A lamb bleats. Another knock, his knuckles on wood sounding like artillery belches in the dense solitude. No response. Rustling noises within, and then a small, feminine voice, "Who is it?" He announces himself, and the surprised maid opens the door.

The door opens into a dark, womb-like interior. The camera seems to be as blind as we are. But we can feel the warmth of her cottage. The silence. It rolls on and on, out into the dark viewing theater. Awkward. Absorbing. Prescient.

Maria's bedroom is a liminal temple. Madonna icons. Ancestors present in old baroque picture frames. A ticking clock—but it ticks differently, more softly; it is a Kairos clock. Time here expands and slows rather than shrinking and speeding up. Alexander processes behind her, a servant abbot. He pauses behind her and blends with her—a *coniunctio* prefigurement. This is that dark annunciation moment. The sacrament was earlier prepared, now it is to be celebrated.

Maria notices Alexander's limp. He explains the fall. She goes for a white pitcher, lifts off its linen cloth cover and tenderly pours pure water into a basin. He washes off the road dirt as she pours the cleansing liquid. Purifying. This is sacramental step three: hand and soul cleansing.

Alexander finds an old pump organ, probably rescued from some rural byway church. He plays old hymns solemnly and slowly and begins to talk. He tells a story, a fable about tending his dying mother's garden, fighting back the neglect and decay and restoring order and rhythm to the wild belligerence of uncontrolled nature. Then, one day, the work was done. Nature controlled into human elegance. He dressed in his Sunday finery for the occasion and rolled his mother out for the review of his heroic accomplishment. And in that instant, he was filled with remorse. He immediately grasped the arrogance and violence of his patriarchal "restoration" of nature's primal elegance and wildness. He grieves, even years later in this late-night retelling—his vesper lamentation a grasping of the arrogance and violence of his empty narcissistic existence. This is the confession.

The gentle Icelandic maid tracks Alexander's story, inquiring, "What about your mother?" The camera finds her face and falls prayer-silent before timeless, iconic beauty. She is Theotokos—mother of all that is godly and divine in the cosmos. She is Mother Maria—a pieta not for a male Christ but for the lost Deep Feminine in Alexander's mother's ravaged garden. Alexander kneels before her on the simple bed under a simple wall crucifix: "Save us, Maria." This is the Kyrie.

Alexander lies in her lap and tells her he knows who she is, that she is a White Witch. She is horrified. She demurs even as she compassionately and accurately connects to his anguish. Caught off guard, Maria flees a bit; goes to the crystal oil lamp lighting the room; touches a warmed hand to her face. Then, this crystal lamp shakes just as the crystal glasses had shaken in Alexander's home. Crystal lives in both worlds, human and divine.

The camera pans to Alexander. He grieves even more deeply as he remembers the night's desperate mission. He is filled with despair. Suddenly he produces a gun—a gun strangely discovered in his son-in-law's medical bag. He must die for past and current crimes of narcissistic entitlement. He puts it to his head. Maria turns, horrified to discover Alexander with a gun to his temple. She rushes to his side, urgently soothing and calming. A real Madonna, like the one on her simple home altar. "You poor man," she says. "What have they done to you? I know her [Adelaide], she is evil."

Maria promises to do anything as Alexander tells her of Otto's strange intercourse prescription. "Yes, yes anything." Banshee jets screech overhead as they lovingly embrace and rise in a counter-clockwise, levitating love-making. Alexander weeps in deep mourning and agony as his inner eye awakens to intercourse-roused visions. At first, he sees horrific visions of a white car disastrously overturned in the midst of people scrambling desperately in urban streets. There is a haunting feminine voice, a siren voice—not a trickster siren, but an anguished siren. We have heard her in the soundtrack all through the film, but never so pronounced as now. There are long tracking shots of coins, water, scarves, detritus—human and natural. There is mud and snow. Little Man's bare feet in snow? Then a baby, face down in a white feather comforter. Alexander is suddenly lying in his wife's lap in the coastal woods of his beloved home, but his wife has Maria's face.

The sacrament is ended. Go in peace.

Alexander startles awake on his second-floor couch, blurting "Mama." He awakens to a color-filled, early-morning room. Adelaide lurks sinisterly around a corner—this is not the dream wife, but the anxious, brittle, real-world wife again. He sits up painfully. What does it all mean? He stands to look around, orient himself. He bangs his left knee on a desk. He limps like Jacob after his midnight encounter by the ford at Jabbok, after his wrestling with the gods. We wonder if he is the Fisher King, wounded and ailing, looking for the Grail—the lost Anima Mundi—as a mournful panpipe plays.

At this point, the film's pace picks up to a mild canter. Alexander calls his editor. Uncertain if this is truly ordinary time again? Call your editor. Yep, the editor is in a crucial meeting and cannot talk just now. Ordinary, distracted, anxious time. Down the now full-color hallway, in the ordinary post-dawn light, we see that Little Man's bed is empty—innocence awakened after the dark-night slaughter of the innocents. "Things always look better in the morning."

Alexander is a dazed man, caught between two space-time worlds. He wakes up from Kairos time and must adapt to Chronos time. Haunting sounds intrude: the tapping of something loose on window glass; a creaky door opening on the mirrored cupboard. Alexander puts on a sleeping robe, the only appropriate garment to connect him to the Kairos dream world. And he begins to weep in his disoriented despair. What is real? What is dream? What is his duty? What was his sacrifice for the absent son? What was his promise, really? He crawls out the second-floor window and down the ladder again—a good Kairos way to leave a scary Chronos room—and climbs down behind a tree. Here is the earth-sky, axial, Anima Mundi tree yet again. Alexander is a shaman climbing up and down the World Tree to seek his teaching and healing guides, to ask for the wisdom of the eagle god at its eight-branched apex.[6]

As Alexander descends, he hears his daughter Julia speaking of "our Victor," who is moving abroad to head a clinic in Australia. The family is gathered around the outside breakfast table. Alexander watches, as he did the night before—a voyeur of his family's life, of his life, of life itself. Victor says he's tired of being a nursemaid. He feels he is a warden to this family. Australia is his way out. We all want to escape our unique, ancestral world sorrows.

The film's canter becomes a slow gallop. Alexander, the wounded Fisher King, stealthily limps off again. He is wearing his silk night robe but, wait, there is an emblem on the back—something samurai maybe? As he enters a yard shed, the emblem clearly shows: a yin-yang mandala. He is samurai. A night warrior defying the day's deceits. He overhears that Little Man has gone to their Japanese tree. As Alexander lurks around the shed to avoid his family's detection, the family walks off to join Little Man. We hear Julia say that Alexander thinks he and his son are both Japanese. The father and son working in the world to blend oppositional wisdoms.

Alexander enters the house, gliding to the breakfast table. He takes a bite of an apple. The fruit of the Tree of Knowledge. He stacks wicker furniture in a first-floor room. He drapes it in white linen. He sets it afire. He visits the second floor one last time, reaches for a glass and drinks, then descends the Kairos ladder once again.

We hear the roar of the fire that Alexander has carefully set. The family races back. They become shocked familial keystone cops, screaming and grieving, running to and fro, screen left to screen right, chasing after Alexander and stumbling over themselves. Alexander's wife, exhausted from her pursuit, collapses in a marsh's mud. We see a disoriented, otherworldly family tableau set against the blazing house, watching as it burns down to blackened beam butts and ash—the sacrifice pledge achieved.

An ambulance with men in white coats come and chase after Alexander. Maria arrives and races to comfort him, but is rebuffed by Adelaide. Alexander is locked into the back of the ambulance and driven off. Maria pursues on bike and observes as the ambulance drives past Little Man, who is awkwardly carrying two buckets of water for his Bonzai tree. He speaks for the first time: "In the beginning was the Word. Why was that, Papa?"

---

6. Eliade, *Shamanism*, 67–75.

The child. The Divine Child. That child that is both of flesh and of earth, of seed and dirt. The child lovingly held in the arms of Mother Tree. All of Tarkovsky's films are sacramental films—films of deep, transforming earth sacrament—but especially this film, his last.

The father, sacrificed. The father's patriarchal house, burned to the ground. The dark, sacrificial night saved by the light of a new day so that a child, this child, can be healed, is healed. He is given back voice, ready to water the next generational turn of the great cosmic Wheel of Being.

A DOCUMENTARY FILM'S ANIMA MUNDI VIEW

Documentary film has made enormous advances in recent decades.[7] Interesting word, "documentary." To document. Implying that this is a more fact-based, reality-close medium of image than narrative film. In a can-do, evidence-based, hard-capitalist society, this realistic appearance—this rawness—provides the ever-present illusion of high cultural value. But just as *The Sacrifice*, a narrative film, documents "real" truth in an honest and essential way, great documentary film knows that it needs to reflect profound narrative art as well. Both cinematic art forms drink from the same deep soul well.

Micha Peled is a contemporary artist of the documentary format who sees the coming apocalypse. In a documentary style that captures a macroscopic global vision through the eyes of impoverished, suffering individuals and families on the microscopic ground level, he engages both our outrage and our compassion. In Peled's decade-in-the-making globalization trilogy, his camera moves from a Walmart in dying middle America to a jeans sweatshop in market-frenzied China. From there, he turns to a suicide-saturated farming village in India, his bloodhound journalism tracking down beastly, planet-killing prey.

With Peled, it's not "follow the green," it's "follow the greed." His trilogy lifts the veneer off the soul-numbing gluttony of mindless greed that is killing the earth and threatening our species with extinction. Peled's lens burrows up from the realm of the collective self to expose the narcissistically damaged collective ego of acquisition driving our cultural and sociopolitical suicide.

I first saw *Bitter Seeds* (2011) at a Telluride Film Festival screening. It was one of the rare occasions in my long film-watching career that I

7. Hurwitz and Klenk, "Decisive Image," 17–34.

experienced the activating immediacy and dark, raw passion of cinematic image turning an everyday audience into an extraordinary mob-like pack.

I believe the fuse for the event was pre-lit by the director's introductory remarks to the screening. He explained that he had just finished editing the final cut of the version we were to see. The film's underwriter, the Public Broadcasting Service (PBS), had asked him to make substantial edits to the film we'd see—particularly the sections exposing the blatant, morally bankrupt behavior of the Monsanto Corporation. He also shared that there would be a discussion panel about film, food, and ecology at another festival venue, the town's 19th-century courthouse, immediately after the screening.

The packed audience (it was the last full festival day and the last major time slot) then watched the extraordinarily moving documentary. At the close of the film, the audience exploded out into the ravishing high alpine, late afternoon light and flooded up to the courthouse, packing every nook and cranny of that venerable justice temple. The room was abuzz with angry, animated, activated citizen cineastes. It was an image-charged, ideological lynch mob in the forming, and the sentence read, "Monsanto: guilty as charged." We were an unruly bunch that gradually subdued itself to hear a modest, thoughtful presentation on the problems facing modern documentarists tracking the global ecological and food-chain crisis. Most of us stood; few could sit down right away, so charged with adrenaline was the assembled hoard. Such is the unmediated power of an image, whether painted in blood on the wall of a Paleolithic cave or projected onto the twilight wall of a Rocky Mountain cinema.

A twilight darkness is again settling on our culture, as it did for our bear-clan forebears and for our subsequent ancestors in innumerable failed empires. The global streets are again filling up with those who feel existentially, economically, culturally disenfranchised. And again, image hopefully and centrally lights the way through the flickering darkness.

Micha Peled's camera lives in that twilight. In many moments, it feels as though the tortured Anima Mundi, the world soul, directs the gaze of the lens, not Peled himself. This seems to be an authentic feature of all depth, auteur craftspeople. It's as though filmmaking becomes an enacted, active imagination event, a moment of living improvisation where other worlds agree to allow the soul to be seen and interacted with.

Peled's prophetic, probing, insistent documentary work awakens our collective compassion to the avoided, buried trauma of our times. Peled is adroit at this liturgy of filmic compassion expansion. He cleverly follows the macrocosmic story through the microcosmic humanity of his carefully chosen human narrators, the tragic global chronicle unfolding before our eyes and within our awed bodies.

The impersonal generally inflicts much more harm in this weary world than intentional evil. It is the crushing force of economic impersonality behind global finance that Peled tackles with such skill in his filmic essays. And the impersonal makes the inventive personal narrative at the core of his documentary design all the more urgently contrasting. It is the bruised face and soul of impersonal evil's victims that haunt and motivate us. It simultaneously arouses our shame as co-participants in the impersonal effects of evil while also constellating our compassion and sorrow. There is rage, as the effect of my first collective viewing of *Bitter Seeds* amply testifies. But ultimately, there is a call to our wider, self-interested, compassionate, literally co-suffering sorrow, a redemptive sorrow that awakens an impulse to intervene for the wider good; a sorrowful intervention that quickly leads to a painful but necessary self-inventory of the ways we collude with the soul-numbing, leveling energies of the impersonal.

Peled's film event is liquid Anima Mundi. We see her in the opening image: several trees at the edge of a verdant field early in the harvest season. Amid a montage of farm carts, work cattle and oxen, villager chatter, and intimate dinner preparations around earthen vessels and rock-enclosed flame, Peled reveals the slow, terrifying cadence of the realities of this ancient farm culture colliding with mass global agri-business. Half of the world's population are farmers, he reminds his urban, first-world viewers. In the last sixteen years, a quarter million Indian farmers have committed suicide, one every thirty minutes. On and on the grim statistics screen scrolls. As we are drawn into deeper love for the family of our 18-year-old narrator, Manjusha Ambarwar, we feel a rising dread. We somehow know this is not going to turn out well, even as we gather around the family dinner circle with story and laughter, ripe-cut tomatoes and dhal, flickering lamp-oil light, lovely folk music, and festivity; we know a dark rider stalks this family, and it begins to stalk the camera and our collective spirit, too. This documentary tale is heading down a dark lane.

A billboard sign for Super Mallika BT, a Monsanto India company, reads:
"Welcome to Green City
This the time for happiness"

We see the Anima Mundi as three generations of village farming women sow cotton into freshly-tilled soil—swaying back and forth as one hand brushes the earth, the other plants the seed. It is a fertility dance. It contrasts poignantly with the darker dance of a single male striding across a green leafy cotton field pumping a canister with one hand and spraying its pesticide poisons with the other.

We see the Anima Mundi in the simple joy of a family meal on the hard-packed earth of a village hut. They are celebrating the sowing of the year's cotton crop. There is a special, festive feast of sweet rice and yogurts. The youngest boy-child jokes about not getting his snot mixed with the food. All roar with humble, fully embodied mirth—the mirth of sweat-sweet, farmer innocence.

The Anima Mundi is in the tear-soaked garland wreathes hung round the neck of a farmer who committed suicide by drinking Monsanto's pesticide poison to escape the crushing Monsanto-generated debt poison visited on these simple, good farmers of the earth.

She is in the fierce-warrior Maat-Yama-goddess justice of Manjusha, a young woman seeking to become a journalist as she tells the story of the epidemic of farmer suicides that has taken the lives of so many innocent, overwhelmed farmers, including her own father.

Peled's walking camera literally falls into the gentle cadence of village life, in sync with its inhabitants' contemplative stroll. The best of image-making matches the beat of its observed hearts, breathing in harmony with their existence. The camera captures the agony of a lower-caste farmer's daughter who has been rejected by a potential suitor's higher-caste family because her poor family cannot raise an acceptable dowry. She is crushed—maybe she can only achieve a "love" marriage, which, in an arranged marriage society, would bring deep shame to her clan.

Sawpa, the daughter, collapses and weeps. Her mother soothes, "Let it go. You are beautiful. The boy looked like a monkey." As is too often the case on a planet besieged by the disease of an out-of-control patriarchy, it is the women who must suffer, soothe, stand their impoverished ground, and endure. Too often, it is these women who have digested the global angst in their bodies, hearts, and souls.

Near the end of the documentary, Peled films a protest rally in Pandharkawada. A regional community organizer introduces our young, very nervous, novice journalist. Manjusha has never spoken in such a public setting before, but her father was one of the first farmer suicides. We have learned that this is the reason for her intense vocational motivation—to understand what happened to him, to her family, to her. She freezes before the mic. The organizer kindly comes to her side and compassionately says, "When Gandhi gave a speech for the first time, he cried. At least Manjusha is not crying." She is re-centered and empowered. Her heart and voice open up:

> "We sow BT cotton and are seeing the negative effects. In the past, farmers were using conventional seeds. They got yields using cow dung. They spent very little and produced a lot. Farmers, please prepare to suffer from now on. Don't build houses; build crema- tion grounds. We won't rest until we drive BT cotton out of India. Please forgive me if I made any mistakes in my speech. Long live India. Long live Maharashtra."

She becomes embodied Anima Mundi. She is primal justice, the force of restorative rage and healing. She is the voice of survival truth for our species. We must build cremation grounds; burn the dead and use the ash to re-soil the coming transformation of earth and community soul.

There is a still point in the film, almost its imagistic center, the calm at the center of the globalization hurricane. A little Indian girl riding a bike on a high wire stretched in a market square. She holds a thick balance bar. Her cherubic face is fierce with the intensity of concentration. Will she fall? Will she make it across? We ride that high wire with her and disastrous peril threatens on all sides.

Indian farmers walk their windrows at dawn and dusk, like my farmer granddad did, and his father and grandfather before him. They say their prayers of gratitude to the sheltering trees of life that keep the fierce winds from stripping away the precious soil. They say a prayer to the Tree of Life, to the Anima Mundi, to the mother of all farmers, to the mother of the All.

CONCLUSION

Disaster is an inevitable ingredient in being. To live is to experience pe- riodic collapse; to be engulfed in episodic catastrophe. This is true on the personal, collective, and cosmic levels. Creation and destruction endlessly flux through both quarks and solar systems.

The trick is in how to interact with disaster. The greatest of the world's historical mythic and spiritual systems seem to be in fairly consistent accord here in positing that the best attitude toward such periodic, devastating upheaval is a contemplative outlook, an attitude of loving indifference that is both compassionately engaged with the crisis and disengaged from anxious, controlling efforts. We don't control our births. We don't control our deaths. And we control scant little in between. What we can control a bit is our attitude of engagement—contemplative inquiry and interaction over panicked denial and avoidance, a repose in renewing liminal realms tinged with memory of our divine origins and destinies.

A Jungian worldview is a contemplative, liminal worldview. It is a technique of psycho-spiritual deepening that seeks an individuation, a more conscious awareness, within the patterns of meaning that weave together creation and destruction, evolution and extinction into a fabric of discovered and revealed significance and context. It seeks a more conscious awareness even in chaos and disaster—maybe, in fact, most of all within the meaning-bearing essence and necessity of chaos and disaster.

Analysis accomplishes this task on the personal plane; cultural artifacts like film accomplish this on a collective plane. Like the clustering synchronisms in individual analysis and depth psycho-spiritual process that increasingly anticipate breakdown moments of devastation and subsequent breakthrough moments of creation and synthesis, film, at its best, is a collective synchronistic transponder that receives and alerts the global commune of incoming disaster and breakthrough moments of liminal recreation and transformation.

A celebrated alchemical image is the *arbor inversus*, the inverted tree.[8] An upside-down tree, its crown in the earth, its roots waving in the air, highlights the paradoxical inversion of reality necessary to expose the inevitable oppositional tensions that exist between all things in the phenomenal world. Nothing is as it first appears, nothing—not love, innocence, or divinity. All heroic light has jet-black feet of clay.

With the challenges of natural and ecological disaster, we frail humans are turned on our heads. Our heads are planted in rich loam, our branched feet waving in airy realms. In a patriarchal culture rendered so dangerously arid by hyper-heady intellectualisms and rationalisms, it is potentially healing to have that head vigorously returned to its dark, moist, deep-feminine origins while its imprisoned and often immobilized Eros-feet are left free to wave in renewing, blustering breezes. Something as irreconcilably dark and evil as natural and ecological disaster demands such a dramatic upending of convenient worldviews. It is Tarkovsky following Alexander's midnight

---

8. Jung. Alchemical Studies, 311–15.

visit to an arctic witch or Peled's underground camera fearlessly document-
ing ominous events in a beleaguered Indian village.

What common ground is tilled by their complementary but genre-
distinct essays on our precarious contemporary predicament? I would like
to suggest four containers of restorative liminal healing embedded in these
cinematic treasures:

Recovery of the Deep Feminine: The Anima Mundi is feminine. She
is the source of what the great medieval mystic Hildegaard called *veriditas,* "the greening." As Jung writes, "God [Her]self dwells in the fiery glow
[*Gloria mundi*—glory of the world] of the sun and appears as the fruit of
the philosophical tree and thus as the product of the opus, whose course
is symbolized by the growth of the tree."[9] She notices everything, *notitia.*
Her care is that deep. She animates everything human and extra human,
interior and exterior.[10]

**Recovery of an Essential and Spirit-Healthy Tribalness, an Origi-
nal Indigeneity**: Stripped to his core in personal and collective crisis, Alexander discovered that family—clan—is the essential vessel in which we
cook and evolve. Similarly, stripped to her core by personal and collective
crisis, Manjusha discovered that her family and tribal village is the essential
vessel of her destiny.

At our core, we are still cave people. When disaster strikes, it is the
clan cave to which we return. Family is the ribcage of our being; within it,
the heart of our soul keeps its protected meter.

**Relationship with Earth and Cosmos—Not Conquest of the Earth
and Cosmos**: This is the crucial dynamic. When we lovingly distance ourselves from the personal and collective identification with natural and ecological disaster, we better grasp the wider horizon of these often volatile and
irrational shaping forces of the planet. They are volatile and irrational, but
purposive in darkly obscure ways that our beings can only faintly apper-
ceive but never fully measure. We can only consciously surrender to them.

Advocacy for Creature Humility and Compassion: And, finally,
disasters—ecological, existential, natural—are necessary and inevitable
shaping life forces. Consciousness can avoid more of our species-generated
varietals of disaster, but not the foundational necessity and inevitability of
them. What is needed here is an achieved philosophical maturity of compassionate and loving indifference. We can incubate a psycho-spirituality

9. Jung, "Philosophical Tree," 311–15.
10. Jung, "Philosophical Tree," 307.

of dark desperation from such a hard reality, or we can incubate one of generative light.

Maybe we all need, especially at moments of personal and collective disaster, to stop climbing, straining, and achieving and just go into the woods and nestle below our Tree of Being and wish upon our star of destiny; to wonder at the deep rich correspondences of being between us and the natural world, between us and the Anima Mundi.

ECHOES

In Nature's temple, living columns rise,
Which oftentimes give tongue to words subdued,
And [Wo]Man traverses this symbolic wood,
Which looks at [her]him with half familiar eyes,

Like lingering echoes, which afar confound
Themselves in deep and sombre unity,
As vast as Night, and like transplendency,
The scents and colours to each other respond.

And scents there are, like infant's flesh as chaste,
As sweet as oboes, and as meadows fair,
And others, proud, corrupted, rich and vast,

Which have the expansion of infinity,
Like amber, musk and frankincense and myrrh,
That sing the soul's and senses' ecstasy.

~ *Charles Baudelaire*[11]

CLOSING CLINICAL POSTSCRIPT: DEUS INCARNATUS AND WATERING THE WORLD TREE

And so this liminal journey comes to its end. But it's a dynamic end, an end that spirals right back to a deeper-cut beginning. The World Tree sinks its roots deep into the flesh soil of us all. The numinous seeps into that root sap every moment of every day of our lives. It's a cosmic IV dripping its immersion into our essence, envious of our capacity to love in a mortal frame,

11. Baudelaire, *Flowers of Evil*, 10.

jealous of our passion for consciousness. *Deus incarnates*: divine essence incarnating into human essence.

A middle-aged professional male full swing in his career is haunted by recurrent doubts about his true creativity and the destiny that creativity requires of him.

> *I dreamed that I was made Pope. Unexpected. Unsought. I am Prot-*
> *estant. I am not baptized a Catholic. Won't that make a difference? I*
> *kneel before close colleagues, the black cap and golden miter of office*
> *in hand. I am humbled. I am moved. I move into this sudden cer-*
> *emony with humble dignity. But don't people see the mistake here?*
> *Oh, I want them to. But they seem to know who I am and feel I still*
> *have no choice. They have definitively chosen. I am the Pope now.*
> *Now, how do I go about bringing more love into this broken world?*

The Self is what happens when the ego is busy making other plans. The self is interested in one thing only—luring, herding, impelling the ego toward a congruent depth relationship with the living divinity in us, the part of us that is part of God, the numinal otherness, the imago dei. When ego is humbled by the immensity of this compassionate tiara-destiny—the destiny of social justice bringing and bearing—the resources, both individual and collective, often seem to fall easily to hand. We can become loving father/mother, loving papa/mama shepherd to our flock of inner and outer lost sheep of being.

This man's mid-life ambitions and doubts were brought to stark, awesome ground in his dream. The broad majesty and mystery of his being, as well as the divine being to which it was anchored, became movingly sober and real to him. He could now serve his true fate with a resolve, clarified and just-hearted.

A woman in similar late-career full stride was filled with ongoing echoes of childhood trauma dreams:

> *I am in Italy, it is evening. In some sort of hotel or apartment build-*
> *ing. Somehow the Pope [Francis] comes by and he's going up to his*
> *room in an apartment, with a woman who seems in her 60s with*
> *him. She's nice looking. The Pope is in his white cossack and little*
> *skullcap.*
>
> *They are going up to his apartment, get on the elevator and*
> *close the metal gate like hotels in Europe used to have. I think that it*
> *is nice that he has a lady friend with him; I think that this is perhaps*
> *why he is such a wonderful guy: because he has this woman in his*
> *life, the influence of the feminine. I wonder if she is just a friend or if,*

perhaps, because he is from Latin America where ecclesial mistresses are very common, she is his mistress. I don't know, but I wonder what their relationship is.

Then the scene changes. It is night. I have a room or an apartment. I encounter the Pope again; seems like we are walking down the hall together, but then he seems to come by my apartment. I let him in. The scene I remember is that he wants me to be really quiet—so people won't know of this Papal impropriety. I have not even locked the door yet; he asks if I can lock the door. He says to run some water to cover our relational sounds. I'm holding stuff at the door, so I say, "you do it." He goes over, turns on the water faucet. Then, after setting down my bundles, I lock the door.

He seems a little nervous to be there, and I wonder if he thinks someone might be coming to my room and could discover us together. It is night, time to go to bed. He indicates that there's perhaps this holy man outside the door, like the guy who serves and guards him and takes care of his stuff. He rather abruptly leaves for his apartment, then goes instead back into a corner of my apartment where there is a curtain into another room next door.

In the other room, there are two beds, and someone—seems like a church functionary—is asleep in one bed. There's an empty bed, so I think he's going to sleep in the other one. I'll go back into my room and get my bed ready to go to sleep; straightening up the pillows on one side. The Pope comes back in and lies down on the side I was planning to sleep on. I say, "Oh, you were going to sleep here?" I wonder about this, he is the Pope, after all. But I go ahead and ask if it was okay with him, would he mind sleeping on the other side? I was planning to sleep there. He says okay. I am pleased that he has come to my room, as I like him and admire him. He seems like a really human person. I wake up and keep musing about the dream.

Unlike the man's papal dream, this woman has a domesticated Pope, not an awesome one. She has Hestia's comfort with any visitors—human or divine. The distance between sacred and temporal worlds has been foreshortened. They sleep in each other's beds, share each other's toilets, eat over the same tables, clean up in the same sinks. In this liminal apartment complex, divine and human have become roommates.

Hopefully, this is what we are evolving toward through all our shared experience. There is deepening of soul going on individually and collectively across the planet, a deepening that turns even a casual visit to Central Park into an Anima Mundi wonder:

POSTLUDE

A client dreams of staring up into the boughs of one of the ancient lovely trees on the west side of Central Park in New York City. It is midafternoon on a partially cloudy day, and the more subdued sky acts as a soft background to the myriad apple-sized, golden balls that fill the tree top to bottom, side to side. She reaches up and touches one, and is delighted that it is not metal but feels like wax coating— soft and supple to the touch. She and the tree harmonically glisten together, inside and out.

BIBLIOGRAPHY

Abrego, Jasmine. "Combat Training: Can Female Marines Get The Job Done?" Interview by
   Tom Bowman. *Early Edition*, National Public Radio, November 24, 2014. Audio, 6:00,
   https://www.npr.org/2014/11/24/365723967/combat-training-can-female-marines
   -get-the-job-done.
Alighieri, Dante. Translated by Henry Wadsworth Longfellow. *The Divine Comedy.*
   Cambridge, Riverside Press, 1886.
Baudelaire, Charles. Translated by William Aggeler. *The Flowers of Evil.* Fresno, CA:
   Academy Library Guild, 1954.
Belah, Robert N. *Religion in Human Evolution: From the Paleolithic to the Axial Age.*
   Cambridge, MA: Harvard University Press, 2011.
Bergson, Henri. *Creative Evolution.* New York: Henry Holt, 1911.
Berman, Morris. *The Twilight of American Culture.* New York: W.W. Norton, 2000.
Bernstein, Jerome S. *Living in the Borderland: The Evolution of Consciousness and the
   Challenge of Healing Trauma.* London: Routledge, 2005.
———. *Power and Politics: The Psychology of Soviet-American Partnership.* San Francisco:
   Shambhala, 1989.
Berry, Wendell. "Wendell Berry, Poet & Prophet." Interview by Bill Moyers. *Moyers &
   Company,* New York Public Affairs Television (WNET), October 4, 2013. Video,
   56:46, http://billmoyers.com/episode/wendell-berry-poet-prophet/.
Bolen, Jean Shinoda. *Crossing to Avalon: A Woman's Midlife Quest for the Sacred Feminine.*
   San Francisco: HarperSanFrancisco, 1994.
Bourgeault, Cynthia. *The Meaning of Mary Magdalen: Discovering the Woman at the Heart
   of Christianity.* Boston: Shambhala, 2010.
Brisson, Luc. *How Philosophers Saved Myths: Allegorical Interpretation and Classical
   Mythology.* Chicago: University of Chicago Press, 2004.
Brooke, Roger. "The Self, the Psyche and the World: A Phenomenological Interpretation."
   Journal of Analytical Psychology 54, no. 5 (November 2009) 601–18.
Brother Lawrence. *The Practice of the Presence of God: The Best Rule of a Holy Life.* New
   York: Fleming H. Revel, 1895.
Buser, Steven, and Leonard Cruz, eds. *A Clear and Present Danger: Narcissism in the Era
   of Donald Trump.* Asheville, NC: Chiron, 2016.
Cambray, Joseph. The Emergence of the Ecological Mind in Hua-Yen/Kegon Buddhism
   and Jungian Psychology," *Journal of Analytical Psychology* 62 (2017) 20–31.
Caruth, Cathy. An Interview with Jean Laplanche. 2001. Retrieved from: http://pmc.iath.
   virginia.edu/text-only/issue.101/11.2caruth.txt.

Cheetham, Tom. *All the World an Icon: Henry Corbin and the Angelic Function of Beings.* Berkeley, CA: North Atlantic, 2012.

Cicero, Marcus Tullius. "On the Laws (De Legibus)." Excerpts from Cicero, *On the Laws,* trans. David Fott. Ithaca: Cornell University Press, 2014. Accessed May 20, 2020, http://www.nlnrac.org/classical/cicero/documents/de-legibus.

Clebsch, William. A., and Charles R. Jaekle. *Pastoral Care in Historical Perspective.* New York: Jason Aronson Inc., 1977.

Clift, John Dalby, and Wallace B. Clift. *The Archetype of Pilgrimage: Outer Action with Inner Meaning.* Eugene, OR: Wipf & Stock, 2004.

Coleman, Warren. "Imagination and the Imaginary." *Journal of Analytical Psychology* 51, no. 1 (February 2006) 21–41.

Corbett, Lionel. *The Religious Function of the Psyche.* New York: Routledge, 1996.

———. *The Sacred Cauldron: Psychotherapy as a Spiritual Practice.* Asheville, NC: Chiron, 2011.

Deloria, Vine, Jr. *C. G. Jung and the Sioux Traditions: Dreams, Visions, Nature and the Primitive.* New Orleans: Spring Journal, 2009.

Dourley, John P. *On Behalf of the Mystic Fool: Jung on the Religious Situation.* London: Routledge, 2009.

———. *Jung and His Mystics: In the End it All Comes to Nothing.* New York: Routledge, 2014.

———. "Jung and the Recall of the Gods." *Journal of Jungian Theory and Practice* 8, no. 1 (2006) 43–53.

Dunbar-Ortiz, Roxanne. *An Indigenous Peoples' History of the United States.* Boston: Beacon, 2014.

Edinger, Edward F. *The Mysterium Lectures.* Toronto: Inner City, 1995.

Eliade, Mircea. *Shamanism: Archaic Techniques of Ecstasy.* Princeton: Princeton University Press, 1964.

Ellis, Joseph. J. *American Sphinx: The Character of Thomas Jefferson.* New York: Vintage, 1998.

Fox, Mathew. *Illuminations of Hildegard of Bingen.* Rochester, VT: Bear, 1985.

Freud, Sigmund. *The Interpretation of Dreams.* Translated by A. A. Brill. New York: McMillan, 1900.

Fuller, Buchminster. "Lecture delivered at Tacoma First Congregational Church." Tacoma, WA, March 4, 1979.

Gambini, Roberto. *Soul and Culture.* College Station: Texas A&M University Press, 2003.

Gauthier, James David. "Martin Heidegger, Emmanuel Levinas, and Politics of Dwelling." PhD diss. Louisiana State University, 2004. Retrieved online from: http://etd,lsu,edu/docs/available/etd-11052004–163310/unrestricted/Gauthier.dis.pdf, 2004.

Gibson, Terrill L. *Private Personal Journal.* Unpublished. 1979–present.

———. "Process and Politics in Pastoral Psychology: A Jungian Perspective on the Transformative Imago Dei in Depth Therapy." *The Journal of Spirituality in Mental Health* 11, no. 1 (2009) 51–65.

Giergerich, Wolfgang. "Enchantment and Disenchantment: The Psyche in Transformation [postmodern and multi-cultural perspectives on analytic craft]." Papers and dialogues from the First Regional Conference of the International Association for Jungian Studies, London, July 15–16, 2011.

———. *Soul Violence.* Vol. 3 of *The Collected English Papers of Wolfgang Giergerich.* New Orleans: Spring Journal, 2008.

Goodwin, Doris Kearns. *The Bully Pulpit: Theodore Roosevelt, Howard Taft and the Golden Age of Journalism.* New York: Simon and Schuster, 2014.

———. *Team of Rivals: The Political Genius of Abraham Lincoln.* New York: Simon and Schuster, 2006.

Grenz, Stanley J. *Reason for Hope: The Systematic Theology of Wolfhart Pannenberg.* New York: Oxford University Press, 1990.

Gros, Frederick. Translated by John Howe. *A Philosophy of Walking.* London: Verso, 2009.

Gross, Terry. "Timothy Spall Takes On Painter J.M.W. Turner, A 'Master Of The Sublime'" Interview by Terry Gross. *Fresh Air*, National Public Radio, December 15, 2014. Audio, 37:05, https://www.npr.org/2014/12/15/370959146/timothy-spall-takes-on-painter-j-m-w-turner-a-master-of-the-sublime.

Grotstein, James. *A Beam of Intense Darkness: Wilfred Bion's Legacy to Psychoanalysis.* New York: Karnac, 2007.

Guggenbuhl-Craig, Adolph. *Marriage: Dead or Alive.* New Orleans: Spring, 1986.

Hauke, Christopher. *Jung and the Postmodern: The Interpretation of Realities.* London: Routledge, 2000.

Heidegger, Martin. Translated by Stadstadter Alfred. *Poetry, Language, Thought.* New York: Harper Perennial, 1971.

Heisig, James W. *Imago Dei: A Study of C. G. Jung's Psychology of Religion.* Lewisburg, PA: Bucknell University Press, 1979.

Henderson, Joseph L. *Thresholds of Initiation.* Middletown, CT: Wesleyan University Press, 1967.

Herrmann, Steven *William James and C. G. Jung.* Oberlin, OH: Analytical Psychology, 2020.

Hill, John. *At Home in the World: Sounds and Symmetries of Belonging.* New Orleans: Spring Journal, 2010.

Hillman, James. *The Dream and the Underworld.* New York: Harper & Row, 1979.

———. *The Soul's Code: In Search of Character and Calling.* New York: Random House, 1996.

Hockley, Luke. *Cinematic Projections: The Analytical Psychology of C. G. Jung.* London: University of Luton Press, 2001.

Hollis, James. *The Archetypal Imagination.* College Station: Texas A&M University Press, 2002.

Homans, Peter. *Jung in Context: Modernity and the Making of a Psychology.* Chicago: University of Chicago Press, 1979.

Homer. *The Odyssey.* Translated by A. S. Kline. 2004. Accessed May 20, 2020. http://www.poetryintranslation.com/PITBR/Greek/Odhome.htm

Hurwitz, Tom, and Margaret Klink. "The decisive image; In documentary film, in Jungian Analysis." In *Jung and Film II: The Return*, edited by Christopher Hauke and Luke Hockley, 17–34. London: Routledge, 2011.

Jaffe, Aniela. *The Myth of Meaning in the Work of C. G. Jung.* Zurich: Daimon Verlag, 1970.

James, William. *The Varieties of Religious Experience: A Study in Human Nature.* 1900. New York: Cosimo, 2007.

Jameson, Fredric. *The Seeds of Time.* New York: Columbia University Press, 1996.

Jaspars, Karl. *The Origin and Goal of History.* New Haven: Yale University Press, 1953.

Johnson, Robert. A. *Balancing Heaven and Earth: A Memoir.* New York: HarperCollins, 2009.

Johnson, William. *The Inner Eye of Love.* New York: Harper and Row, 1975.

Jung, Carl Gustav. *Alchemical Studies*. Vol. 13 of *The Collected Works of C. G. Jung*, edited by Gerhard Adler. Princeton: Princeton University Press, 1967.

————. *The Archetypes and the Collective Unconscious*. Vol. 9, part 1 of *The Collected Works of C. G. Jung*, edited by Gerhard Adler. Princeton: Princeton University Press, 1959.

————. *C. G. Jung Letters*. Edited by Gerhard Adler. 2 vols. New York: Routledge, 1976.

————. *Memories, Dreams and Reflections*. New York: Pantheon, 1963.

————. *Modern Man in Search of a Soul*. New York: Harcourt Harvest, 1933.

————. *Notes of the Seminar Given in 1928-30*. Vol. 1 of *Dream Analysis*, edited by William McGuire. New York: Routledge, 1972.

————. "The Philosophical Tree." In *Alchemical Studies*, edited by Gerhard Adler, 251–342. Vol. 13 of *The Collected Works of C. G. Jung*. Princeton: Princeton University Press, 1969.

————. "Psychological Commentary on 'The Tibetan Book of the Great Liberation." In *Psychology and Religion: West and East*, edited by Gerhard Adler, 509–28. Vol. 11 of *Collected Works of C. G. Jung*. Princeton: Princeton University Press, 1939.

————. *Psychological Types*. Vol. 6 of *The Collected Works of C. G. Jung*, edited by Gerhard Adler. Princeton: Princeton University Press, 1976.

————. *On Psychological and Visionary Art: Notes from C. G. Jung's Lecture on Gerald D. Nerval's Aurelia*. Edited by Craig E. Stephenson. Princeton: Princeton University Press. 2015.

————. *The Red Book*. Edited by Sonu Shamdusani, New York: W. W. Norton, 2009.

————. "The Spiritual Problem of Modern Man." In *Civilization in Transition*, edited by Gerhard Adler, 74–94. Vol. 10 of *The Collected Works of C. G. Jung*. Princeton: Princeton University Press, 1964.

————. *Structure and Dynamics of the Psyche*. Vol. 8 of *The Collected Works of C. G. Jung*. Princeton: Princeton University Press, 1970.

————. *Symbols of Transformation*. Vol. 5 of *The Collected Works of C. G. Jung*. Princeton: Princeton University Press, 1977.

————. "The Transcendent Function." In *The Structure and Dynamics of the Psyche*, edited by Gerhard Adler, 67–91. Vol. 8 of *The Collected Works of C. G. Jung*. Princeton: Princeton University Press, 1958.

————. *Two Essays on Analytical Psychology*. Vol. 7 of *The Collected Works of C. G. Jung*, edited by Gerhard Adler. Princeton: Princeton University Press, 1966.

————. *The Visions Seminars*. 2 vols. New Orleans: Spring, 1976.

Kalsched, Donald. *Trauma and the Soul: A Psycho-Spiritual Approach to Human Development and Its Interruption*. New York: Routledge, 2014.

Kawai, Hayao. *Buddhism and the Art of Psychotherapy*. College Station, TX: Texas A&M University Press, 2008.

Kaylo, Janet. "Imagination and the Mundus Imaginalis." *Spring: A Journal of Archetype and Culture* 77 (Spring 2007) 107–24.

Kelsey, Morton. *Dreams: The Dark Speech of the Soul*. New York: Doubleday, 1968.

————. *Encounter with God: A Theology of Christian Experience*. Minneapolis: Bethany Fellowship Inc., 1972.

Kerr, Michael. E. and Murray Bowen. *Family Evaluation: An Approach Based on Bowen Theory*. New York: W. W. Norton, 1988.

King, Martin Luther. *Why We Can't Wait*. New York: New American Library, 2002.

Kingsley, Peter. *In the Dark Places of Wisdom*. Point Reyes Station, CA: The Golden Sufi Center, 2004.

———. *Reality*. Point Reyes Station, CA: The Golden Sufi Center, 2004.

Klein, Naomi. *The Shock Doctrine: The Rise of Disaster Capitalism*. New York: MacMillan, 2007.

———. *This Changes Everything: Climate and Capitalism*. New York: Simon and Schuster, 2014.

Kolbert, Elizabeth. *The Sixth Extinction: An Unnatural History*. New York: Henry Holt and Co, 2014.

Kugler Paul. *Raids on the Unthinkable: Freudian and Jungian Psychoanalyses*. New Orleans: Spring Journal Books, 2006.

Lammers, Ann Conrad and Adrian Cunningham, eds. *The Jung-White Letters*. New York: Routledge, 2007.

Lamon, Ward Hill. *Recollections of Abraham Lincoln, 1847–1865*. Lincoln: University of Nebraska Press, 1994.

Leopold, Aldo. *A Sand County Almanac*. New York: Ballantine, 1986.

Lovelock, James. *The Vanishing Face of Gaia*. New York: Hachette Book Group, 2009.

Malabou, Catherine. *What Should We Do with Our Brain?* New York: Fordham University Press, 2008.

Marcus, Paul. *In Search of the Good Life: Emmanuel Levinas, Psychoanalysis and the Art of Living*. London: Karnac, 2010.

Marlan, Stanton. *The Black Sun: The Alchemy and Art of Darkness*. College Station, TX: Texas A&M University Press, 2008.

Masters, Edgar Lee. *Spoon River Anthology*. Urbana: University of Illinois Press, 2005.

Mathews, Washington. *The Night Chant, A Navajo Ceremony*. Washington D. C.: Volume VI of the Memoirs of the American Museum of Natural History, May, 1902.

McCullough, David. *Truman*. New York: Simon and Schuster, 1992.

Miró, Joan. *Miró: The Experience of Seeing*. Exhibit. February 13–May 26, 2014. Seattle: Seattle Art Museum.

Moore, Thomas. *The Re-enchantment of Everyday Life*. New York: Harper Perennial, 1997.

Muir, John. *The Mountains of California*. New York: Penguin, 1985.

Nichols, Sally. *Jung and Tarot: An Archetypal Journey*. Boston: WeiserBooks, 1980.

Otto, Rudolf. Translated by John W. Harvey. *The Idea of the Holy: An Inquiry Into the Non Rational Factor in the Idea of the Divine*. London: Kessinger, 2004.

Patha, Camille. *A Punch of Color: Fifty Years of Painting by Camille Patha*. Exhibit. February 1–May 25, 2014. Tacoma: Tacoma Art Museum.

Raff, Jeffrey, and Linda Bonnington Vocatura. *Healing the Wounded God: Finding Your Personal Guide on Your Way to Individuation and Beyond*. York Beach, ME: Nicolas-Hays, 2002.

Raff, Jeffrey. *Jung and the Alchemical Imagination*. York Beach, ME: Nicolas-Hays, 2000.

Rasche, Joerg, and Thomas Singer. *Europe's Many Souls: Exploring Cultural Complexes and Identities*. New Orleans: Spring Journal, 2016.

Riedel, Eberhard. "A Depth Psychological Approach to Collective Trauma in Eastern Congo." *Psychological Perspectives* 57, no. 3 (2014) 249–77.

Roesler, Christian. "Are Archetypes Transmitted More by Culture Than Biology? Questions Arising from Conceptualizations of the Archetype." *Journal of Analytical Psychology* 57, no. 2 (April 2012) 223–46.

———. "Evidence for the Effectiveness of Jungian Psychotherapy: A Review of Empirical Studies." *Behavioral Science* 3, no. 4 (December 2013) 562–75.

Roszak, Theodore, Mary E. Gomes, and Allen D. Kanner. *Ecopsychology: Restoring the Earth, Healing the Mind*. San Francisco: Sierra Club, 1995.

Samuel, Andrew. "The Trickster." Paper presented at Rebirth and Renewal—Conference of the International Association for Jungian Studies, Phoenix, June 28, 2014.

Sandner, Donald F., and Steven. H. Wong, eds. *The Sacred Heritage: The Influence of Shamanism on Analytical Psychology*. London: Routledge, 1996.

Sabini, Meredith. *The Earth Has a Soul: C. G. Jung on Nature, Technology and Modern Life*. New York: Random House, 2001.

Safina, Carl. *The View from Lazy Point: A Natural Year in an Unnatural World*. New York: Picador, 2012.

Sardello, Robert. S. *Facing the World with Soul: The Reimagination of Modern Life*. New York: HarperCollins, 1994.

Saxton, Libby. "Fragile Faces: Levinas and Lanzmann," *Film-Philosophy* 11, no. 2 (August 2007) 1–14.

Scranton, Roy. "'Star Wars' and the Fantasy of American Violence." *The New York Times*. July 2, 2016. https://www.nytimes.com/2016/07/03/opinion/sunday/star-wars-and-the-fantasy-of-american-violence.html.

Shamdusani, Sonu. *Jung and the Making of Modern Psychology: The Dream of a Science*. Cambridge: Cambridge University Press, 2005.

Sheikh, Fazal. *Portraits*. Gottingen: Steidl Photography International. Seattle Art Museum exhibit, 2011.

Sheldrake, Rupert. *Morphic Resonance: The Nature of Formative Causation*. London: London Park Street, 2009.

Shirazi, Faegheh, ed. *Muslim Women in War and Crisis*. Austin: University of Texas Press, 2010.

Singer, Thomas. *The Vision Thing: Myth, Politics and Psyche in the World*. New York: Routledge, 2000.

Singer, Thomas, and Samuel L. Kimbles, eds. *The Cultural Complex: Contemporary Jungian Perspectives on Psyche and Society*. New York: Routledge, 2004.

Soelle, Dorothee. *The Silent Cry: Mysticism and Resistance*. New York: Fortress, 2001.

Stein, Murry. *The Red Book I and II*. DVD. Asheville, NC: Asheville Jung Center, 2010.

Suh, Do Ho, curator. *Luminous, The Art of Asia*. Exhibit. October 13, 2011–January 8, 2012. Seattle: Seattle Art Museum.

Swimme, Brian. *The Universe Is a Green Dragon: A Cosmic Creation Story*. Santa Fe: Bear, 1984

Tacey, David. *Edge of the Sacred: Jung, Psyche, Earth*. Zurich: Daimon Verlag, 2012.

Taibbi, Mark. *The Divide: American Injustice in the Age of the Wealth Gap*. New York: Random House, 2014.

Tarnas, Richard. *Cosmos and Psyche: Intimations of a New World View*. New York: Viking, 2006.

Turner, Victor. "Myth and Symbol." In *International Encyclopedia of Social Science* vol. 10, edited by David L. Sills, 576–82. New York: MacMillan and Free, 1968.

———. *The Ritual Process: Structure and Anti-Structure*. New York: Aldine de Gruyter, 1995.

Ulanov, Ann Belford. *Religion and Spirituality in Carl Jung*. Mahwah, NJ: Paulist, 1999.

Van Gennep, Arnold. *Rites of Passage*. 1909. Chicago: University of Chicago Press, 1961.

Vine, David. "Defeat was inevitable: This was a corrupt war to its core." *The Guardian*, August 19, 2021 [online edition].

Von Franz, Marie-Louise. *Puer Aeternus: A Psychological Study of the Adult Struggle With the Paradise of Childhood.* New York: Sigo, 1997.

Wilder, Thornton. *Our Town.* New York: Harper Perennial Modern Classics, 1998.

Wilkinson, Margaret. *Changing Minds in Therapy: Emotion, Attachment, Trauma, and Neurobiology.* New York: W.W. Norton, 2010.

Williams, Terry Tempest. *The Open Space of Democracy.* Eugene, OR: Wipf & Stock, 2004.

Winnicott, D. W. *Playing and Reality.* London: Tavistock, 1971.

Woods, Richard. *Mysterion: An Approach to Mystical Spirituality.* New York: Thomas Moore, 1981.

Wordsworth, William. *Intimations of Immortality: From Recollections of Early Childhood and Other Poems.* New York: Houghton, Mifflin, 1895.

Worster, Donald. *The Wealth of Nature: Environmental History and the Ecological Imagination.* New York: Oxford University Press, 1994.

Yalom, Irving, et al. "The Many Faces of Wisdom: Perspectives on Therapy's Questions." *Psychotherapy Networker* (March/April, 2013). https://www.psychotherapynetworker. org/magazine/article/190/the-many-faces-of-wisdom.

Zinn, Howard. "The Optimism of Uncertainty." *The Nation.* September 2, 2004. https:// www.thenation.com/article/optimism-uncertainty/.

Zornberg, Avivah Gottlieb. *The Murmuring Deep: Reflections on the Biblical Unconscious.* New York: Knopf-Doubleday, 2009.